T0384323

THE BIG FAT GEOMETRY WORKBOOK

WORKMAN PUBLISHING
NEW YORK

Workman Kids
Workman Publishing
Hachette Book Group, Inc.
1290 Avenue of the Americas
New York, NY 10104
workman.com

Workman Kids is an imprint of Workman Publishing,
a division of Hachette Book Group, Inc.
The Workman name and logo are registered
trademarks of Hachette Book Group, Inc.

Designed by Abby Dening
Illustrations by Kim Ku
Written by Robert Vigneri
Reviewed by Dr. Steven J. Warner

Workman books may be purchased in bulk for business, educational,
or promotional use. Special editions or book excerpts can also be created
to specification. For information, please contact your local bookseller or the
Hachette Book Group Special Markets Department at special.markets@hbgusa.com.

ISBN 978-1-5235-2376-4

First Edition September 2024

Printed in China on responsibly sourced paper.

10 9 8 7 6 5 4 3 2 1

WELCOME TO THE BIG FAT GEOMETRY WORKBOOK.

This workbook is designed to support you as you work your way through *Everything You Need to Ace Geometry in One Big Fat Notebook* or through your Geometry class. Consider the *Notebook* your main source and this *Workbook* extra practice.

Each chapter in this workbook supports the content of a corresponding chapter in the study guide. It begins with a brief recap of the key concepts, followed by an example solved step by step. Then there's a series of extra practice problems for you to solve that will help you really master the concept.

The solution process section in the back of the book guides you through every step of finding the solution for each question. No more trying to figure out where you went wrong. The path to the correct answer is clearly laid out.

Whether you're reviewing for a test, need to strengthen your problem-solving skills, or are just looking for extra practice, look no further than this companion workbook. You'll encounter the same fun approach to math and easy-to-understand language that you love in *Everything You Need to Ace Geometry in One Big Fat Notebook*.

Both books provide you with everything you need to ace that Geometry class!

CONTENTS

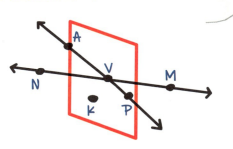

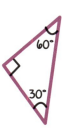

UNIT 5: GEOMETRIC TRANSFORMATIONS **137**

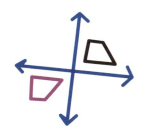

UNIT 6: SIMILARITY **175**

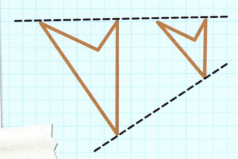

UNIT 7: RIGHT TRIANGLES and TRIGONOMETRY **211**

x

Unit 1

Basics of Geometry

POINTS, LINES, AND PLANES

Here are some key concepts and basic terms used in geometry:

POINT: indicates a location	**LINE**: a straight path extending infinitely in opposite directions. A line is **one-dimensional**.	**LINE SEGMENT**: part of a line with two endpoints
RAY: part of a line that starts at a point and extends infinitely in one direction	**PARALLEL LINES**: lines that are always the same distance apart. They *never* meet.	**PERPENDICULAR LINES**: lines that intersect to form four right angles (angles that measure 90°)
VERTEX: the point of intersection of two or more line segments, rays, or lines	**ANGLE**: formed by two rays with the same endpoint, the vertex	**TRIANGLE**: a shape with three sides, three angles, and three vertices

CONGRUENT LINE SEGMENTS: line segments that have the same length	**MIDPOINT**: the halfway point of a line segment. It divides the line segment into two congruent segments.	**PLANE**: a flat surface that extends infinitely in all directions
SEGMENT BISECTOR: a line, ray, segment, or plane that passes through a segment at its midpoint (bisects it)	**COLLINEAR**: points lie on the same line	**INTERSECTION**: the point or line where lines or planes pass through or lie across each other
	COPLANAR: points lie on the same plane	

PROOFS are logical reasons used to confirm an idea. **POSTULATES** and **THEOREMS** are used to support proofs.

A *postulate* is a statement that is accepted as fact, without proof. A *theorem* is a statement that has been proven to be true using other theorems, definitions, and/or postulates.

EXAMPLE: If A is between M and T, MA = 4x, AT = 18, and MT = 54, find the value of x.

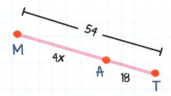

To find the value of x, use the **Segment Addition Postulate**: If A is a point on line segment MT, then MA + AT = MT.

MA + AT = MT

$4x + 18 = 54$ Substitute. Then use the
                Properties of Equality.

$4x + 18 = 54$

$\underline{\quad - 18 = -18}$ Subtraction Property of Equality

$4x + 0 = 36$

$4x = 36$

$\dfrac{4x}{4} = \dfrac{36}{4}$ Division Property of Equality

$x = 9$

So, the value of x is 9.

EXAMPLE: Use the given figure to answer the following statements.

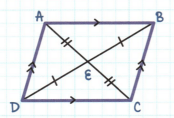

▶ Name the line segments that are congruent, or equal in length. (Hint: Look at the tick marks.)

$\overline{DE} \cong \overline{EB}$ and $\overline{AE} \cong \overline{EC}$

$\overline{AB}$ = name of the line segment

AB = length of the line segment

▶ Name the point of intersection for $\overline{AC}$ and $\overline{DB}$.

The point of intersection for $\overline{AC}$ and $\overline{DB}$ is point E.

▶ Name line segments that are parallel. Then name line segments that are perpendicular.

$\overline{AB} \parallel \overline{DC}$ and $\overline{AD} \parallel \overline{BC}$

There are *no* line segments that are perpendicular or intersect to form right angles (angles that measure 90°).

FOR QUESTIONS 1 THROUGH 4, USE THIS FIGURE.

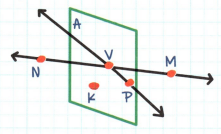

1. What are six other names for plane A?

2. Name three coplanar points.

3. Name the intersection of the line $\overleftrightarrow{NM}$ and plane A.

4. Name three collinear points.

FOR QUESTIONS 5 AND 6, USE THIS FIGURE.

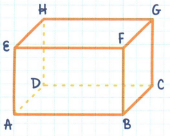

5. How many planes are shown in the figure?

6. What is the intersection of plane EFG and plane EAD?

7. Use the line segment given below to explain the Segment Addition Postulate.

8. Find the length of $\overline{AC}$.

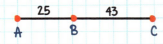

9. Find the value of x.

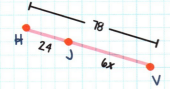

10. Which figures illustrate lines that are parallel? Select all that apply. Explain how you know the lines are parallel.

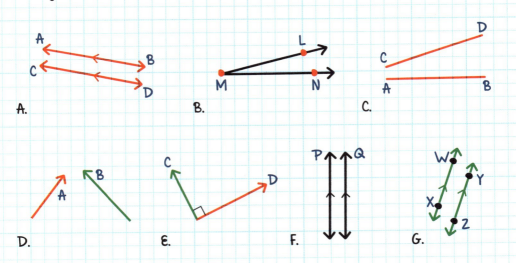

11. Which figures illustrate lines that are perpendicular? Select all that apply. Explain how you know the lines are perpendicular.

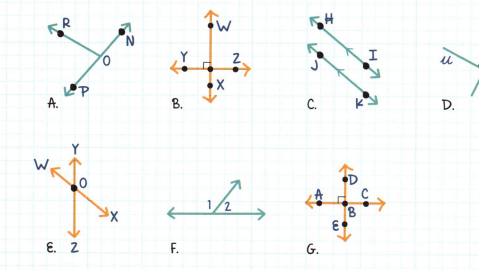

A. B. C. D.

E. F. G.

12. Using the figures given below, explain what a segment bisector is.

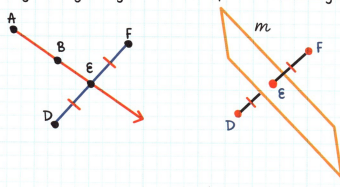

13. Write congruence statements for the congruent segments in the figure below.

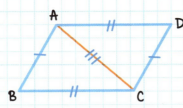

14. Jonathan writes the theorem below in his notebook. He says this statement is accepted as fact because it is obvious that two lines would intersect at one point. Is Jonathan correct? Explain your reasoning.

Theorem: If two lines intersect, then they intersect in exactly one point.

Chapter 2 ANGLES

An **ANGLE** (∠) is formed by two **RAYS** with a common **ENDPOINT**, called the **VERTEX**.

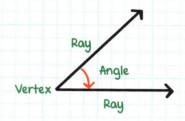

Three ways to name an angle:

1. the vertex: ∠A

2. three points, with the vertex in the middle: ∠BAC or ∠CAB

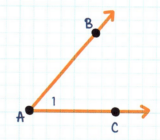

3. the number inside the angle: ∠1

The space around an angle can be classified as **interior** or **exterior**.

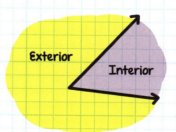

ANGLE MEASURE

The **MEASURE** of ∠A (the size of the angle) is written as m∠A.

DEGREES (°) measure the size of an angle.

TYPES OF ANGLES	
ANGLE(S)	**DEFINITION**
RIGHT ANGLE	Measures *exactly* 90°
ACUTE ANGLE	Measures *greater than* 0° but *less than* 90°
OBTUSE ANGLE	Measures *greater than* 90° but *less than* 180°
STRAIGHT ANGLE (straight line)	Measures *exactly* 180°

ANGLE(S)	DEFINITION
ADJACENT ANGLES	Angles that lie in the same plane, have a common (the same) vertex, share a common side, and have no common interior points
NON-ADJACENT ANGLES	Angles that do not have a vertex or a side in common
CONGRUENT ANGLES	Angles that are equal in measure

EXAMPLE: Look at the figure. m∠ABE = 180° and m∠CBD = 90°.

Find the value of x.

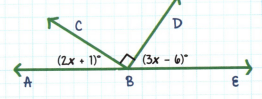

To find the value of x, use the **Angle Addition Postulate:** Add the measures of the smaller angles to find the measure of the larger angle.

STEP 1: Substitute.

m∠ABC + m∠CBD + m∠DBE = m∠ABE

$(2x + 1)° + 90° + (3x − 6)° = 180°$

STEP 2: Use the Properties of Equality to solve for x.

$(2x + 1)° + 90° + (3x − 6)° = 180°$

$(2x + 3x) + (1 + 90 − 6) = 180$ Combine like terms.

$\quad 5x \quad + \quad 85 \quad = 180$

$5x + 85 = 180$

$\underline{- 85 = - 85}$ Subtraction Property of Equality

$5x + 0 = 95$

$5x = 95$

$\dfrac{5x}{5} = \dfrac{95}{5}$ Division Property of Equality

$x = 19$ So, the value of x is 19.

List all the congruent angles in the given figure.

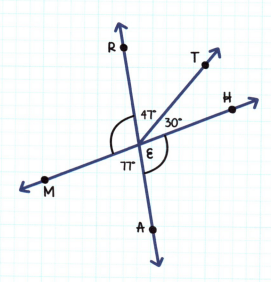

▶ Look at the matching angle marks. They show any angles that are congruent: ∠MER ≅ ∠AEH

▶ Is ∠MEA ≅ ∠REH?

Use the Angle Addition Postulate. This will show that the angles are equal in measure.

m∠REH = m∠RET + m∠TEH

m∠REH = 47° + 30°

m∠REH = 77°

Since ∠MEA and ∠REH both measure 77°, they are congruent.

Congruent angles: ∠MER ≅ ∠AEH and ∠MEA ≅ ∠REH

USE WHAT YOU KNOW ABOUT ANGLES TO ANSWER THE QUESTION.

1. Give the three names for the shaded angle.

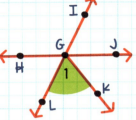

FOR QUESTIONS 2 THROUGH 5, CLASSIFY THE ANGLES AS STRAIGHT, RIGHT, ACUTE, OR OBTUSE.

2.

3.

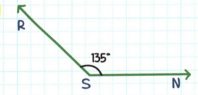

4.

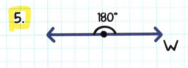

5.

6. Given the measure of $\angle CAE$ is $102°$, determine the value of x.

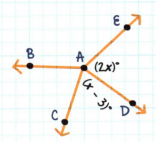

7. Given ∠NSP is a straight angle, find the measure of ∠NSH.

Hint: Find the value of x first.

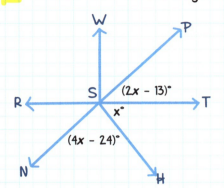

FOR QUESTIONS 8 THROUGH 11, USE THE GIVEN FIGURE.

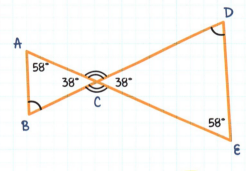

8. ∠ABC ≅ _____

9. ∠DCE ≅ _____

10. ∠CAB ≅ _____

11. ∠ACD ≅ _____

ANGLE PAIRS

ANGLE PAIRS are related to each other by their measures or orientations.

Angle Pair	Definition
ADJACENT ANGLES	Angles that lie in the same plane, have a common vertex, share a common side, and have no common interior points
VERTICAL ANGLES	Angles that are nonadjacent and opposite each other. They are formed when two lines intersect. They share the same vertex. Vertical angles are congruent.
COMPLEMENTARY ANGLES	Two angles whose sum is 90°
SUPPLEMENTARY ANGLES	Two angles whose sum is 180°
LINEAR PAIR	Two angles that are adjacent and supplementary whose sum is 180°

ANGLE BISECTORS

An **ANGLE BISECTOR** is a line, ray, or line segment that divides an angle into two congruent angles.

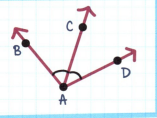

If $\overrightarrow{AC}$ is the angle bisector of $\angle BAD$, then $\angle BAC \cong \angle CAD$.

PERPENDICULAR BISECTORS

A **PERPENDICULAR BISECTOR** is a line, ray, or line segment that divides a line segment into two congruent segments and forms right angles with it.

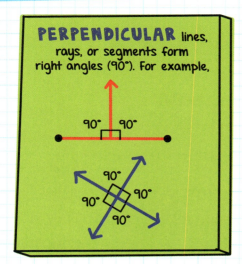

PERPENDICULAR lines, rays, or segments form right angles (90°). For example,

two congruent segments

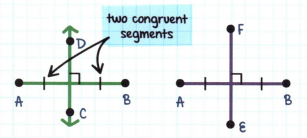

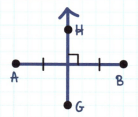

$\overrightarrow{CD}$, $\overleftrightarrow{EF}$, and $\overrightarrow{GH}$ are all perpendicular bisectors of $\overline{AB}$.

EXAMPLE: $\overrightarrow{BD}$ is an angle bisector of $\angle ABC$, $m\angle ABD = (4x - 16)°$, and $m\angle DBC = (2x + 4)°$. Find $m\angle ABC$.

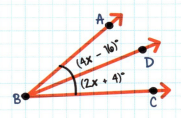

First, find the value of x.

The angle bisector $\overrightarrow{BD}$ divides $\angle ABC$ into two congruent angles, and congruent angles have equal measures.

So, $m\angle ABD = m\angle DBC$.

$(4x - 16)° = (2x + 4)°$

$4x - 16 + 16 = 2x + 4 + 16$ Add 16 to both sides of the equation.

$4x = 2x + 20$

$4x - 2x = 2x - 2x + 20$ Subtract $2x$ from both sides of the equation.

$2x = 20$

$2x \div 2 = 20 \div 2$ Divide both sides of the equation by 2.

$x = 10$

So, $m\angle ABD = (4x - 16)° = (4 \cdot 10 - 16)° = 24°$

$m\angle DBC = (2x + 4)° = (2 \cdot 10 + 4)° = 24°$

Now there is enough information to find $m\angle ABC$. Use the Angle Addition Postulate.

$m\angle ABC = m\angle ABD + m\angle DBC$

$= 24° + 24°$ Substitute.

$= 48°$

So, $m\angle ABC = 48°$.

EXAMPLE: Line ℓ is a perpendicular bisector of $\overline{JP}$, $JH = 6x - 2$, $\overline{HP} = 3x + 25$, and $m\angle KHP = (5y + 40)°$. Find the values of x and y.

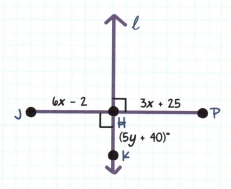

The perpendicular bisector, ℓ, divides $\overline{JP}$ into two congruent line segments, and congruent segments have equal length.

So, $JH \cong HP$.

$6x - 2 = 3x + 25$

$6x - 2 + 2 = 3x + 25 + 2$ Add 2 to both sides of the equation.

$6x = 3x + 27$

$6x - 3x = 3x - 3x + 27$ Subtract $3x$ from both sides of the equation.

$3x = 27$

$3x \div 3 = 27 \div 3$ Divide both sides of the equation by 3.

$x = 9$

The perpendicular bisector, ℓ, forms four right angles with $\overline{JP}$.

So, $m\angle KHP = 90°$.

$m\angle KHP = 90°$

$5y + 40 = 90$ Substitute.

$5y + 40 - 40 = 90 - 40$ Subtract 40 from both sides of the equation.

$5y = 50$

$5y \div 5 = 50 \div 5$ Divide both sides of the equation by 5.

$y = 10$

So, the value of x is 9 and the value of y is 10.

FOR QUESTIONS 1 THROUGH 5, USE THE FIGURE BELOW TO COMPLETE THE ANGLE PAIRS.

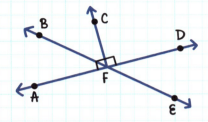

1. Vertical angles: ∠EFD and _____

2. Complementary angles: ∠BFC and _____

3. Supplementary angles: ∠CFD and _____

4. Linear pair: ∠DFE and _____

5. Vertical angles: ∠AFE and _____

6. Find the values of x and y in the figure below.

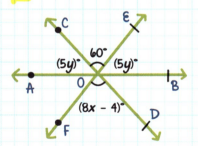

7. If ∠1 and ∠2 form a linear pair, and m∠1 = 118°, find m∠2.

8. Two complementary angles have a positive difference of 32°. What are the measures of the two angles?

9. Explain angle bisectors using the figure below.

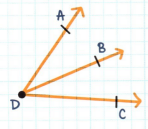

10. In the figure below, m is a perpendicular bisector of $\overline{ST}$, SR = $8y - 14$, RT = $3y - 4$, and m∠PRT = $(7x + 6)$°. Find the values of x and y.

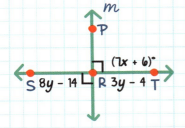

4. CONSTRUCTIONS

CONSTRUCTING PERPENDICULAR LINES

There are two ways to construct a perpendicular bisector.

One way:

1. Set compass width.

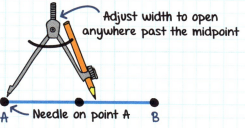

Adjust width to open anywhere past the midpoint

Needle on point A

2. Draw a large arc across segment $\overline{AB}$.

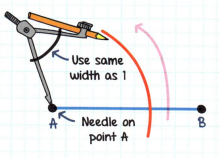

Use same width as 1

Needle on point A

3. Repeat on the right side.

4. Draw a vertical line to connect the intersections of the two arcs.

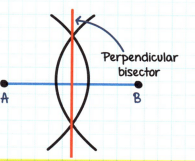

Perpendicular bisector

Another way:

1. Draw two small arcs on $\overline{AB}$.

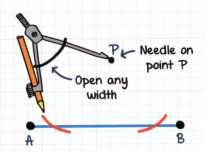

Needle on point P

Open any width

A   B

2. Draw an arc below $\overline{AB}$.

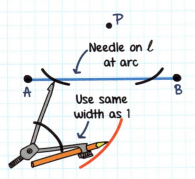

•P

Needle on ℓ at arc

Use same width as 1

A   B

3. Repeat on the right side.

4. Draw a vertical line to connect point P and the intersection of the bottom two arcs.

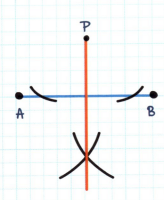

P

A   B

CONSTRUCTING PARALLEL LINES

To construct a line through point P and parallel to ℓ:

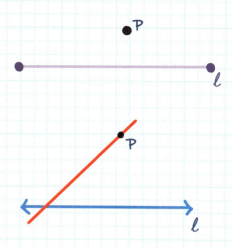

1. Use a straightedge to draw a long line through P and any point on ℓ.

2. Draw an arc through the two lines.

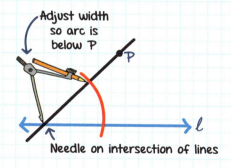

Adjust width so arc is below P

Needle on intersection of lines

3. Move the compass needle to P, and draw a second arc above P.

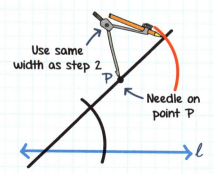

Use same width as step 2

Needle on point P

4. Set the compass width to match the two intersecting points of the first arc.

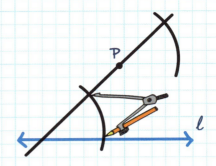

5. Use that width to draw a third small arc on the upper arc. Draw a point at the intersection.

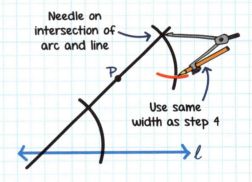

Needle on intersection of arc and line

Use same width as step 4

6. Draw a line that connects **P** and the point made in step 5. The new line is parallel to line ℓ.

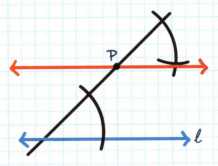

CONSTRUCTING ANGLES

To construct an angle congruent to ∠G:

1. Draw a ray.

2. Draw a large arc on ∠G. Draw it again on the ray.

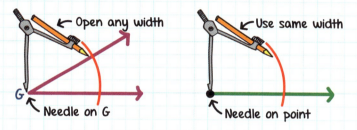

3. On the ray, draw a small arc across the first arc.

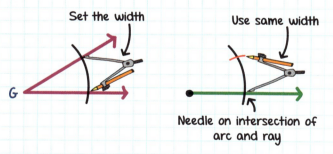

4. Draw a ray from the point through the intersection of the small and large arcs.

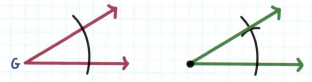

CONSTRUCTING ANGLE BISECTORS

To construct an angle bisector of ∠M:

1. Draw a large arc that intersects both rays.

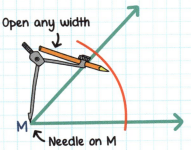

Open any width

Needle on M

2. Draw a small arc across the center of the angle.

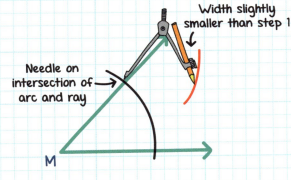

Width slightly smaller than step 1

Needle on intersection of arc and ray

M

3. Repeat on the opposite ray. Draw an arc to intersect with the arc made in step 2.

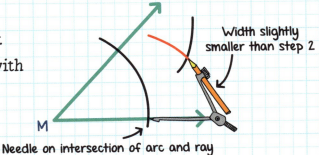

Width slightly smaller than step 2

M

Needle on intersection of arc and ray

4. Draw a ray from the vertex of ∠M through the intersection of the two small arcs.

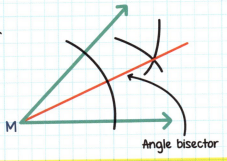

M

Angle bisector

COPY THE FIGURE IN EACH EXERCISE AND USE A COMPASS AND STRAIGHTEDGE TO CONSTRUCT THE FOLLOWING:

1. A perpendicular bisector to $\overline{GW}$.

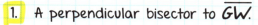

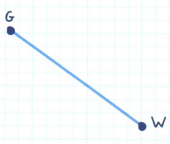

2. A perpendicular bisector to $\overline{ST}$.

3. A perpendicular line from point Q to line m.

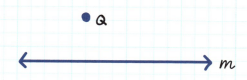

4. A perpendicular line from point W to line *n*.

5. A line through point H and parallel to line *b*.

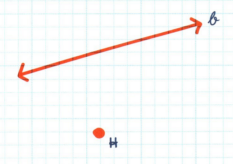

6. An angle that is congruent to ∠M.

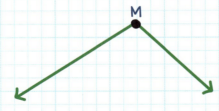

7. An angle that is congruent to ∠Q.

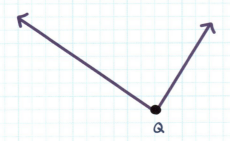

8. The angle bisector of ∠P.

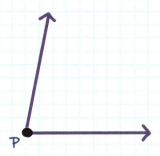

9. The angle bisector of ∠D.

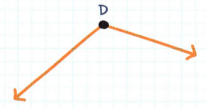

10. Given: Point A on line k.

    Construct: $\overline{BA} \perp k$ at A.

5 LOGIC AND REASONING

INDUCTIVE REASONING is used to form hypotheses (possible explanations) based on a set of observations. The explanation, or conclusion, is called a **CONJECTURE**.

Inductive reasoning involves:

1. Examining a few examples

2. Observing a pattern

3. Assuming that the pattern will always hold

An exception to the observation.

To prove that a conjecture is *false*, we need to find one counterexample.

EXAMPLE: Prove the following conjecture is false.

The product of two positive real numbers is always greater than either factor.

STEP 1: Examining a few examples

Factor	Factor	Product
2	3	6
15	12	180
200	195	39,000

It appears the conjecture is correct. In the examples, the product is always greater than either factor.

STEP 3: Does the pattern hold? Is there a counterexample?

Counterexample

Factor	Factor	Product
$\frac{1}{2}$	4	2

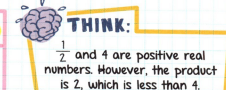

THINK: $\frac{1}{2}$ and 4 are positive real numbers. However, the product is 2, which is less than 4.

The pattern does not hold; we have found a counterexample.

So, the conjecture is *false*.

CONDITIONAL STATEMENTS are statements that have the form **if . . . then**.

Conditional statements are written as: **If p, then q**, or p ⟶ q.

hypothesis ⟶ p   conclusion ⟶ q

The **CONVERSE** of a conditional statement is formed by *switching* the hypothesis and the conclusion, q ⟶ p.

The converse of a true conditional statement is *not* always true.

Conditional statement: If a figure is a square, then it is a quadrilateral.

True. A quadrilateral is a four-sided plane figure. Since a square is a plane figure with four sides, it is a quadrilateral.

Converse statement: If a figure is a quadrilateral, then it is a square.

False. A quadrilateral is a four-sided plane figure, but not *all* quadrilaterals are squares.

A **BICONDITIONAL STATEMENT** is a combination of a conditional statement and its converse. The biconditional is true when the conditional and converse have the same truth value (both true or both false), and it is false otherwise.

The most important usage of the biconditional is the following:

> True Conditional + True Converse = True Biconditional

A biconditional statement is written as:

p if and only if q (written as p if q or p $\longleftrightarrow$ q)

This means: **if p, then q,** and **if q, then p.** [p $\longrightarrow$ q and q $\longrightarrow$ p]

Conditional statement: If C is a right angle, then m∠C = 90°.

Converse: If m∠C = 90°, then C is a right angle.

Biconditional statement: C is a right angle *if* and *only if* m∠C = 90°.

DEDUCTIVE REASONING uses given facts and statements to reach a conclusion logically.

LAWS OF DEDUCTIVE REASONING

Law of Detachment

If the statements $p \longrightarrow q$ and p are true, then the statement q is true.

1. If $\angle x$ and $\angle y$ form a linear pair, then the angles form a straight line.

2. $\angle x$ and $\angle y$ form a linear pair.

Using the **LAW OF DETACHMENT**, we can conclude that the statement

The angles form a straight line is true.

Law of Syllogism

If the statements $p \longrightarrow q$ and $q \longrightarrow r$ are both true, then the statement $p \longrightarrow r$ is also true.

1. **True:** If I draw a ray that is an angle bisector, then I divide an angle into two congruent angles.

2. **True:** If I divide an angle into two congruent angles, then the resulting two angles will be equal in measure.

Using the **LAW OF SYLLOGISM**, we can conclude that:

If I draw a ray that is an angle bisector, then the resulting two angles will be equal in measure.

ANSWER THE QUESTIONS USING WHAT YOU KNOW ABOUT LOGIC AND REASONING.

1. Identify whether the example indicates inductive reasoning or deductive reasoning. Then explain your choice.

Based on the chart below, Mateo concludes that the sum of the two odd positive natural numbers in each row is even.

Addend	Addend	Sum
1	9	10
3	11	14
21	35	56
25	61	86
73	39	112
77	25	102

A. Inductive Reasoning   B. Deductive Reasoning

2. Prove the following conjecture is false using a counterexample.

The sum of two fractions is a whole number.

CHAPTER 5

3. Write the following as a conditional statement.

   All pairs of lines that are perpendicular form right angles.

4. Write the converse of the following conditional statement and determine if it is true.

   If two angles are supplementary, then the angles form a straight line.

5. Write the converse of the conditional statement. Then form a biconditional statement using the conditional statement and its converse.

   Conditional statement: If a polygon is a triangle, then it has three sides.

6. Given the following true statements, write a logical conclusion using the Law of Detachment.

If ∠C and ∠D are complementary angles, then the sum of their measures equals 90°.

∠C and ∠D are complementary angles.

7. Given the following true statements, write a logical conclusion using the Law of Syllogism.

If the school marching band raises $2,000, then the band will purchase new instruments.

If the school marching band purchases new instruments, then the band will perform at the annual homecoming parade.

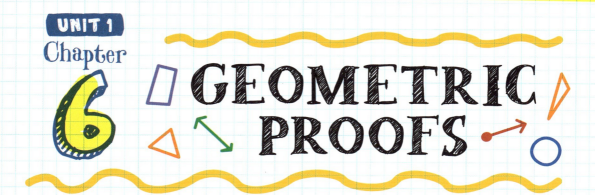

GEOMETRIC PROOFS

PROOF, or logical argument, can be used to show why a conjecture is true. We use **Properties of Equality** and **Properties of Congruence** to show proofs. ⌐ Whatever you do to one side of an equation, do to the other.

A **TWO-COLUMN PROOF** is a proof that is arranged in a two-column table. It starts with the given statement and follows steps to reach the statement being proven. For each **statement** in the left column, the **reason** for that step is in the right column.

Reasons can be:

▶ given information ▶ definitions ▶ theorems
▶ properties ▶ postulates

A **FLOWCHART PROOF** is a diagram that uses boxes and arrows to show the logical order of each statement leading to a conclusion.

A **PARAGRAPH PROOF** explains why a conjecture is true in paragraph form. It still follows logical steps and gives reasons for them.

EXAMPLE: Given: ∠M and ∠N are complementary.

∠P and ∠N are complementary.

Prove: ∠M ≅ ∠P

Use a two-column proof.

STATEMENTS	REASONS
1. ∠M and ∠N are complementary ∠P and ∠N are complementary	**1.** Given
2. m∠M + m∠N = 90° m∠P + m∠N = 90°	**2.** Definition of Complementary Angles
3. m∠M + m∠N = m∠P + m∠N	**3.** Symmetric Property of Equality Transitive Property of Equality
4. m∠M + m∠N − m∠N = m∠P + m∠N − m∠N m∠M = m∠P	**4.** Subtraction Property of Equality
5. ∠M ≅ ∠P	**5.** Definition of Congruent Angles

EXAMPLE: Given: $\overleftrightarrow{RT}$

m∠VST = 35°

Prove: m∠RSV = 145°

Use a flowchart.

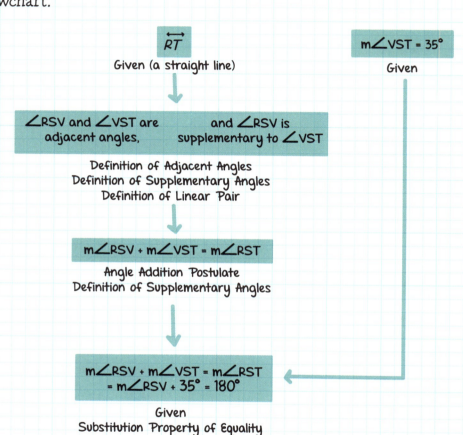

$\overleftrightarrow{RT}$

Given (a straight line)

m∠VST = 35°

Given

∠RSV and ∠VST are adjacent angles,   and ∠RSV is supplementary to ∠VST

Definition of Adjacent Angles
Definition of Supplementary Angles
Definition of Linear Pair

m∠RSV + m∠VST = m∠RST

Angle Addition Postulate
Definition of Supplementary Angles

m∠RSV + m∠VST = m∠RST
= m∠RSV + 35° = 180°

Given
Substitution Property of Equality
Definition of a Straight Angle

m∠RSV + m∠VST = m∠RST
m∠RSV + 35° – 35° = 180° – 35°
m∠RSV = 145°

Subtraction Property of Equality

USE WHAT YOU KNOW ABOUT PROOFS TO ANSWER THESE QUESTIONS.

1. Complete the two-column proof below.

Given: m∠1 = m∠3
m∠2 = m∠4

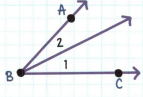 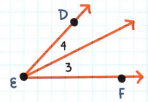

Prove: m∠ABC = m∠DEF

Statements	Reasons
1.	1.
2. m∠1 + m∠2 = m∠3 + m∠2	2. Addition Property of Equality
3. m∠1 + m∠2 = m∠3 + m∠4	3.
4. m∠1 + m∠2 = m∠ABC m∠3 + m∠4 = m∠DEF	4.
5. m∠ABC = m∠DEF	5.

2. Complete the proof below using a two-column format.

Given: Points A, B, and C

$\overline{AB} \cong \overline{BC}$

AB = 6x – 8

BC = 7x – 12

AC = 32

Prove: AB + BC = AC

Statements	Reasons

3. Fill in the missing steps in the flowchart to prove that $\overline{RS} \cong \overline{SU}$.

Given: $\overline{SU}$ bisects $\overline{RT}$

SU = ST

Prove: RS = SU

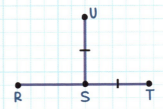

Given

$\overline{SU} \cong \overline{ST}$

_____

$\overline{RS} \cong \overline{ST}$

Angle Addition Postulate

Definition of Congruence

Definition of Congruence

CHAPTER 6

WORK SPACE

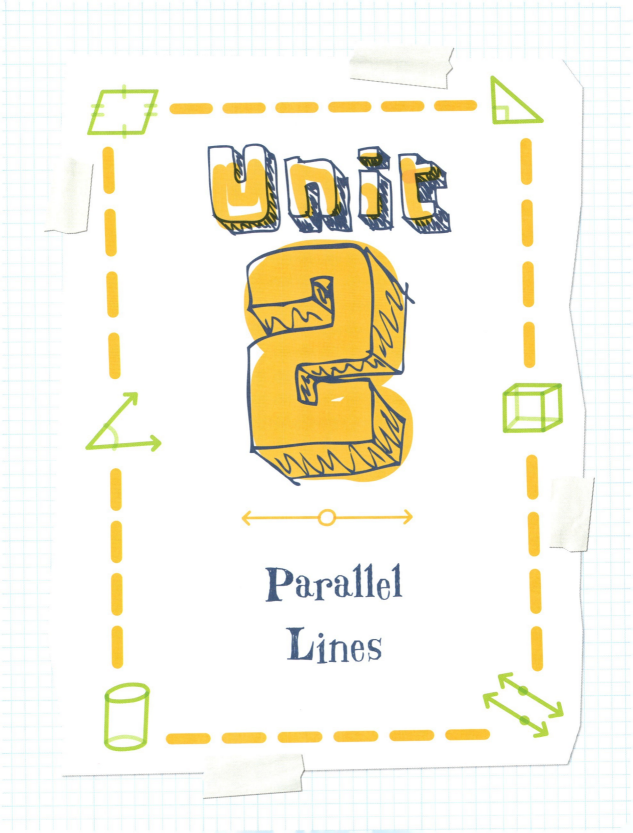

Unit 2

Parallel Lines

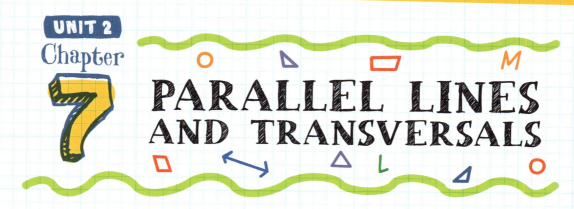

PARALLEL LINES AND TRANSVERSALS

PARALLEL LINES are lines on the same plane that *never* meet (intersect). They are indicated with arrows.

SKEW LINES are two lines that are not parallel and do not intersect.

PARALLEL PLANES are two planes that never intersect.

TRANSVERSALS

A **TRANSVERSAL** is a line that intersects two or more lines.

INTERIOR ANGLES are all the angles between the lines intersected by the transversal.

EXTERIOR ANGLES are all the angles that are not between the lines intersected by the transversal.

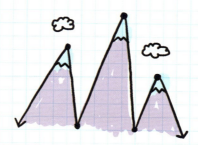

TRANSVERSAL ANGLE PAIRS

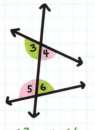

∠3 and ∠6
∠4 and ∠5

ALTERNATE INTERIOR ANGLES

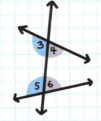

∠3 and ∠5
∠4 and ∠6

SAME-SIDE INTERIOR ANGLES

(Corresponding interior angles)

∠1 and ∠8
∠2 and ∠7

ALTERNATE EXTERIOR ANGLES

∠1 and ∠5
∠2 and ∠6
∠3 and ∠7
∠4 and ∠8

CORRESPONDING ANGLES

EXAMPLES:

1. Name all pairs of alternate interior, same-side interior, alternate exterior, and corresponding angles in the given figure.

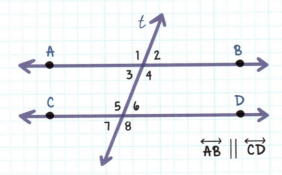

$\overleftrightarrow{AB} \parallel \overleftrightarrow{CD}$

ALTERNATE INTERIOR ANGLES		SAME-SIDE INTERIOR ANGLES	
∠3 and ∠6	∠3 ≅ ∠6	∠3 and ∠5	
∠4 and ∠5	∠4 ≅ ∠5	∠4 and ∠6	supplementary angles
ALTERNATE EXTERIOR ANGLES		**CORRESPONDING ANGLES**	
∠1 and ∠8	∠1 ≅ ∠8	∠1 and ∠5	∠1 ≅ ∠5
∠2 and ∠7	∠2 ≅ ∠7	∠2 and ∠6	∠2 ≅ ∠6
		∠3 and ∠7	∠3 ≅ ∠7
		∠4 and ∠8	∠4 ≅ ∠8

2. Name the alternate interior angle pairs in the given figure.

There are four transversals:
k, h, p, and t.

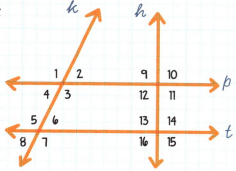

The alternate interior angle pairs are:

∠4 and ∠6, transversal k ∠2 and ∠12, transversal p

∠3 and ∠5, transversal k ∠3 and ∠9, transversal p

∠12 and ∠14, transversal h ∠6 and ∠16, transversal t

∠11 and ∠13, transversal h ∠7 and ∠13, transversal t

FOR QUESTIONS 1 THROUGH 4, USE THIS FIGURE.

The figure is made up of
quadrilaterals with right angles.

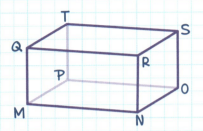

1. Name two parallel planes.

2. Name two skew segments.

3. Name two segments parallel to $\overline{TS}$.

4. Name two segments parallel to $\overline{QM}$.

FOR QUESTIONS 5 THROUGH 8, USE THIS FIGURE.

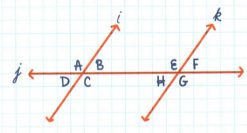

5. Name all alternate interior angle pairs.

6. Name all same-side interior angle pairs.

7. Name all alternate exterior angle pairs.

8. Name all corresponding angle pairs.

FOR QUESTIONS 9 THROUGH 12, USE THIS FIGURE.

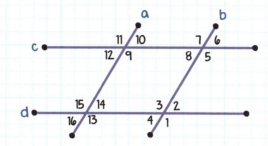

9. Find all same-side interior angles that are numbered.
   Name the transversal that connects each pair.

10. Find all alternate interior angles that are numbered.
    Name the transversal that connects each pair.

11. Find all alternate exterior angles that are numbered.
    Name the transversal that connects each pair.

12. Find all corresponding angles that are numbered.
    Name the transversal that connects each pair.

Chapter 8 PROVING SPECIAL ANGLE PAIRS

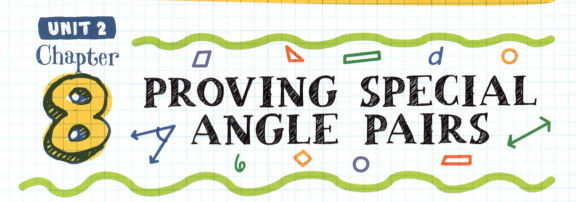

When two parallel lines are cut by a transversal, some of the **special angle pairs** formed have specific properties.

CORRESPONDING ANGLES POSTULATE

If two parallel lines are cut by a transversal, their corresponding angles are congruent.

lie on the same side of the transversal

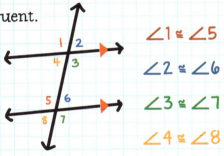

∠1 ≅ ∠5

∠2 ≅ ∠6

∠3 ≅ ∠7

∠4 ≅ ∠8

ALTERNATE INTERIOR ANGLES THEOREM

If two parallel lines are cut by a transversal, then their alternate interior angles are congruent.

∠1 ≅ ∠3

∠2 ≅ ∠4

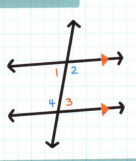

ALTERNATE EXTERIOR ANGLES THEOREM

If two parallel sides are cut by a transversal, then their alternate exterior angles are congruent.

$\angle 1 \cong \angle 3$

$\angle 2 \cong \angle 4$

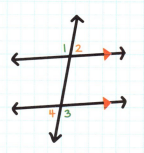

SAME-SIDE INTERIOR ANGLES THEOREM

If two parallel lines are cut by a transversal, then their same-side interior angles are supplementary.

$m\angle 1 + m\angle 4 = 180°$

$m\angle 2 + m\angle 3 = 180°$

Important note! To use the postulate and theorems given above, the lines that are cut by the transversal *must* be parallel.

Given the figure below, find the value of x and y. State the theorem, postulate, definition, or property you used to find those values.

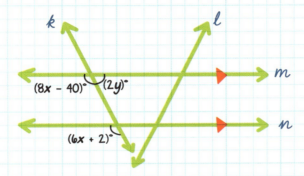

STEP 1: Find the value of x.

Use the **Corresponding Angles Postulate**.
The measures of these angles are equal.

$(8x - 40)° = (6x + 2)°$ Corresponding Angles Postulate

$8x - 40 + 40 = 6x + 2 + 40$ Addition Property of Equality

$8x = 6x + 42$

$8x - 6x = 6x - 6x + 42$ Subtraction Property of Equality

$2x = 42$

$2x ÷ 2 = 42 ÷ 2$ Division Property of Equality

$x = 21$

STEP 2: Find the value of y.

Use the Definition of a Straight Angle.
The sum of $(8x - 40)°$ and $(2y)°$ must be $180°$.

$8x - 40 + 2y = 180$ Definition of Straight Angle

$8(21) - 40 + 2y = 180$ $x = 21$; Substitution Property
                                              of Equality

$168 - 40 + 2y = 180$ Subtract to combine like terms

$128 + 2y = 180$

$128 - 128 + 2y = 180 - 128$ Subtraction Property of Equality

$2y = 52$

$2y ÷ 2 = 52 ÷ 2$ Division Property of Equality

$y = 26$

So, the value of x is 21, and the value of y is 26.

FOR QUESTIONS 1 THROUGH 5, USE THE FIGURE
BELOW. NAME THE THEOREM, POSTULATE,
DEFINITION, OR PROPERTY YOU USED TO FIND
EACH MEASURE.

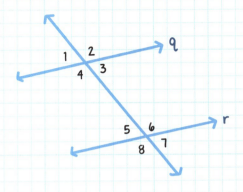

Given: q ∥ r

1. m∠1 = 50°. What is m∠5?

2. m∠3 = 50°. What is m∠6?

3. m∠2 = 130°. What is m∠8?

4. m∠3 = 50°. What is m∠7?

5. m∠6= 130°. What is m∠4?

FOR QUESTIONS 6 THROUGH 9, USE THE FIGURE BELOW. STATE ALL THE THEOREMS, POSTULATES, DEFINITIONS, OR PROPERTIES YOU USED TO FIND THE UNKNOWN VALUE.

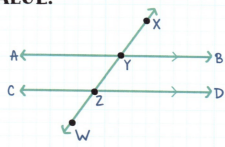

6. If $m\angle XYB = (3x + 38)°$ and $m\angle CZW = (8x - 77)°$, what is the value of x?

7. If $m\angle BYZ = (9y - 33)°$ and $m\angle DZY = (5y + 3)°$, what is the value of y?

8. If $m\angle AYX = (5z + 75)°$ and $m\angle DZY = (13z - 21)°$, what is the value of z?

9. If $m\angle CZW = (8k - 24)°$ and $m\angle DZW = (5k + 35)°$, what is the value of k?

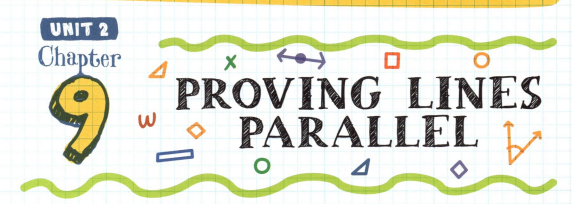

PROVING LINES PARALLEL

The converses of the parallel line theorems and postulates are true.

CONVERSE OF CORRESPONDING ANGLES POSTULATE

If corresponding angles are congruent, then the lines are parallel.

CONVERSE OF ALTERNATE INTERIOR ANGLES THEOREM

If alternate interior angles are congruent, then the lines are parallel.

CONVERSE OF SAME-SIDE INTERIOR ANGLES THEOREM

If same-side angles are supplementary, then the lines are parallel.

CONVERSE OF ALTERNATE EXTERIOR ANGLES THEOREM

If alternate exterior angles are congruent, then the lines are parallel.

Determine whether lines ℓ and m are parallel and state the reasoning.

Use the **Converse of Same-Side Interior Angles Theorem** to determine if the lines ℓ and m are parallel.

In this figure, the same-side interior angles are supplementary. (The sum of the angle measures is 180°: 74° + 106° = 180°.)

So, lines ℓ and m are parallel.

Determine whether lines r and s are parallel and state the reasoning.

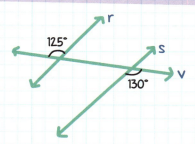

Use the **Converse of Alternate Exterior Angles Theorem** to determine if the lines r and s are parallel.

In this figure, the alternate exterior angles are *not* congruent. (The angle measures are not equal: 125° ≠ 130°.)

So, lines r and s are *not* parallel.

EXAMPLE:

Given: $a \parallel b$

$\angle 3 \cong \angle 2$

Prove: $c \parallel d$

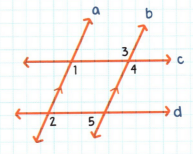

Use a two-column proof to prove $c \parallel d$.

STATEMENTS	REASONS
1. $a \parallel b$	**1.** Given
2. $\angle 3 \cong \angle 2$	**2.** Given
3. $m\angle 3 = m\angle 2$	**3.** Definition of Congruent Angles
4. $\angle 1 \cong \angle 3$	**4.** Alternate Interior Angles Theorem
5. $m\angle 1 = m\angle 3$	**5.** Definition of Congruent Angles
6. $\angle 1 \cong \angle 2$	**6.** Transitive Property of Equality: If $\angle 1 \cong \angle 3$ and $\angle 3 \cong \angle 2$, then $\angle 1 \cong \angle 2$.
7. $c \parallel d$	**7.** Converse of Corresponding Angles Postulate

FOR QUESTIONS 1 THROUGH 7, USE THE FIGURE
BELOW. IDENTIFY THE PARALLEL LINES AND
EXPLAIN HOW YOU KNOW THEY ARE PARALLEL.

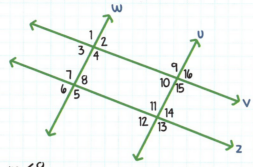

1. Given: m∠2 = m∠8.

   Parallel lines:

2. Given: m∠3 = m∠16.

   Parallel lines:

3. Given: m∠10 = m∠14.

   Parallel lines:

4. Given: m∠4 = m∠9.

   Parallel lines:

5. Given: m∠11 + m∠10 = 180°.

   Parallel lines:

6. Given: $m\angle 4 + m\angle 10 = 180°$.

Parallel lines:

7. Given: $m\angle 7 = m\angle 5$ and $m\angle 1 = m\angle 5$.

Parallel lines:

8. Examine the figure. Which lines are parallel? Explain your reasoning.

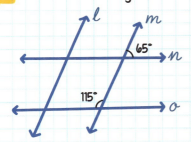

9. Complete each statement and reason for the following proof.

Given: $\angle 1 \cong \angle 2$

Prove: $m\angle 4 + m\angle 2 = 180°$

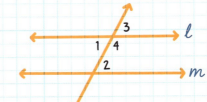

Statements	Reasons
1. $\angle 1 \cong \angle 2$	1. Given
2. $m\angle 1 = m\angle 2$	2.
3. $\angle 1 \cong \angle 3$	3.
4.	4. Definition of Congruent Angles
5. $m\angle 2 = m\angle 3$	5.
6.	6.
7.	7. Converse of Corresponding Angles Postulate
8. $m\angle 4 + m\angle 2 = 180°$	8.

10. Use a paragraph proof to show that if m∠2 + m∠5 = 180°, then ℓ || m.

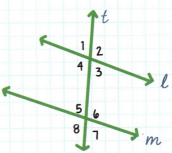

11. Examine the figure. Is e || f? Explain how you know.

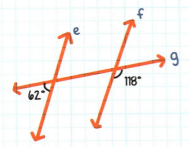

WORK SPACE

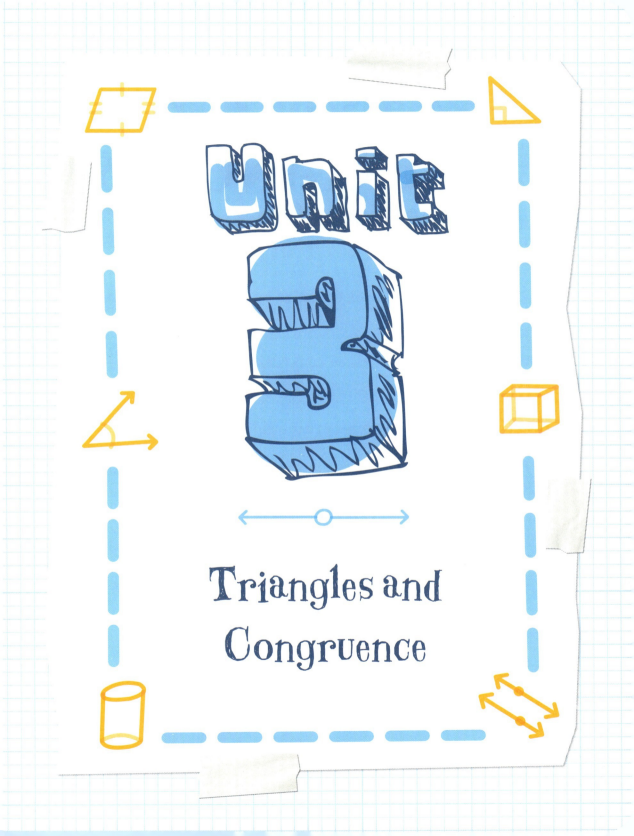

Unit 3

Triangles and Congruence

CLASSIFYING TRIANGLES

We can **CLASSIFY** (or organize) triangles by the **number of congruent sides** or **angles**.

Equilateral Triangle: three congruent sides, three congruent angles

Isosceles Triangle: two congruent sides, two congruent angles

Scalene Triangle: zero congruent sides, zero congruent angles

We can also classify triangles by their **types of angles**.

Acute Triangle: three acute angles (all angles less than 90°)

Obtuse Triangle: one obtuse angle (one angle greater than 90°)

Right Triangle: one right angle (one angle at 90°)

Equiangular Triangle: three congruent angles (each angle at 60°)

We can combine both systems of classification to describe a triangle more precisely.

EXAMPLE: Classify the triangles.

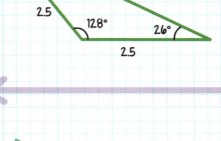

Angles: There are two congruent angles.
         There is one obtuse angle.

Sides: There are two congruent sides.

Type: An obtuse isosceles triangle

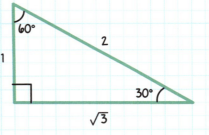

Angles: There is a right angle.

Sides: No two sides are congruent.

Type: A scalene right triangle.

ISOSCELES TRIANGLES

In an **ISOSCELES TRIANGLE**, the sides that are equal in length are called the **legs**. The third side is called the **base**. The angles opposite the legs are called the **base angles**.

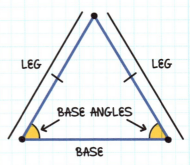

ISOSCELES TRIANGLE THEOREM

If two sides of a triangle are congruent, then the angles opposite those sides are congruent.

CONVERSE OF ISOSCELES TRIANGLE THEOREM

If two angles of a triangle are congruent, then the sides opposite those angles are also congruent.

EXAMPLE:

Reardon says that the value of y in $\triangle ABC$ must be 45. Is he correct? How do you know? Classify this triangle.

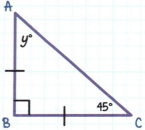

Reardon is correct. According to the Isosceles Triangle Theorem, if two sides (legs) of a triangle are congruent, then the angles opposite those sides are congruent. $\overline{AB} \cong \overline{BC}$, therefore $\angle C \cong \angle A$.

If $\angle C \cong \angle A$, then $m\angle A = m\angle C = 45°$, and therefore y must equal 45.

This triangle contains one right (90°) angle. Additionally, it contains opposite sides equal in length and opposite angles equal in measure.

So, this triangle is an isosceles right triangle.

FOR QUESTIONS 1 THROUGH 4, CLASSIFY EACH
TRIANGLE BY ITS NUMBER OF CONGRUENT SIDES
AND ANGLES.

1.

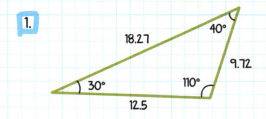

2.

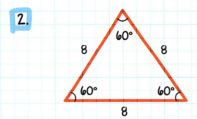

3.

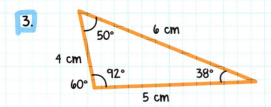

4.

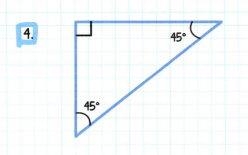

5. Find the value of z in the triangle shown. Then find the lengths of $\overline{CD}$ and $\overline{DE}$.

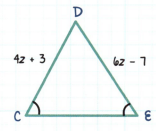

6. Find the values of w, x, and y in the triangle shown. Explain how you determined each value.

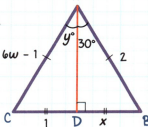

7. Marti says that an equilateral triangle has a right angle. Is she correct? Explain your reasoning.

INTERIOR AND EXTERIOR ANGLES

The angles inside a triangle are the **INTERIOR ANGLES**.

> ### TRIANGLE ANGLE-SUM THEOREM
>
> The sum of the measures of the three interior angles is $180°$.

The angles on the outside of the triangle are the **EXTERIOR ANGLES**.

∠2, ∠3, and ∠4 are interior angles.

∠1 is an exterior angle of △ABC.

∠1 and ∠2 are supplementary to each other.

m∠1 + m∠2 = $180°$

exterior angle

EXAMPLE: Find m∠A and m∠C in △ABC.

TRIANGLE ANGLE-SUM THEOREM:
the measures of the three interior angles in a triangle add up to $180°$.

m∠B = $90°$

$(2x - 1)°$

$(5x + 7)°$

STEP 1: Write an equation.

$m\angle A + m\angle B + m\angle C = 180°$

$(2x - 1)° + 90° + (5x + 7)° = 180°$ Substitute.

$2x + (-1) + 90 + 5x + 7 = 180$ Combine like terms.

$7x + 96 = 180$

$7x + 96 - 96 = 180 - 96$ Subtraction Property of Equality

$7x = 84$

$7x \div 7 = 84 \div 7$ Division Property of Equality

$x = 12$

STEP 2: Substitute $x = 12$ into each angle measure.

$m\angle A = (2x - 1)° = [2(12) - 1]° = 23°$

$m\angle C = (5x + 7)° = [5(12) + 7]° = 67°$

So, $m\angle A = 23°$ and $m\angle C = 67°$.

STEP 3: Check your work.

$m\angle A + m\angle B + m\angle C = 180° \rightarrow 23° + 90° + 67° = 180°$

$180° = 180°$ ✓

EXAMPLE:

Find m∠Q and m∠P in △NPQ.

The measure of an exterior angle is equal to the sum of the measures of the two nonadjacent interior angles.

So, the sum of m∠Q and m∠P is 161°.

STEP 1: Write an equation.

$m\angle Q + m\angle P = 161°$

$(5w - 3)° + (18w + 3)° = 161°$　　Substitute.

$5w + (-3) + 18w + 3 = 161$　　Combine like terms.

$23w + 0 = 161$
$23w = 161$

$23w \div 23 = 161 \div 23$　　Division Property of Equality

$w = 7$

STEP 2: Substitute $w = 7$ into each angle measure.

$m\angle Q = (5w - 3)° = [5(7) - 3]° = 32°$

$m\angle P = (18w + 3)° = [18(7) + 3]° = 129°$

STEP 3: Check your work.

$m\angle P + m\angle Q = 161° \longrightarrow 129° + 32° = 161°$

$161° = 161°$ ✓

USE WHAT YOU KNOW ABOUT EXTERIOR AND INTERIOR ANGLES TO ANSWER THE QUESTIONS.

1. Find the measure of ∠F in △FGH.

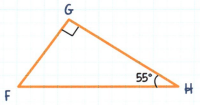

2. Find the measure of ∠A in △CHA.

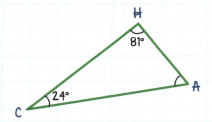

3. Find the measures of ∠R, ∠S, and ∠T in △RST.

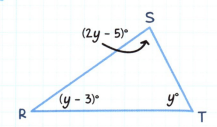

4. Find the measure of ∠KLO exterior to △PLK. Then find the measure of ∠KLP in △PLK.

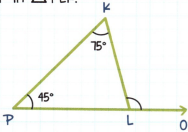

5. Find the measure of ∠BCA in △BAC.

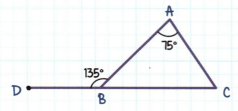

6. Find the value of *h* in the figure below.

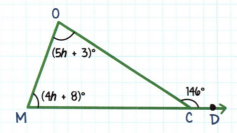

7. Find the measures of ∠NOP, ∠NOR, ∠NPO, and ∠PNO. Then find the value of *y*.

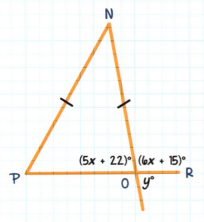

SIDE-SIDE-SIDE AND SIDE-ANGLE-SIDE CONGRUENCE

CONGRUENCE

Congruent polygons have the *same* shape and size.

Their **CORRESPONDING ANGLES** (angles in the same relative position on each figure) and **CORRESPONDING SIDES** are congruent.

If $\triangle ABC$ and $\triangle DEF$ are congruent, the corresponding angles are congruent:

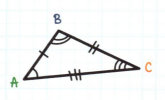

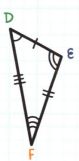

$\angle A \cong \angle D$, $\angle B \cong \angle E$, $\angle C \cong \angle F$

Also, the corresponding sides are congruent:

$\overline{AB} \cong \overline{DE}$, $\overline{BC} \cong \overline{EF}$, $\overline{AC} \cong \overline{DF}$

The congruence statement is $\triangle ABC \cong \triangle DEF$.

> **IMPORTANT:** Make sure the corresponding congruent angles are listed in the same order.

SIDE-SIDE-SIDE (SSS) CONGRUENCE POSTULATE

If the three sides of one triangle are congruent to the three sides of another triangle, then the triangles are congruent.

If the corresponding sides are congruent, then the angles are also congruent.

SIDE-ANGLE-SIDE (SAS) CONGRUENCE POSTULATE

If two sides and the included angle of one triangle are congruent to two sides and the included angle of another triangle, then the triangles are congruent.

EXAMPLE: Write a two-column proof to prove the two triangles are congruent.

Given: $\overline{MN} \cong \overline{MP}$ and $\overline{NO} \cong \overline{PO}$

Prove: $\triangle MNO \cong \triangle MPO$

STATEMENTS	REASONS
1. $\overline{MN} \cong \overline{MP}$ and $\overline{NO} \cong \overline{PO}$	1. Given
2. $\overline{MO} \cong \overline{MO}$	2. Reflexive Property of Congruence
3. $\triangle MNO \cong \triangle MPO$	3. Side-Side-Side Congruence Postulate

EXAMPLE: Triangles △XYZ and △BAC are congruent by SIDE-SIDE-SIDE (SSS) Congruence Postulate. What value of x ensures this congruence?

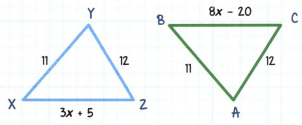

Given: XY = 11 and BA = 11

ZY = 12 and CA = 12

So, two sides are congruent:

$\overline{XY} \cong \overline{BA}$ and $\overline{ZY} \cong \overline{CA}$

Verify: $\overline{XZ} \cong \overline{BC}$

$XZ = BC$

$3x + 5 = 8x - 20$

$3x - 3x + 5 = 8x - 3x - 20$ Subtraction Property of Equality

$5 = 5x - 20$

$5 + 20 = 5x - 20 + 20$ Addition Property of Equality

$25 = 5x$

$25 \div 5 = 5x \div 5$ Division Property of Equality

$5 = x$

$3(5) + 5 = 8(5) - 20$ Substitute $x = 5$

$20 = 20$ ✓

So, $\overline{XY} \cong \overline{BA}$, $\overline{ZY} \cong \overline{CA}$, and $\overline{XZ} \cong \overline{BC}$.

The three sides of △XYZ are congruent to the three sides of △BAC. Therefore, according to the Side-Side-Side Congruence Postulate, the two triangles are congruent.

△XYZ ≅ △BAC

FOR QUESTIONS 1 THROUGH 4, IDENTIFY THE POSTULATE (SSS OR SAS) THAT TELLS WHY THE TRIANGLES ARE CONGRUENT. WRITE A CONGRUENCE STATEMENT AND EXPLAIN YOUR REASONING.

1.
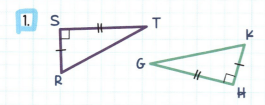

2.
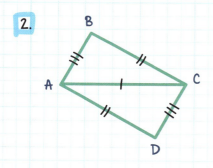

3.
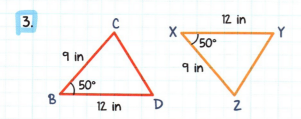

4.

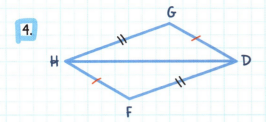

FOR QUESTIONS 5 THROUGH 8, DETERMINE IF THE GIVEN TRIANGLES ARE CONGRUENT. IF SO, WRITE A CONGRUENCE STATEMENT AND INCLUDE THE POSTULATE (SSS OR SAS) IT DEMONSTRATES.

5. △OAD ≅ △OBC

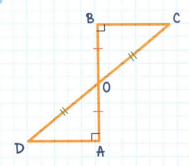

6. △BAC ≅ △FED

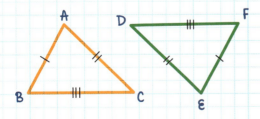

CHAPTER 12

7. △ABC ≅ △LMN

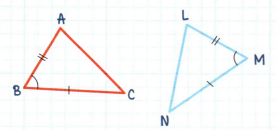

8. △PQR ≅ △TSV

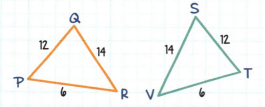

9. Gwen says that the given triangles are congruent by the Side-Angle-Side Postulate. Is she correct? Explain your reasoning.

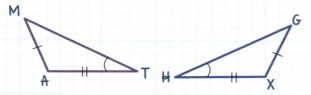

UNIT 3
Chapter 13
ANGLE-SIDE-ANGLE AND ANGLE-ANGLE-SIDE CONGRUENCE

Additional ways to determine if triangles are congruent:

ANGLE-SIDE-ANGLE (ASA) CONGRUENCE POSTULATE

If two angles and the included side of one triangle are congruent to two angles and the included side of another triangle, then the triangles are congruent.

ANGLE-ANGLE-SIDE (AAS) CONGRUENCE THEOREM

If two angles and the nonincluded side of one triangle are congruent to two angles and the nonincluded side of another triangle, then the triangles are congruent.

HYPOTENUSE-LEG THEOREM

specifically for right triangles

If the hypotenuse and a leg of one right triangle are congruent to the hypotenuse and a leg of another right triangle, then the triangles are congruent.

Write a two-column proof to prove the two triangles are congruent.
Use the Angle-Side-Angle (ASA) Congruence Postulate.

Given: $\overline{DC} \parallel \overline{AB}$

Prove: $\triangle ADC \cong \triangle CBA$

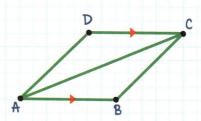

STATEMENTS	REASONS
1. $\overline{DC} \parallel \overline{AB}$	**1.** Given
2. $\angle ACD \cong \angle CAB$	**2.** When parallel lines are cut by a transversal, alternate interior angles are congruent.
3. $\angle DAC \cong \angle ACB$	**3.** When parallel lines are cut by a transversal, alternate interior angles are congruent.
4. $\overline{AC} \cong \overline{AC}$	**4.** Reflexive Property
5. $\triangle ADC \cong \triangle CBA$	**5.** Angle-Side-Angle (ASA) Congruence Postulate

Write a two-column proof to prove
the two triangles are congruent.
Use the Angle-Angle-Side Congruence
(AAS) Theorem.

Given: $\overline{FE}$ is an angle bisector of $\angle E$

   $\angle D \cong \angle G$

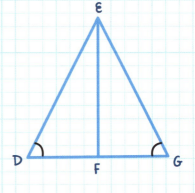

Prove: $\triangle DEF \cong \triangle GEF$

STATEMENTS	REASONS
1. $\overline{FE}$ is an angle bisector of $\angle E$ $\angle D \cong \angle G$	**1.** Given
2. $\angle DEF \cong \angle GEF$	**2.** Definition of Angle Bisector
3. $\overline{FE} \cong \overline{FE}$	**3.** Reflexive Property of Equality
4. $\triangle DEF \cong \triangle GEF$	**4.** Angle-Angle-Side (AAS) Congruence Theorem

THERE IS NO SIDE-SIDE-ANGLE
OR ANGLE-ANGLE-ANGLE
POSTULATE OR THEOREM.

FOR QUESTIONS 1 THROUGH 5, STATE THE
CONGRUENCE POSTULATE OR THEOREM THAT
WOULD BE USED TO PROVE THE TRIANGLES ARE
CONGRUENT. IF NONE EXISTS, ANSWER "NONE."

1.

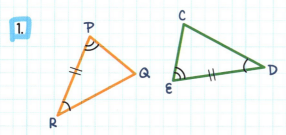

2.

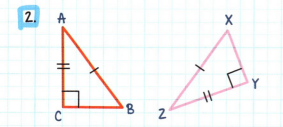

3.

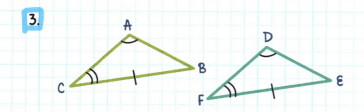

4.

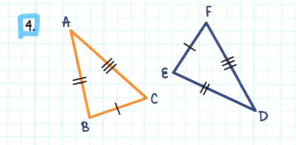

5.

6. Write a two-column proof to prove the two triangles are congruent.

Given: $\overline{HR}$ bisects ∠CRT

∠CHR ≅ ∠THR

Prove: △CRH ≅ △TRH

Statements	Reasons

7. Find the value of y that would make $\triangle PQR \cong \triangle STR$.

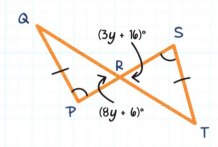

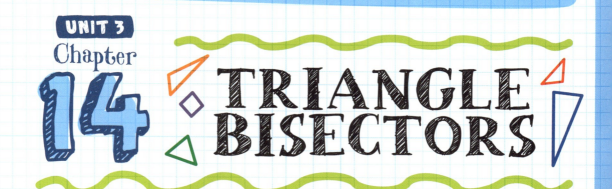

TRIANGLE BISECTORS

PERPENDICULAR BISECTORS

Perpendicular bisectors always cross a line segment at a right angle and divide it into two equal parts.

PERPENDICULAR BISECTOR THEOREM

If a point is on the perpendicular bisector of a line segment, then the point is equidistant to the segment's endpoints.

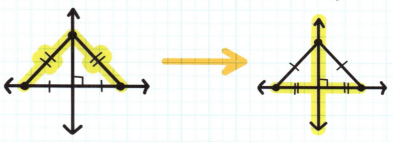

CONVERSE OF PERPENDICULAR BISECTOR THEOREM

If a point is equidistant to the endpoints of a segment, then it is on the perpendicular bisector of that segment.

Find the value of x and y in the figure.

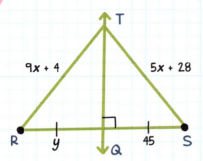

Since $\overrightarrow{TQ}$ is a perpendicular bisector of $\overline{RS}$, T is equidistant to R and S.

$\overline{RT} \cong \overline{TS}$

$9x + 4 = 5x + 28$

$9x - 5x + 4 = 5x - 5x + 28$ Subtraction Property of Equality

$4x + 4 - 4 = 28 - 4$ Subtraction Property of Equality

$4x \div 4 = 24 \div 4$ Division Property of Equality

$x = 6$

$9(6) + 4 = 5(6) + 28$ Substitution

$58 = 58$

Since RQ = QS, $y = 45$.

When three or more lines intersect at one point, they are **CONCURRENT**. Their point of intersection is called the **POINT OF CONCURRENCY**.

CIRCUMCENTER

In a triangle, there are three perpendicular bisectors that all meet at one point, the **CIRCUMCENTER**.

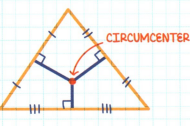

CIRCUMCENTER

The circumcenter can be outside or inside the triangle.

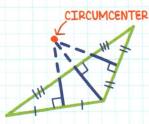

CIRCUMCENTER

CIRCUMCENTER THEOREM

The circumcenter of a triangle is equidistant to the vertices.

EXAMPLE: In △ABC, BD = 2z + 15 and DC = 3z + 10. Find the value of AD.

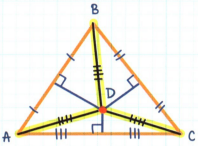

By the Circumcenter Theorem, the circumcenter is equidistant to the vertices, so BD = AD = DC.

STEP 1: Find the value of z.

BD = DC

2z + 15 = 3z + 10

2z − 2z + 15 = 3z − 2z + 10   Subtraction Property of Equality

15 − 10 = z + 10 − 10   Subtraction Property of Equality

5 = z

STEP 2: Find the value of BD (or DC, since they are the same length).

BD = 2z + 15   DC = 3z + 10
BD = 2(5) + 15 Substitution   DC = 3(5) + 10 Substitution
BD = 25   DC = 25

So, by the Circumcenter Theorem, AD = 25.

In a triangle, the angle bisectors of the three interior angles all meet at one point, the INCENTER.

INCENTER THEOREM

The incenter is equidistant to the sides of the triangle.

EXAMPLE: If G is the incenter of $\triangle$BAC, GF = $10y - 9$, and GD = $7y + 3$, find GE.

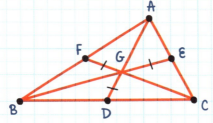

By the Incenter Theorem, the incenter is equidistant to the sides, so GF = GD = GE.

STEP 1: Find the value of y.

GF = GD

$10y - 9 = 7y + 3$

$10y - 7y - 9 = 7y - 7y + 3$ Subtraction Property of Equality

$3y - 9 + 9 = 3 + 9$ Addition Property of Equality

$3y \div 3 = 12 \div 3$ Division Property of Equality

$y = 4$

STEP 2: Find the value of GF (or GD, since they are the same length).

GF = 10y − 9   GD = 7y + 3
GF = 10(4) − 9   Substitution   GD = 7(4) + 3   Substitution
GF = 31   GD = 31

So, by the Incenter Theorem, GE = 31.

The **MEDIAN** of a triangle is a line from a vertex to the midpoint of the opposite side.

Every triangle has three medians, which meet at a point called the **CENTROID**.

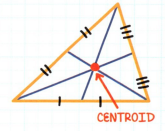

CENTROID

CENTROID THEOREM

The centroid is $\frac{2}{3}$ of the distance from each vertex to the midpoint of the opposite side.

EXAMPLE: In the given triangle, RY = 126. Find the measures of RU and UY.

By the Centroid Theorem:

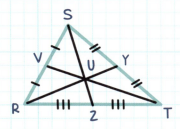

$RU = \frac{2}{3} RY$

$RU = \frac{2}{3} \cdot 126$

$RU = 84$

Now find UY using the **Segment Addition Postulate**:

$RY = RU + UY$

$126 = 84 + UY$

$126 - 84 = 84 - 84 + UY$

$42 = UY$

So, the measure of RU is 84 and the measure of UY is 42.

REMEMBER:

Segment Addition Postulate

If **B** is a point on a segment AC, then AB + BC = AC.

An **ALTITUDE** of a triangle is a line segment from a vertex to the opposite side, and perpendicular to that side. An altitude can be outside or inside the triangle. Every triangle has three altitudes.

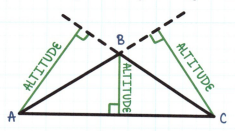

The point where the three altitudes meet is called the **ORTHOCENTER**. The orthocenter can be inside or outside the triangle.

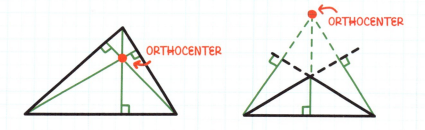

A way to help remember the term that matches each point of concurrency:

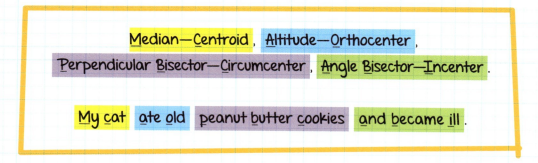

Median—Centroid, Altitude—Orthocenter, Perpendicular Bisector—Circumcenter, Angle Bisector—Incenter.

My cat ate old peanut butter cookies and became ill.

FOR QUESTIONS 1 THROUGH 5, DETERMINE IF
POINT H IS THE INCENTER, CIRCUMCENTER,
CENTROID, OR ORTHOCENTER OF THE TRIANGLE.
EXPLAIN HOW YOU KNOW.

1.

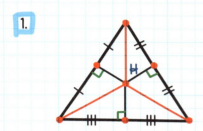

2.

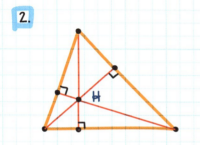

3.

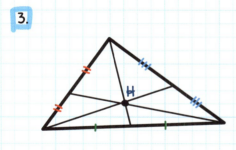

4.

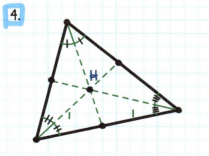

5.

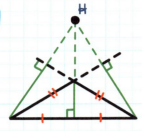

6. For the triangles below, state whether $\overline{RS}$ is a perpendicular bisector, median, or altitude. Tell how you know.

A.

B.

C.

7. Find the value of x.

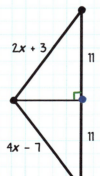

8. In △ABC, GD = 6y − 8 and DE = 5y + 6. Find the value of y.

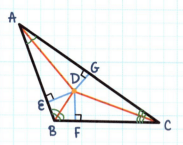

9. In △ANK, NM = 10. Find the measures of MG and NG.

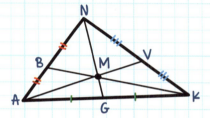

10. In △VXZ, XU = 12a + 4 and UZ = 5a + 18. Find the value of UV.

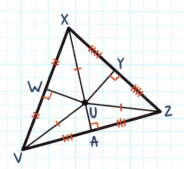

TRIANGLE INEQUALITIES

COMPARING SIDES AND ANGLES

The angle opposite the longer side is *larger than* the angle opposite the shorter side.

If AB > BC, then m∠C > m∠A.

The side opposite the larger angle is *longer than* the side opposite the smaller angle.

If m∠C > m∠A, then AB > BC.

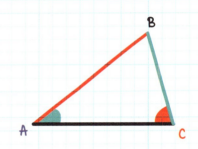

TRIANGLE INEQUALITY THEOREM

The sum of the lengths of any two sides in a triangle is greater than the length of the third side.

AB + BC > AC

BC + AC > AB

AB + AC > BC

Gio is designing a triangular table. His drawing shows two sides with lengths of 6.75 feet and 14.5 feet. What is the range of possible lengths Gio can draw for the third side?

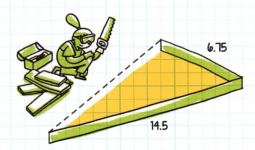

6.75

14.5

To find the range of possible lengths for the third side, assign the variable x for the third side. According to the Triangle Inequality Theorem, x must satisfy these conditions:

$x + 6.75 > 14.5$	$6.75 + 14.5 > x$	$14.5 + x > 6.75$
$x + 6.75 - 6.75$ $> 14.5 - 6.75$	$21.25 > x$	$14.5 - 14.5 + x$ $> 6.75 - 14.5$
$x > 7.75$	$x < 21.25$	$x > -7.75$

Since this calculation gives us a negative range, we can ignore it.

So, the length of the third side must be *greater than* 7.75 feet and *less than* 21.25 ft.

$7.75 < x < 21.25$

USE WHAT YOU KNOW ABOUT TRIANGLE INEQUALITIES TO ANSWER THE QUESTIONS.

1. List the sides in △ABC from *shortest* to *longest*.

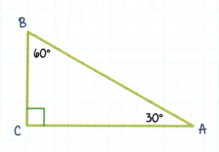

2. List the sides in △RST from *longest* to *shortest*.

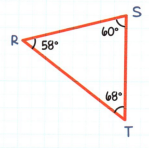

FOR QUESTIONS 3 THROUGH 5, STATE WHETHER IT IS POSSIBLE TO FORM A TRIANGLE WITH THE GIVEN SIDE LENGTHS.

3. 10, 18, 25

4. 8, 10, 16

5. 6.6, 10.4, 17.5

6. A triangle has two sides with lengths of 8.9 centimeters and 12.5 centimeters. Find the range of possible values for the third side.

7. A triangle has two sides with lengths of $6\frac{1}{4}$ inches and $15\frac{5}{8}$ inches. Find the range of possible values for the third side.

Unit 4

Quadrilaterals and Polygons

PARALLELOGRAMS

PROPERTIES OF PARALLELOGRAMS

Parallelograms have the following properties:

▶ congruent opposite sides

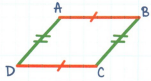

▶ congruent opposite angles

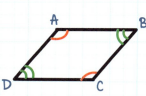

▶ consecutive angles that are supplementary

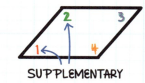

▶ diagonals bisect each other

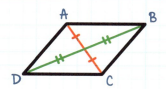

▶ each diagonal divides the parallelogram
  into two congruent triangles

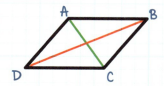

EXAMPLE: ABCD is a parallelogram. Find the measures of ∠A, ∠B, ∠C, and ∠D.

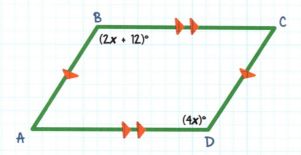

Use the properties of parallelograms:

▶ Opposite angles are congruent.

▶ Consecutive angles are supplementary (180°).

STEP 1: Find the value of x.

∠B and ∠D are opposite angles, so they are congruent.

$m\angle B = m\angle D$

$2x + 12 = 4x$

$2x - 2x + 12 = 4x - 2x$ Subtraction Property of Equality

$12 = 2x$

$12 \div 2 = 2x \div 2$ Division Property of Equality

$6 = x$

STEP 2: Since ∠B and ∠D are congruent, substitute $x = 6$ into the expressions to find the angle measures. Both expressions should have the same value.

$4x = ?$ $2x + 12 = ?$

$4(6) = 24$ $2(6) + 12 = 24$

So, m∠B = m∠D = 24°.

STEP 3: Write an equation to find the measures of ∠A and ∠C. Since consecutive angles are supplementary (180°), you can write two equations:

m∠A + m∠B = 180°
m∠C + m∠D = 180°

Substitute: 24°

m∠A + m∠B = 180°   m∠C + m∠D = 180°

m∠A + 24° = 180°   m∠C + 24° = 180°

m∠A + 24° − 24° = 180° − 24°   m∠C + 24° − 24° = 180° − 24°

m∠A = 156°   m∠C = 156°

So, m∠A = m∠C = 156°.

You can use these theorems to prove that a quadrilateral is a parallelogram:

> If both pairs of opposite sides are congruent, then it is a parallelogram.

> If both pairs of opposite angles are congruent, then it is a parallelogram.

> If an angle is supplementary to both of its consecutive angles, then it is a parallelogram.

> If a quadrilateral has diagonals that bisect each other, then it is a parallelogram.

> If a quadrilateral has one pair of sides that is both congruent and parallel, then it is a parallelogram.

EXAMPLE: Prove that RSTV is a parallelogram.

Given: $\overline{RT}$ bisects $\overline{SV}$

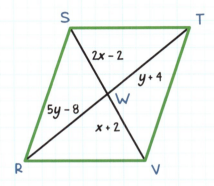

To prove RSTV is a parallelogram, you can write a two-column proof and use the theorem: **If a quadrilateral has diagonals that bisect each other, then it is a parallelogram.**

STATEMENTS	REASONS
1. $\overline{RT}$ bisects $\overline{SV}$	**1.** Given
2. Diagonal $\overline{RT}$	**2.** Given
3. RW = WT	**3.** $5y - 8 = y + 4$ Given expressions
	$5y - 8 + 8 = y + 4 + 8$
	Addition Property of Equality
	$5y = y + 12$
	$5y - y = y - y + 12$
	Subtraction Property of Equality
	$4y = 12$
	$4y \div 4 = 12 \div 4$
	Division Property of Equality
$5(3) - 8 = (3) + 4$	$y = 3$
$7 = 7$	
4. Diagonal $\overline{SV}$	**4.** Given

STATEMENTS	REASONS
5. SW = WV	**5.** $2x - 2 = x + 2$ Given expressions
	$2x - 2 + 2 = x + 2 + 2$ Addition Property of Equality
	$2x = x + 4$
	$2x - x = x - x + 4$ Subtraction Property of Equality
$2(4) - 2 = (4) + 2$ $6 = 6$	$x = 4$
6. RSTV is a parallelogram	**6.** $\overline{RW} \cong \overline{WT}$ and $\overline{SW} \cong \overline{WV}$ If a quadrilateral has diagonals that bisect each other, then it is a parallelogram.

USE WHAT YOU KNOW ABOUT QUADRILATERALS TO ANSWER THE QUESTIONS.

1. **Given:** Rhombus MRHP. Find all the missing lengths and angle measures.

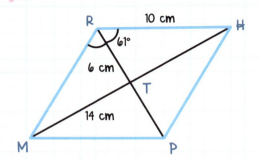

$\overline{MP}$ = _____ $\overline{TH}$ = _____

$\overline{MR}$ = _____ $\overline{TP}$ = _____

$\overline{HP}$ = _____

m∠M = _____ m∠R = _____ m∠H = _____ m∠P = _____

FOR QUESTIONS 2 THROUGH 5, WRITE ALL POSSIBLE QUADRILATERALS FOR EACH DESCRIPTION.

2. four congruent sides: _____

3. exactly one pair of parallel sides: _____

4. two pairs of parallel sides: _____

5. a parallelogram with four right angles: _____

6. ABCD is a parallelogram. Find the value of z.

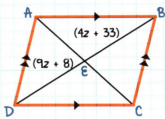

7. ABCD is a parallelogram. Find the measures of ∠A, ∠B, ∠C, and ∠D.

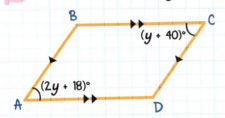

8. Find the values of x and y that would make ABCD a parallelogram.

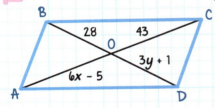

9. ABCD is a parallelogram. Find the measures of ∠C and ∠D.

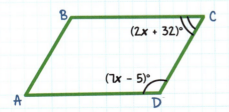

115

RHOMBUSES, RECTANGLES, AND SQUARES

Rhombuses, rectangles, and squares are quadrilaterals that are also parallelograms.

A **RHOMBUS** is a parallelogram with four congruent sides. Rhombuses have all the properties of a parallelogram, plus:

▶ Rhombuses have diagonals that are perpendicular.

▶ Each diagonal in a rhombus bisects a pair of opposite angles.

You can use these theorems to determine if a parallelogram is a rhombus:

> If a parallelogram has perpendicular diagonals, then it is a rhombus.

> If a parallelogram has one diagonal that bisects a pair of opposite angles, then it is a rhombus.

> If a parallelogram has one pair of consecutive congruent sides, then it is a rhombus.

EXAMPLE: Determine if ABCD is a rhombus.

Use a two-column proof and what you know about parallel lines, parallelograms, and rhombuses to prove ABCD is a rhombus.

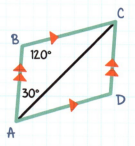

STATEMENTS	REASONS
1. ABCD is a parallelogram.	**1.** Properties of a Parallelogram (both pairs of opposite sides are parallel; $\overline{BC} \parallel \overline{AD}$ and $\overline{AB} \parallel \overline{DC}$)
2. $\angle CAB \cong \angle ACD$	**2.** Alternate Interior Angles Theorem
3. $m\angle CAB = m\angle ACD$	**3.** Definition of Congruence $m\angle ACD = m\angle CAB = 30°$
4. $m\angle ACB = 30°$	**4.** Triangle Angle-Sum Theorem (the sum of the measures of the interior angles of $\triangle ABC$ must equal 180°) $m\angle ACB + 120° + 30° = 180°$ $m\angle ACB + 150° = 180°$ $m\angle ACB + 150° - 150° = 180° - 150°$ $m\angle ACB = 30°$

STATEMENTS	REASONS
5. ∠ACB ≅ ∠CAD	**5.** Alternate Interior Angles Theorem
6. m∠ACB = m∠CAD	**6.** Definition of Congruence m∠CAD = m∠ACB = 30°
7. m∠BAD = m∠BCD	**7.** m∠BAD = 30° + 30° = 60° m∠BCD = 30° + 30° = 60°
8. $\overline{AC}$ bisects ∠BAD and ∠BCD	**8.** Definition of Angle Bisector
9. ABCD is a rhombus	**9.** Since a diagonal of ABCD bisects a pair of opposite angles, it is a rhombus.

A **RECTANGLE** is a parallelogram with four right angles.

▶ If a parallelogram is a rectangle, then its diagonals are congruent.

▶ The converse of this is also true: If a parallelogram has congruent diagonals, then it is a rectangle.

EXAMPLE: Given that ABCD is a rectangle, AC = $18y - 20$, and BD = $9y + 25$, find the values of y, AC, and BD.

Given: Rectangle ABCD

$$AC = 18y - 20$$
$$BD = 9y + 25$$

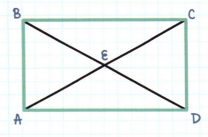

Rectangles have diagonals that are congruent. That means AC = BD.

STEP 1: Write an equation and solve for y.

AC = BD

$18y - 20 = 9y + 25$

$18y - 20 + 20 = 9y + 25 + 20$ Addition Property of Equality

$18y = 9y + 45$

$18y - 9y = 9y - 9y + 45$ Subtraction Property of Equality

$9y = 45$

$9y \div 9 = 45 \div 9$ Division Property of Equality

$y = 5$

STEP 2: Substitute $y = 5$ into each expression for AC and BD.

AC = $18y - 20$	BD = $9y + 25$
AC = $18(5) - 20$	BD = $9(5) + 25$
AC = 70	BD = 70

So, the value of y is 5, and AC = BD = 70.

A **SQUARE** is a parallelogram with four right angles and four congruent sides.

A square is both a rectangle *and* a rhombus.

EXAMPLE: Given that RSTV is a square, find the values of x and y.

Given: Square RSTV
RV = $4x + 3$
RS = 27
$m\angle S = (2y + 8)°$

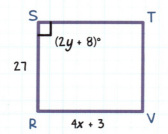

A square has four congruent sides. That means $\overline{RV} \cong \overline{RS}$.

A square has four right angles. That means $m\angle S = 90°$.

STEP 1: Write an equation to solve for x.

RV = RS

$4x + 3 = 27$

$4x + 3 - 3 = 27 - 3$ Subtraction Property of Equality

$4x = 24$

$4x \div 4 = 24 \div 4$ Division Property of Equality

$x = 6$

STEP 2: Write an equation to solve for y.

$m\angle S = 90°$

$(2y + 8)° = 90°$

$2y + 8 - 8 = 90 - 8$ Subtraction Property of Equality

$2y = 82$

$2y \div 2 = 82 \div 2$ Division Property of Equality

$y = 41$

So, the value of x is 6 and the value of y is 41.

FOR QUESTIONS 1 THROUGH 4, INDICATE WHETHER THE STATEMENT IS *TRUE* OR *FALSE*. IF YOUR ANSWER IS *FALSE*, EXPLAIN YOUR REASONING.

1. All quadrilaterals are rectangles.

2. All squares are rectangles.

3. A square and a rectangle have two pairs of adjacent sides that are congruent.

4. All rhombuses are not squares.

5. Name all possible quadrilaterals that have two pairs of congruent sides.

6. Name all possible quadrilaterals that have two pairs of parallel sides.

7. Name all possible quadrilaterals that have four congruent sides and four congruent angles.

8. Given that CRST is a rhombus, find the value of w and the length of $\overline{RT}$.

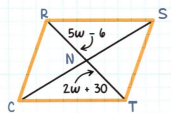

Explain how you determined the value of w and the measure of $\overline{RT}$.

Given: Rhombus CRST

RN = $5w - 6$

TN = $2w + 30$

9. Determine if GFHJ is a rhombus.

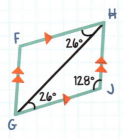

10. Find the values of a and b and the lengths of $\overline{KL}$ and $\overline{LM}$. Explain how you determined the values and lengths of the sides.

Given: Square KLMN

KL = $3a + 11$

LM = $10a - 3$

m∠N = $(6b)°$

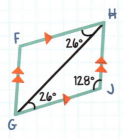

11. Find the value of y in rhombus TUVW below. Explain how you determined the value of y.

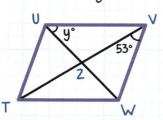

12. Find the measure of ∠ABD and the lengths of $\overline{AB}$ and $\overline{CD}$. Explain how you determined the angle measure and side lengths.

Given: Rectangle ABCD

AB = 6x - 20

CD = x + 15

m∠DBC = 44°

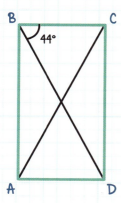

UNIT 4
Chapter
18 TRAPEZOIDS AND KITES

Trapezoids and kites are quadrilaterals that are not parallelograms.

A **TRAPEZOID** is a quadrilateral with exactly *one pair* of parallel sides.

The parallel sides are called bases, and the nonparallel sides are called legs.

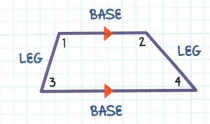

The angles adjacent to a base are called base angles.

∠1 and ∠2 are base angles to the *top base*.

∠3 and ∠4 are base angles to the *bottom base*.

The **MIDSEGMENT** of a trapezoid is a line segment that *bisects both legs* and is parallel to the bases.

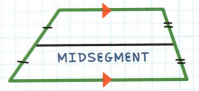

You can find the length of the midsegment by averaging the lengths of the two bases.

An **ISOSCELES TRAPEZOID** has congruent legs.

> If a trapezoid is isosceles,
> then it has two pairs of congruent base angles.

> A trapezoid is isosceles if and only if its diagonals
> are congruent.

A **KITE** is a quadrilateral with *two pairs* of
adjacent congruent sides.

> If a quadrilateral is a kite, then its diagonals
> are perpendicular.

> If a quadrilateral is a kite, then at least one pair
> of opposite angles are congruent.

EXAMPLE:

Given trapezoid DABC
with midsegment $\overline{FE}$,
find the lengths of $\overline{AB}$ and $\overline{DC}$.

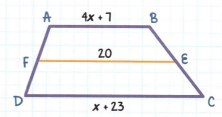

Since the length of the midsegment is found by averaging the lengths of the two bases, you can write an equation to find the value of x.

Equation: Length of Midsegment = $\dfrac{\text{Base 1} + \text{Base 2}}{2}$

Substitute: Midsegment = 20; Base 1 = $4x + 7$; Base 2 = $x + 23$

$20 = \dfrac{(4x + 7) + (x + 23)}{2}$

$20 = \dfrac{5x + 30}{2}$ Combine like terms

$20\,(2) = \dfrac{5x + 30}{2}\,(2)$ Multiplication Property of Equality

$40 = 5x + 30$

$40 - 30 = 5x + 30 - 30$ Subtraction Property of Equality

$10 = 5x$

$10 \div 5 = 5x \div 5$ Division Property of Equality

$2 = x$

To find the lengths of $\overline{AB}$ and $\overline{DC}$, substitute $x = 2$ into each expression.

Top Base: $\overline{AB}$	Bottom Base: $\overline{DC}$
$4x + 7$	$x + 23$
$4(2) + 7$	$2 + 23$
15	25

So, the length of $\overline{AB}$ is 15, and the length of $\overline{DC}$ is 25.

CHAPTER 18

USE WHAT YOU KNOW ABOUT TRAPEZOIDS AND KITES TO ANSWER THE QUESTIONS.

1. Explain why a trapezoid cannot be a parallelogram.

2. Jaquez says every kite is a rhombus. Is she correct? Explain your reasoning.

3. Trapezoid ABCD has two pairs of congruent base angles. One of the angles measures 128°. What are the measures of the other angles? Explain how you know.

4. Given: $\overline{PQ}$ is a midsegment. Find the value of x.

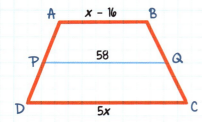

5. Find the measures of ∠M, ∠N, and ∠P.

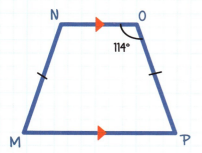

6. The diagonals of an isosceles trapezoid have lengths of 6z + 14 and 5z + 22.

Find the value of z.

7. Find the value of h.

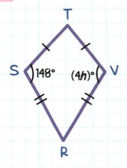

8. Given kite FJHK, find the measures of ∠HKE, ∠HJE, and ∠JHE.

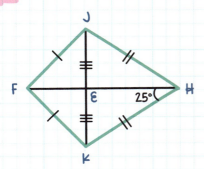

UNIT 4
Chapter
19
ANGLE MEASURES IN POLYGONS

A **POLYGON** is a closed plane figure with at least three straight sides. A regular polygon has all congruent sides and all congruent angles.

Polygons are named by the number of sides they have.

INTERIOR ANGLE MEASURES

The interior angles of a polygon are found inside the boundaries of the shape.

The interior angles of a triangle have measures that add up to 180°.

The interior angles of a quadrilateral have measures that add up to 360°.

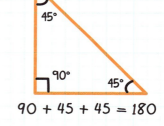

$$90 + 45 + 45 = 180$$

Rule: Each time you *add* a side to a polygon, *add* another $180°$ to the total of the sum of the measures of the interior angles.

To find the **sum of the interior angles of a polygon,** always use this formula:

sum of interior angles = $(n - 2) \cdot 180°$, where n equals the number of sides

THINK: This means "the number of triangles that make up the polygon times 180°."

To find the measure of each interior angle in a regular polygon, divide the total angle measure *by* the number of sides.

EXAMPLE: A regular octagon has **8 congruent sides** and **8 congruent angles**.

Sum of interior angles = $(n - 2) \cdot 180°$

$= (8 - 2) \cdot 180°$

$= 6 \cdot 180°$

$= 1,080°$

So, each angle's measure in a regular octagon is

$\dfrac{1,080°}{8} = 135°$.

total interior angle measure

number of sides

EXTERIOR ANGLE MEASURES

An exterior angle is an angle between the side of a polygon and a line extended from the next side.

> ## POLYGON EXTERIOR ANGLE-SUM THEOREM
>
> The sum of the exterior angles of a polygon is always 360 degrees, no matter how many sides the polygon has.

Note: Use only one exterior angle at each vertex when calculating the sum of exterior angles.

The two exterior angles at each vertex have the same measure.

∠2 and ∠3 are both exterior angles for ∠1.

∠2 ≅ ∠3 (Vertical angles are congruent.)

vertical angles

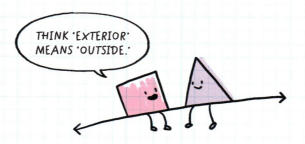

THINK "EXTERIOR" MEANS "OUTSIDE."

The given figure is a regular pentagon. What is the measure of each interior angle, the measure of each exterior angle, and the length of each side?

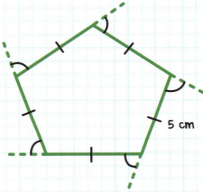

5 cm

In a regular polygon, all interior angles have the same measure, all exterior angles have the same measure, and all sides have the same length.

STEP 1: Find the sum of the measures of all interior angles.

Use the formula for the sum of interior angles.

Sum of interior angles = $(n - 2) \cdot 180°$

$= (5 - 2) \cdot 180°$

$= 3 \cdot 180°$

$= 540°$

STEP 2: To find the measure of each angle, divide the sum of the interior angles by 5, the number of sides in the figure.

So, each interior angle's measure in a regular pentagon is

$\dfrac{540°}{5} = 108°$.

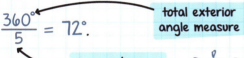

total interior
angle measure

number
of sides

STEP 3: To find the measure of each exterior angle, use the Polygon Exterior Angle-Sum Theorem.

The measures of all exterior angles sum to 360°.

So, each exterior angle measure in a regular pentagon is

$\dfrac{360°}{5} = 72°$.

total exterior
angle measure

number
of sides

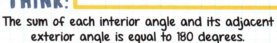

THINK:

The sum of each interior angle and its adjacent exterior angle is equal to 180 degrees.

Interior Angle + Exterior Angle = Straight Angle

108° + 72° = 180°

STEP 4: Identify the length of all sides.

The length of one side of this regular polygon is 5 cm, so all sides have a length of 5 cm.

Therefore, the measure of each interior angle is 108°, the measure of each exterior angle is 72°, and the length of each side of the pentagon is 5 cm.

USE WHAT YOU KNOW ABOUT POLYGONS TO ANSWER THE QUESTIONS.

1. Find the sum of the measures of the interior angles of a 12-sided polygon.

2. What is the measure of the sum of the exterior angles in the given polygon?

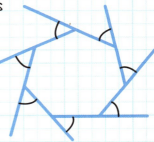

3. Kyle determines that the sum of the measures of a regular polygon is 1,620°. How many sides does the polygon have?

4. What is the measure of the sum of the exterior angles in a heptagon?

CHAPTER 19

5. Find the measure of the exterior angle in each polygon.

A.)

B.)

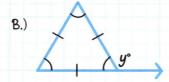

6. Find the value of x.

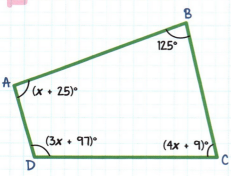

7. Find the value of a.

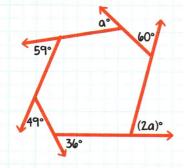

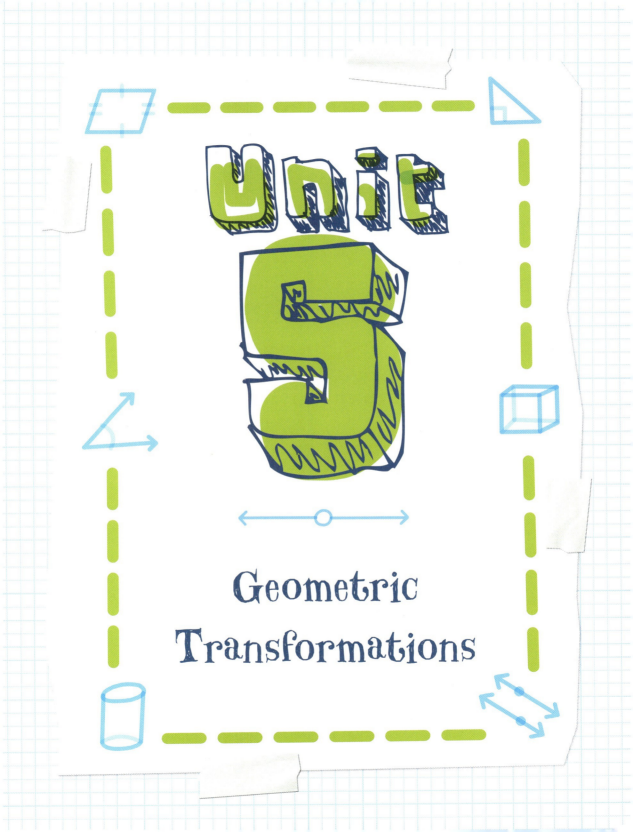

Unit 5

Geometric Transformations

20 REFLECTIONS

A geometric **TRANSFORMATION** is a change in the position or size of a figure. A transformation of a figure creates a new figure that is related to the original.

If the shape and the size of a figure remain the same after a transformation, the movement is called a **RIGID MOTION** or **CONGRUENCE TRANSFORMATION**.

There are three types of rigid motions: reflections, translations, and rotations.

A **REFLECTION** is a type of transformation that flips an image over a *line of reflection*, so that the image appears backward, like in a mirror.

A reflection is a rigid motion: The shape and size of the image do *not* change.

In any transformation, the original figure is called the **PREIMAGE**, and the new figure is called the **IMAGE**.

△ABC is the preimage, and △A'B'C' is the image.

The mark (') is called **PRIME**.
The prime mark (') represents the
new position of a point of the preimage.

△A'B'C' is read as "triangle A prime,
B prime, C prime."

Line l is the **LINE OF REFLECTION**.
We say △ABC is *reflected* across line l.

The reflection maps each point on △ABC to a corresponding
point on △A'B'C'.

A maps to A'   B maps to B'   C maps to C'

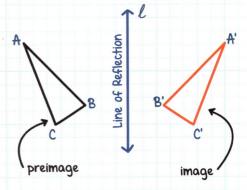

REFLECTIONS ON THE COORDINATE PLANE

Reflections can be shown on the coordinate plane.
The red line is the line of reflection. This one is
written as $x = 1$.

$x = 1$ means that all points on this line
of reflection have an x-coordinate of 1.

For example, points on the line $x = 1$
include (1, -1), (1, 0), and (1, 2).

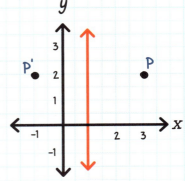

Point P, written as P(3, 2), is 2 units to the right of the line of reflection.

Point P', written as P'(-1, 2), is 2 units to the left of the line of reflection.

We say that P(3, 2) *maps* to P'(-1, 2). We show this with an arrow: P(3, 2) → P'(-1, 2).

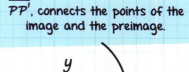

$\overline{PP'}$, connects the points of the image and the preimage.

The line of reflection is the PERPENDICULAR BISECTOR of the line segment that connects the corresponding points of the image and preimage.

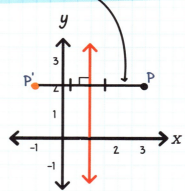

The line $x = 1$ (line of reflection) is the perpendicular bisector of $\overline{PP'}$.

Line of Reflection Rules

LINE OF REFLECTION	RULE	
x-axis	$(x, y) \rightarrow (x, -y)$	multiply the y-coordinate by -1.
y-axis	$(x, y) \rightarrow (-x, y)$	multiply the x-coordinate by -1.
$y = x$	$(x, y) \rightarrow (y, x)$	reverse the order of the coordinates

the same as $y = 1x + 0$

EXAMPLE:

Reflect the triangle RST on the coordinate plane across line $y = -2$.

Since the line of reflection is the perpendicular bisector of $\overline{RR'}$, $\overline{SS'}$, and $\overline{TT'}$, each point on the line of reflection will be equidistant from R and R', S and S', and T and T'.

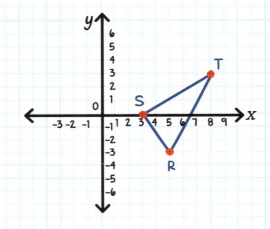

STEP 1: Count how many units away from $y = -2$ (the line of reflection) each point is.

▶ R is at point (5, -3), 1 unit below the line of reflection. R' will be at point (5, -1), 1 unit above the line of reflection. R(5, -3) → R'(5, -1).

▶ S is at point (3, 0), 2 units above the line of reflection. S' will be 2 units below the line of reflection. S(3, 0) → S'(3, -4).

▶ Point T(8, 3) is 5 units above the line of reflection. T' will be 5 units below the line of reflection. T(8, 3) → T'(8, -7).

STEP 2: Plot and label each image point.

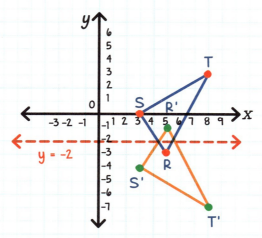

FOR QUESTIONS 1 THROUGH 4, DRAW THE IMAGE OF THE KITE LMJK, WHERE L(1, 2), M(1, 5), J(4, 5), AND K(5, 1) ARE REFLECTED ACROSS THE FOLLOWING AXES OR LINES.

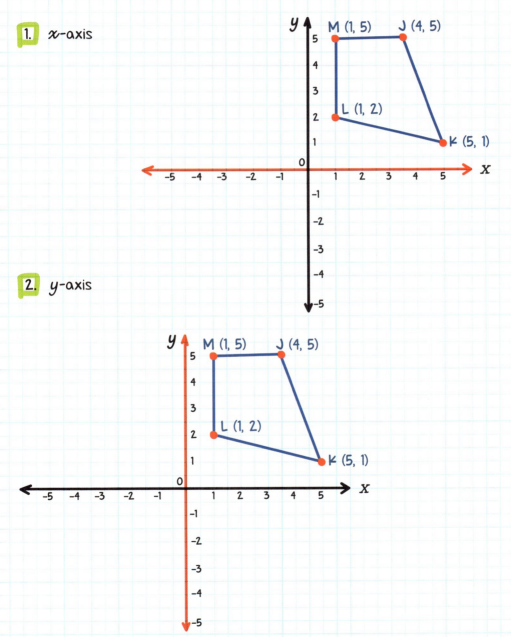

1. x-axis

2. y-axis

CHAPTER 20

3. $x = -1$

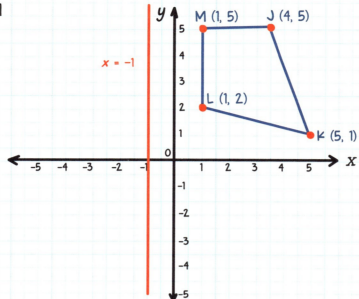

4. $y = -2$

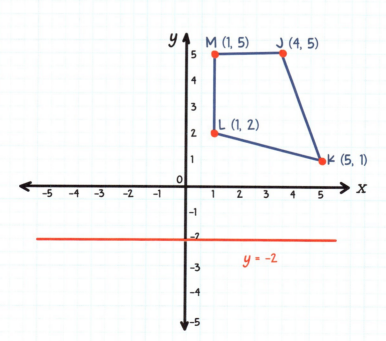

5. Reflect the triangle on the coordinate plane across the line $y = x$.

Preimage points: W(-3, -3), U(-4, 4), and V(-1, 1)

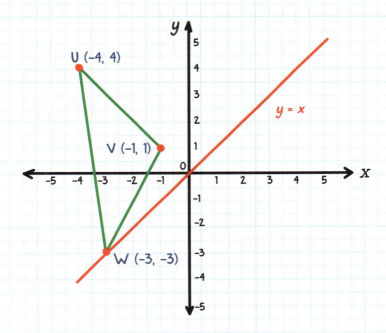

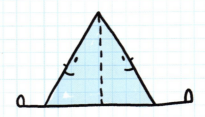

TRANSLATIONS

A **TRANSLATION** is a type of rigid motion that slides a figure a certain distance horizontally (to the left or right), vertically (up or down), or both.

Each point in the figure slides *the same distance* in *the same direction.*

> In a translation, the figure's shape, size, and orientation remain the same.

A translation on the coordinate plane moves all the points in the image the same distance and in the same direction.

In △ABC, each point moves:

    4 units right (*x* direction)
    2 units up (*y* direction)

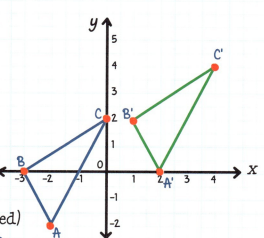

Translations can be defined (described) by using a **TRANSLATION VECTOR**, which states how many units each point in the graph moves in the translation.

The translation vector in this figure is (4, 2).

> 4 units in the x direction
>
> 2 units in the y direction

If a translation vector moves a points a units along the x-axis and b units along the y-axis, then the translation vector is (a, b).

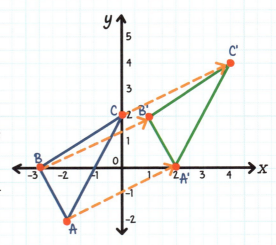

The translation rule is:

$(x, y) \longrightarrow (x + a, y + b)$, where (a, b) is the translation vector.

EXAMPLE:

Graph the translation of △ABC, given a translation vector of (4, -9).

Translation vector: (4, -9)

Move each vertex 4 units to the right and 9 units down.

Translation rule: $(x, y) \longrightarrow (x + 4, y - 9)$

STEP 1: Write the preimage coordinates.

A(-6, 1), B(-2, 7), and C(3, 5)

STEP 2: Determine each translated point.

Preimage Points	Translation $(x + 4, y - 9)$	Image Points
A(−6, 1)	(−6 + 4, 1 − 9)	A'(−2, −8)
B(−2, 7)	(−2 + 4, 7 − 9)	B'(2, −2)
C(3, 5)	(3 + 4, 5 − 9)	C'(7, −4)

STEP 3: Plot, label, and connect the image points. This is △A'B'C'.

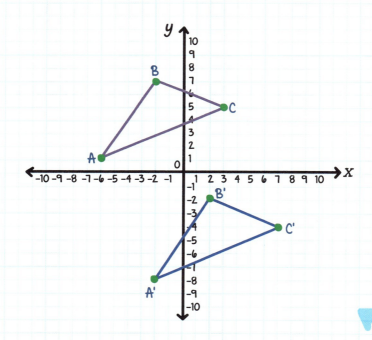

EXAMPLE:

What are the translation vector and translation rule that describe the translation of quadrilateral HEFG ⟶ H'E'F'G'?

Each point, H, E, F, and G, moves 3 units to the left and 6 units down to H', E', F', and G', respectively.

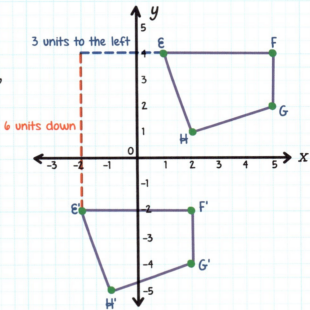

The translation vector is $(-3, -6)$.

The translation rule is: $(x, y) \rightarrow (x - 3, y - 6)$.

Preimage Points	Translation $(x - 3, y - 6)$	Image Points
H(2, 1)	(2 − 3, 1 − 6)	H'(-1, -5)
E(1, 4)	(1 − 3, 4 − 6)	E'(-2, -2)
F(5, 4)	(5 − 3, 4 − 6)	F'(2, -2)
G(5, 2)	(5 − 3, 2 − 6)	G'(2, -4)

USE WHAT YOU KNOW ABOUT TRANSLATIONS TO ANSWER THE QUESTIONS.

1. What is the translation vector that translates A to A'?

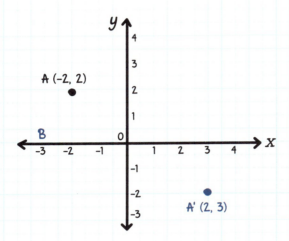

FOR QUESTIONS 2 THROUGH 5, STATE WHETHER OR NOT THE GRAPH ILLUSTRATES A TRANSLATION. IF IT IS A TRANSLATION, STATE THE TRANSLATION VECTOR AND THE TRANSLATION RULE.

2.

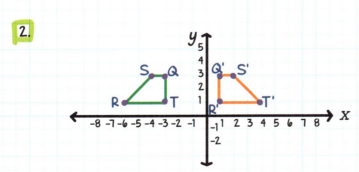

3.

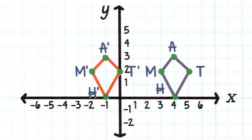

4.

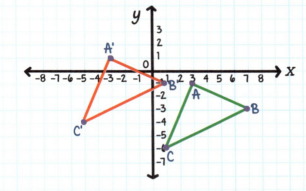

5.

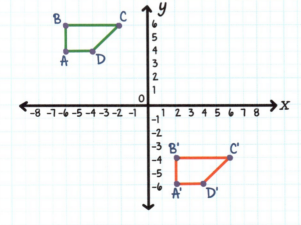

6. Graph the translation of △XYZ, given a translation vector of (3, −1).

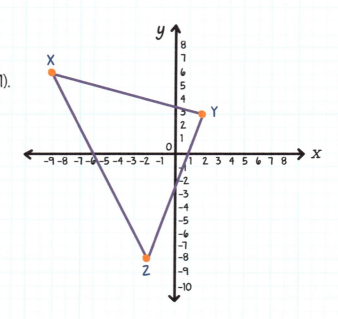

7. Graph the translation of the rectangle ABCD, given a translation vector of (−7, −6).

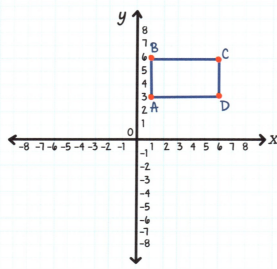

8. Graph a polygon with the following points: M (2, 1), A (2, 4), T (5, 4), and H (5, 2). Then illustrate a transformation using the translation rule:

$(x, y) \longrightarrow (x - 4, y + 5)$.

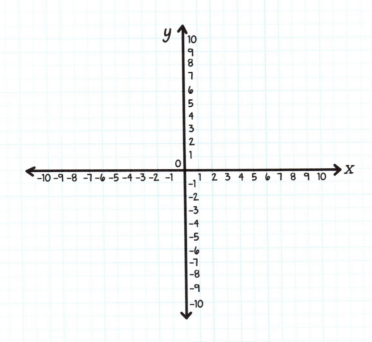

UNIT 5
Chapter
22 ROTATIONS

ROTATIONS are transformations that turn a figure around a fixed point.

Rotations are rigid motions. The shape, size, and measures of angles of the figure *stay the same*, but the orientation changes.

A rotation includes a(n):

CENTER OF ROTATION—the point around which a figure is turned. The center of rotation can be located outside the figure or anywhere inside or along the figure.

ANGLE OF ROTATION—the number of degrees each point on the figure is turned. Rotation can be *clockwise* or *counterclockwise*.

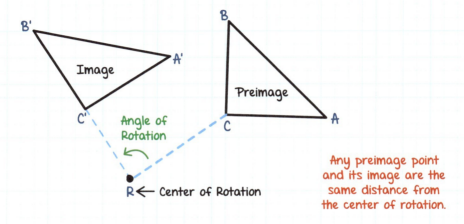

Any preimage point and its image are the same distance from the center of rotation.

DRAWING ROTATIONS

You can use a protractor and a ruler to draw a rotation about a point.

EXAMPLE: Rotate point K 70° counterclockwise about point P.

STEP 1: Draw a line from P to K.

STEP 2: Use a protractor to draw a 70-degree angle counterclockwise, left from $\overline{PK}$.

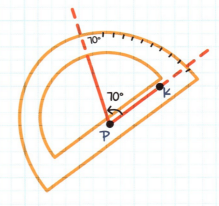

STEP 3: Measure the length of $\overline{PK}$. Draw a new point, labeled K', the same distance from P on the new line.

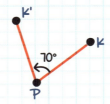

FINDING THE ANGLE OF ROTATION

You can find an angle of rotation with a protractor and ruler.

EXAMPLE: A figure is rotated counterclockwise about a point located at (-1, 0).

Point (2, 2) is rotated to (-3, 3). Find the angle of rotation.

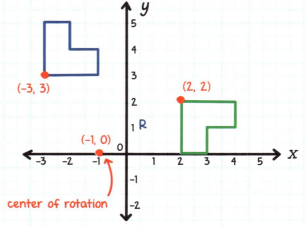

STEP 1: Draw a line from the center of the rotation through each point (2, 2) and (-3, 3).

STEP 2: Use a protractor to measure the angle.

So, the angle of rotation is **90°**.

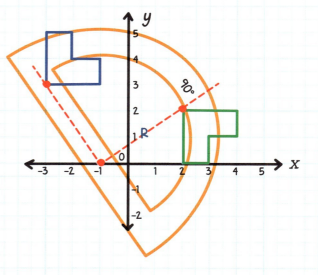

FINDING THE CENTER OF ROTATION

To find the center of rotation between the two figures below, follow these steps.

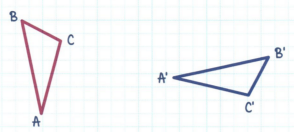

STEP 1: Draw a line to connect A and A'.

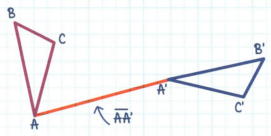

STEP 2: Construct a perpendicular bisector through AA'.

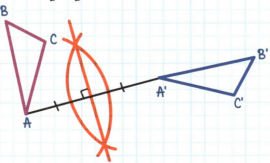

STEP 3: Repeat Steps 1 and 2 on points B and B′.

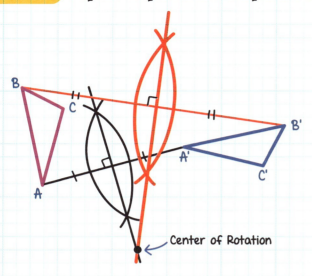

Center of Rotation

The intersection of the two perpendicular bisectors is the center of rotation.

Rules of Rotation

90°: $(x, y) \rightarrow (-y, x)$ Multiply the y coordinate by -1 and reverse coordinate order.

180°: $(x, y) \rightarrow (-x, -y)$ Multiply the x and y coordinates by -1.

270°: $(x, y) \rightarrow (y, -x)$ Multiply the x coordinate by -1 and reverse coordinate order.

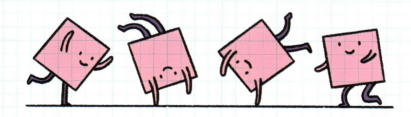

EXAMPLE: Rotate the polygon RSTW 180° counterclockwise around the origin (the center of rotation).

STEP 1: Write the coordinates of the preimage shape:

R(1, 2), S(1, 5), T(4, 4), W(4, 2)

STEP 2: Rotate each point 180°, or two quadrants counterclockwise.

Preimage	Image
R(1, 2)	R'(–1, –2)
S(1, 5)	S'(–1, –5)
T(4, 4)	T'(–4, –4)
W(4, 2)	W'(–4, –2)

 **THINK:**
All coordinates become negative because the rotation brings the points R'S'T'V' into quadrant III.

STEP 3: Plot and connect the points. Then label the image R'S'T'W'.

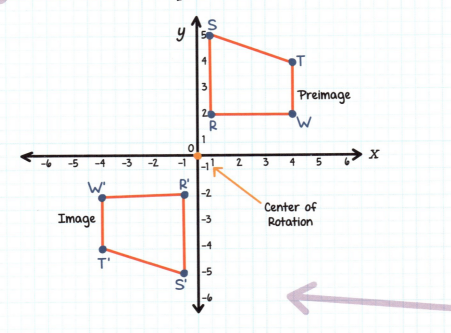

FOR QUESTIONS 1 THROUGH 4, INDICATE WHETHER THE STATEMENT IS *TRUE* OR *FALSE*. IF THE STATEMENT IS FALSE, EXPLAIN WHY IT IS *NOT* TRUE.

1. Rotations are not rigid motions, unlike translations, which *are* rigid motions.

2. To rotate a figure on the coordinate plane 270° counterclockwise, multiply the x-coordinate by –1 and reverse the order of the coordinates.

3. The center of rotation can be located only outside the figure.

4. Point H is rotated $x°$ counterclockwise about point R. The center of rotation is R. The angle of rotation is x. This rotation tells that RH ≠ RH'.

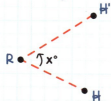

5. Rotate the triangle 90° clockwise about the center of rotation, P.

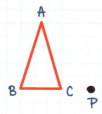

6. Use a protractor to draw the rotation of point B 60° counterclockwise about point A.

B

A

7. Draw the center of rotation that rotates △ABC to △A'B'C'.

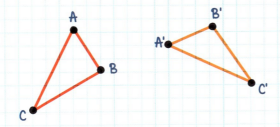

8. Graph a polygon with the following points: M(1, −3), A(1, −6), T(4, −6), and H(4, −2). Then rotate it 270° counterclockwise around the origin.

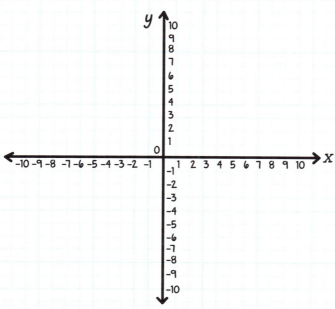

9. Graph a triangle with the following points: R(−2, 5), S(−2, 1), and T(−5, 1). Then rotate it 90° counterclockwise around the origin.

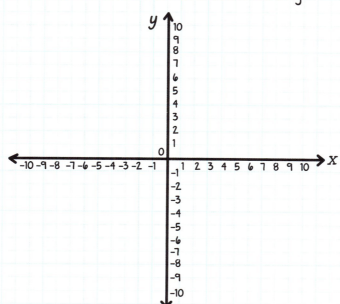

COMPOSITIONS

COMPOSITIONS OF TRANSFORMATIONS

combine two or more transformations to form a new transformation.

In a composition, you perform the second transformation on the image of the first transformation.

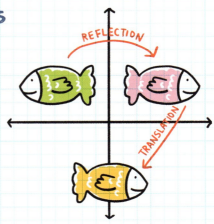

A **COMPOSITION OF TRANSLATIONS** combines two or more translations.

A **GLIDE REFLECTION** is a composition of a translation and a reflection. The reflection line is parallel to the direction of the translation.

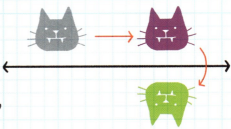

The gray cat translates to the purple cat, which then reflects to the green cat.

COMPOSITIONS OF REFLECTIONS

Parallel: A composition of **two reflections** across **two parallel lines** results in a translation.

Intersection: A composition of **two reflections** across **two intersecting** lines results in a rotation about the point of intersection.

EXAMPLE: Draw the graph of the polygon MATH rotated 180° counterclockwise about the origin, and then translate the figure 6 units to the right.

This is a composition of transformations. First we rotate, then we translate.

STEP 1: Rotate the polygon MATH 180° counterclockwise about the origin.

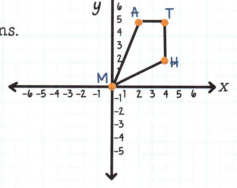

Use the rule $(x, y) \rightarrow (-x, -y)$ to find the vertices of the rotated polygon.

▶ M(0, 0) $\rightarrow$ M'(0, 0)
▶ A(2, 5) $\rightarrow$ A'(−2, −5)
▶ T(4, 5) $\rightarrow$ T'(−4, −5)
▶ H(4, 2) $\rightarrow$ H'(−4, −2)

Connect the vertices of the polygon. Label M'A'T'H'.

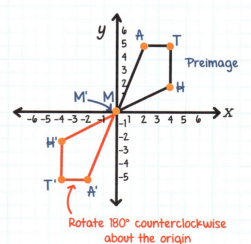

Rotate 180° counterclockwise about the origin

STEP 2: Translate M'A'T'H'.

Each point, M', A', T', and H', moves **6 units to the right**.

The translation vector is **(6**, 0).

The translation rule is
$(x, y) \longrightarrow (x + 6, y + 0)$.

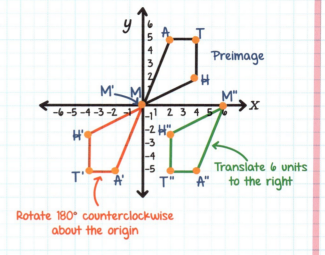

Preimage

M' M   M"

Translate 6 units
to the right

Rotate 180° counterclockwise
about the origin

Preimage	Image
M' (0, 0)	M" (6, 0)
A' (−2, −5)	A" (4, −5)
T' (−4, −5)	T" (2, −5)
H' (−4, −2)	H" (2, −2)

Connect the vertices of the polygon. Label M"A"T"H".

 **THINK:**

The size of the transformed polygon is the same as that
of the original polygon. Similarly, the angle measures of the
transformed polygon are the same as those of the original.
However, since we rotated the image, the orientation of the
transformed polygon is *not* the same as that of the original.

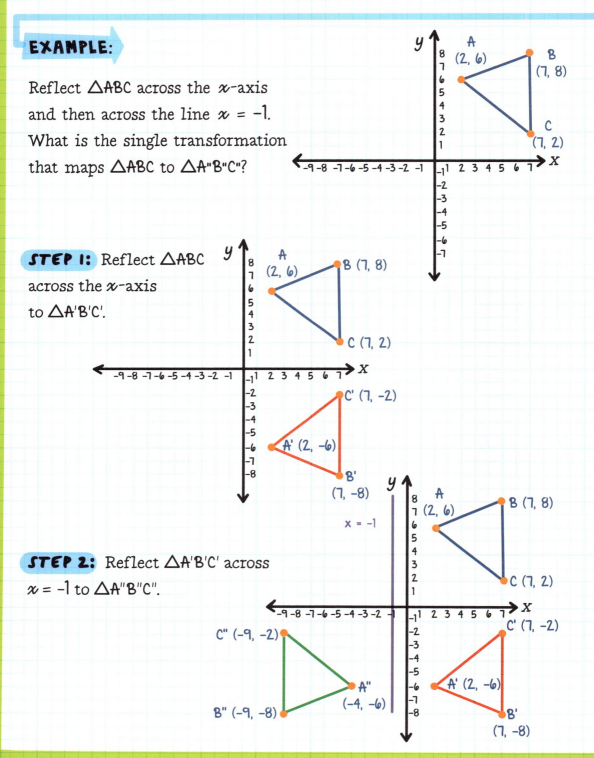

EXAMPLE:

Reflect △ABC across the x-axis and then across the line $x = -1$. What is the single transformation that maps △ABC to △A"B"C"?

A (2, 6)
B (7, 8)
C (7, 2)

STEP 1: Reflect △ABC across the x-axis to △A'B'C'.

A (2, 6)   B (7, 8)
C (7, 2)
C' (7, −2)
A' (2, −6)
B' (7, −8)

STEP 2: Reflect △A'B'C' across $x = -1$ to △A"B"C".

x = −1
A (2, 6)   B (7, 8)
C (7, 2)
C' (7, −2)
A' (2, −6)
B' (7, −8)
C" (−9, −2)
B" (−9, −8)
A" (−4, −6)

Since this transformation is a composition of two reflections across two intersecting lines, the x-axis and $x = -1$, it forms a rotation about the point of intersection (-1, 0).

So, the single transformation that maps △ABC to △A"B"C" is a counterclockwise rotation 180° around the point (-1, 0).

If a figure is reflected across a line and the new figure is unchanged, then the figure has **line symmetry**.

The line of reflection is called a **line of symmetry**.

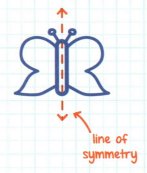

line of symmetry

A line of symmetry divides a figure into two mirror images. Sometimes a figure can have more than one line of symmetry.

If a figure is rotated between 0 degrees and 360 degrees about its center and the figure remains the same, then it has **rotational symmetry**. The point of rotation is called the **center of rotation**.

USE WHAT YOU KNOW ABOUT COMPOSITIONS TO ANSWER THE QUESTIONS.

1. Graph the composition of $\overline{AB}$ rotated 270° counterclockwise about the origin to $\overline{A'B'}$ and then reflected across $y = x$ to $\overline{A''B''}$.

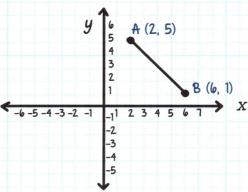

2. What is the composition of two reflections across two intersecting lines?

3. Complete the sentence.

   A composition of two _____ across two parallel lines

   forms a _____.

FOR QUESTIONS 4 THROUGH 6, INDICATE WHETHER THE STATEMENT IS *TRUE* OR *FALSE*.

4. The orientation of a scalene triangle will *not* change if you perform a translation first and then a rotation.

5. If a figure is rotated between 0° and 360° about its center and the resulting figure looks exactly the same then the figure is said to have rotational symmetry.

6. The center of rotation can be located only inside the figure.

7. A.) Reflect polygon RSTW across the y-axis and then across x-axis.

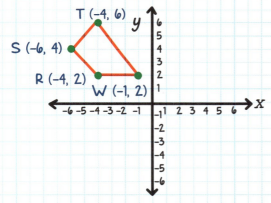

B.) What is the single transformation that maps polygon RSTW to polygon R"S"T"W"?

8. Do the given figures have line symmetry? If so how many lines of symmetry does each figure have?

24 CONGRUENCE

Two figures are **CONGRUENT** if a sequence of rigid motions can map one figure directly onto the other.

EXAMPLE:

Is △ABC congruent to △DEF?

If there is a rigid motion that takes △ABC to △DEF, then the triangles are congruent.

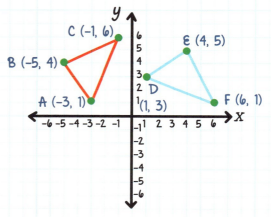

STEP 1: Observe the transformation.

STEP 2: It appears there is a rotation 270° counterclockwise.
Check whether that observation is correct.

Rule: For a 270° counterclockwise rotation, (x, y) becomes $(y, -x)$.

△ABC		△DEF
A(-3, 1)	→	D(1, 3)
B(-5, 4)	→	E(4, 5)
C(-1, 6)	→	F(6, 1)

Checking all the points verifies that a rotation of 270° counterclockwise maps △ABC to △DEF.

Therefore, △ABC is congruent to △DEF: △ABC ≅ △DEF.

FOR QUESTIONS 1 THROUGH 4, DETERMINE IF THE
FIGURES ARE CONGRUENT. IF THEY ARE, WRITE A
CONGRUENCE STATEMENT.

1.

2.

3.

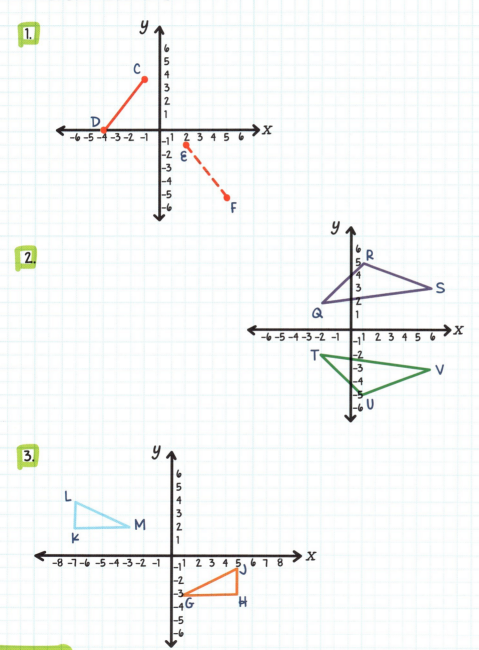

4.

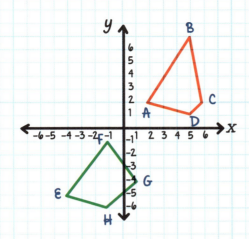

5. The coordinates of △ABC are (–5, –2), (–1, –2), and (–4, –4).
   The coordinates of △RST are (2, –5), (2, –1), and (4, –4).
   Is △ABC ≅ △RST? Explain your reasoning.

6. The coordinates of parallelogram MATH are M(1, –1), A(5, –1), T(9, 3), and
   H(5, 3). The coordinates of parallelogram PNRO are P(–3, –7), N(1, –7),
   R(5, –3), and O(1, –3). Is MATH ≅ PNRO? Explain your reasoning.

WORK SPACE

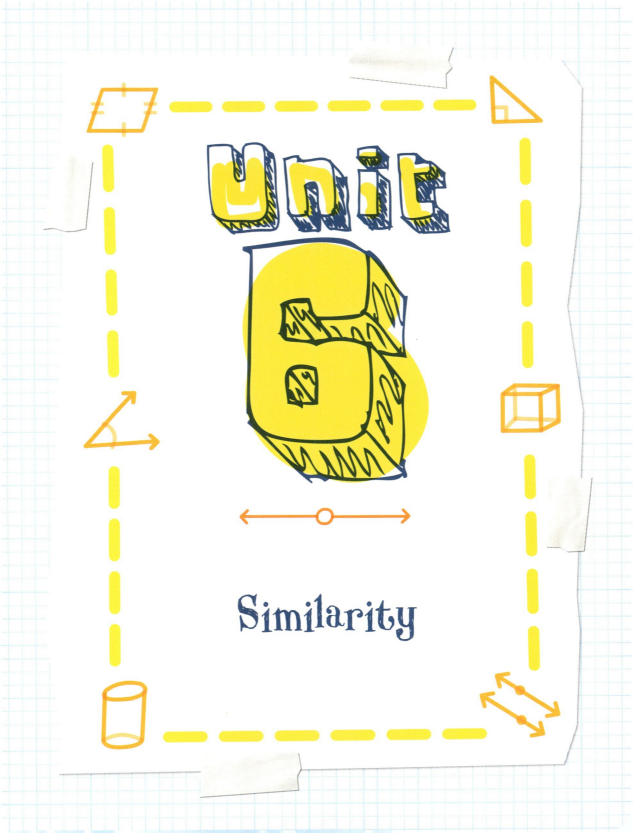

Unit 6

Similarity

RATIO AND PROPORTION

A **RATIO** is a comparison of two or more quantities.

An **EXTENDED RATIO** compares more than two quantities.

For example, if we are comparing three quantities a, b, and c, then we can write $a{:}b{:}c$.

A **PROPORTION** is an equation where two ratios are equal.

It can be written as: $\dfrac{a}{b} = \dfrac{c}{d}$ or $a{:}b = c{:}d$.

In the proportion $\dfrac{a}{b} = \dfrac{c}{d}$, multiply $a \cdot d$ and $b \cdot c$ and set them equal to each other.

$a \,/\, b = c \,/\, d$

$ad = bc$

$\dfrac{a}{b} \times \dfrac{c}{d}$

> Two ratios that form a proportion are called **EQUIVALENT FRACTIONS**.

$ad = bc$

176

You can check whether two ratios form a proportion by using **CROSS PRODUCTS**.

To find cross products, set the two ratios next to each other, then multiply diagonally. If the two products *are equal to each other*, then the two ratios are equal and form a proportion.

We can use a proportion to find an unknown quantity.

EXAMPLE: Solve: $\dfrac{4}{21} = \dfrac{12}{3x}$ ← Use a variable such as x to represent the unknown quantity.

STEP 1: Cross multiply.

$$\dfrac{4}{21} \diagdown \dfrac{12}{3x}$$

$4 \cdot 3x = 21 \cdot 12$ Cross multiply.

$12x = 252$

$12x \div 12 = 252 \div 12$ Division Property of Equality

$x = 21$

STEP 2: Check your answer.

Substitute $x = 21$ into the proportion.

$$\dfrac{4}{21} = \dfrac{12}{3 \cdot 21}$$

$4 \cdot 3 \cdot 21 = 21 \cdot 12$ Cross multiply.

$252 = 252$ ✔   The cross products are equal.

So, the proportion is equal too: $\dfrac{4}{21} = \dfrac{12}{63}$.

USE WHAT YOU KNOW ABOUT RATIOS TO ANSWER THE QUESTIONS.

1. What is the ratio of the rectangular prism's height *to* length *to* width?

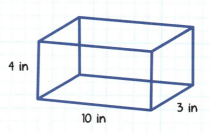

4 in

10 in

3 in

2. Which proportions are true proportions? Explain your reasoning.

$\frac{5}{7} \overset{?}{=} \frac{50}{75}$	$\frac{10}{15} \overset{?}{=} \frac{20}{30}$	$\frac{5}{7} \overset{?}{=} \frac{25}{45}$	$\frac{8}{12} \overset{?}{=} \frac{32}{60}$

FOR QUESTIONS 3 THROUGH 6, FIND THE VALUE OF x.

3. $\frac{x}{14} = \frac{32}{56}$

4. $\frac{28}{63} = \frac{4}{x}$

5. $\frac{4x}{57} = \frac{8}{6}$

6. $\frac{7}{11} = -\frac{x}{33}$

SOLVE THE PROBLEMS.

7. A bread dough recipe requires 2 teaspoons of dry yeast for every 3 cups of flour. If the baker is multiplying the recipe and uses 14 teaspoons of dry yeast, how many cups of flour will the recipe require?

8. An athlete joins a health club for 24 months. The health club's membership cost is $305 for 8 months. How much does the athlete pay for 24 months of membership?

Chapter 26 DILATIONS

A **DILATION** is a transformation that is *not* a rigid motion. Dilations change the size of a figure. The shape remains the same.

A dilation is either: an **enlargement** or **magnification**—the image is larger than the preimage or a **reduction**—the image is smaller than the preimage.

Dilations have a center, O, which is a fixed point. All the points expand *or* shrink from the center by a **scale factor**.

SCALE FACTOR is a ratio (*a:b*) that determines how much bigger or smaller the image is compared to the preimage.

ENLARGE A FIGURE	SHRINK A FIGURE	SCALE FACTOR OF 1
The scale factor is *greater than* 1.	The scale factor is *less than* 1.	The figure stays the same size: 100%.
The image is larger than the preimage.	The new, dilated figure will be *a fraction* of the original size.	A scale factor of 2 means the figure is *200% larger*.

Methods for Finding the Scale Factor

EXAMPLE: Figure ABCD maps to (corresponds to) A'B'C'D'. Determine the scale factor of this dilation.

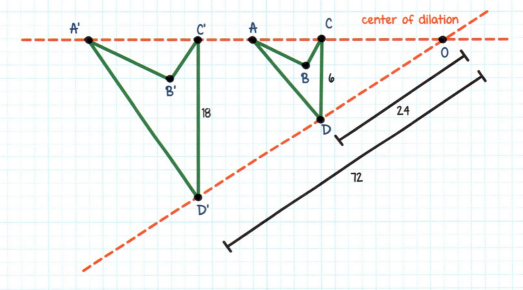

Method 1:	Method 2:
To find the scale factor, divide a side length of the image, A'B'C'D', by the corresponding side length of the preimage, ABCD.	To find the scale factor, divide the distance from O (the center of dilation) to D by the distance from O to D'.
This is the ratio of corresponding side lengths.	This is the ratio of the distance of corresponding points from O.
Scale factor $(r) = \dfrac{C'D'}{CD}$	Scale factor $(r) = \dfrac{OD'}{OD}$
$r = \dfrac{18}{6} = 3$	$r = \dfrac{72}{24} = 3$

So, the scale factor is 3. The image is an enlargement since the scale factor is *greater than* 1.

DRAWING DILATIONS

Draw the image of △ABC under a dilation with center O and scale factor 3.

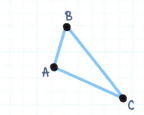

STEP 1: Draw rays from O through each vertex.

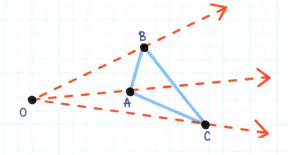

STEP 2: Draw A'.

Use a ruler or compass to measure the length of $\overline{OA}$.

$\overline{OA}$ = 1 cm

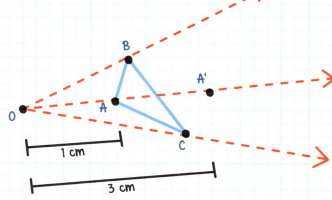

Multiply $\overline{OA}$ by scale factor 3 to get $\overline{OA'}$.

$\overline{OA'} = 3 \cdot \overline{OA} = 3 \cdot (1 \text{ cm}) = 3 \text{ cm}$

So, $\overline{OA'}$ = 3 cm.

On the ray $\overline{OA}$, draw A' 3 cm from O.

STEP 3: Repeat step 2 for points B and C.

$$\overline{OB'} = 3 \cdot \overline{OB} = 3 \cdot (2 \text{ cm}) = 6 \text{ cm}$$

$$\overline{OC'} = 3 \cdot \overline{OC} = 3 \cdot (3 \text{ cm}) = 9 \text{ cm}$$

STEP 4: Connect the points to draw the new triangle.

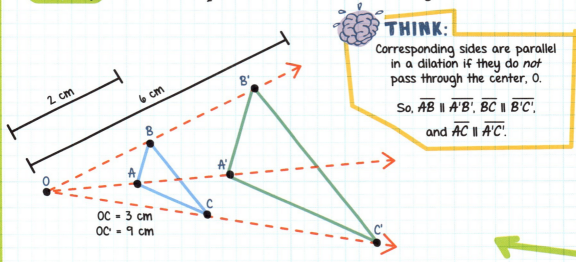

THINK:

Corresponding sides are parallel in a dilation if they do *not* pass through the center, O.

So, $\overline{AB} \parallel \overline{A'B'}$, $\overline{BC} \parallel \overline{B'C'}$, and $\overline{AC} \parallel \overline{A'C'}$.

OC = 3 cm
OC' = 9 cm

DILATIONS ON THE COORDINATE PLANE

To find the image of a dilation on the coordinate plane with the center at the origin $(0, 0)$, multiply each x-coordinate and y-coordinate by the scale factor, r.

If a dilation has a scale factor, r, then $P(x, y) \longrightarrow P'(rx, ry)$.

EXAMPLE: Quadrilateral RSTV maps to R'S'T'V' under a dilation with a scale factor of **50%** and the center at the origin $(0, 0)$. Find the coordinates of the vertices after the dilation.

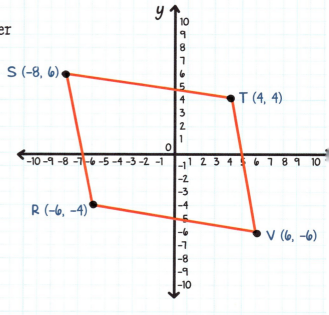

STEP 1: Write the coordinates of the preimage quadrilateral.

STEP 2: Since the center of dilation is the origin $(0, 0)$, multiply each x-coordinate and y-coordinate by the scale factor of **50%** or $\frac{1}{2}$ or **0.5**.

$R(-6, -4) \longrightarrow R'(0.5 \cdot -6, 0.5 \cdot [-4]) = (-3, -2)$

$S(-8, 6) \longrightarrow S'(0.5 \cdot -8, 0.5 \cdot 6) = (-4, 3)$

$T(4, 4) \longrightarrow T'(0.5 \cdot 4, 0.5 \cdot 4) = (2, 2)$

$V(6, -6) \longrightarrow V'(0.5 \cdot 6, 0.5 \cdot [-6]) = (3, -3)$

STEP 3: Plot and label the new image as R'S'T'V'.

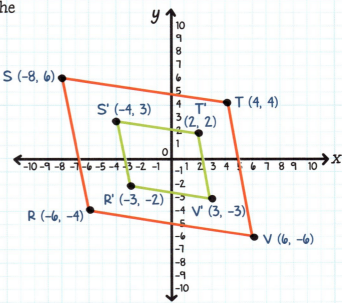

Notice that because the scale factor is *less than* 1, the quadrilateral shrinks.

So, the coordinates of the vertices after the dilation are R'(–3, –2), S'(–4, 3), T'(2, 2), and V'(3, –3).

USE WHAT YOU KNOW ABOUT DILATIONS TO ANSWER THE QUESTION.

1. State whether the given scale factor indicates a reduction, an enlargement, or no change.

   A. Scale factor: 125%

   B. Scale factor: 75%

   C. Scale factor: 1

   D. Scale factor: 0.65

   E. Scale factor: 4

   F. Scale factor: $\frac{1}{5}$

FOR QUESTIONS 2 THROUGH 4, DETERMINE THE SCALE FACTOR UNDER A DILATION WITH THE CENTER AT THE ORIGIN. THEN STATE THE TYPE OF DILATION.

2. $P(-4, -12) \longrightarrow P'(-1, -3)$

3. $P(6, 15) \longrightarrow P'(18, 45)$

4. $P(-1, 5) \longrightarrow P'(-0.5, 2.5)$

FOR QUESTIONS 5 THROUGH 7, DETERMINE THE SCALE FACTOR OF THE DILATION THAT MAPS A TO A' WITH CENTER O. STATE WHETHER THE DILATION IS AN ENLARGEMENT OR A REDUCTION.

5.

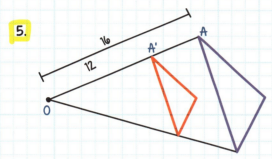

6.

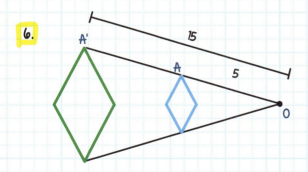

7.

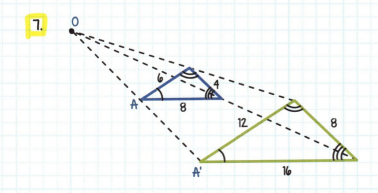

FOR QUESTIONS 8 AND 9, DRAW THE DILATION OF THE FIGURE THROUGH POINT O WITH THE GIVEN SCALE FACTOR, R.

8. r = 3

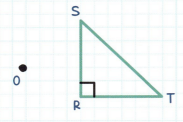

9. r = $\frac{1}{2}$

10. Draw the quadrilateral with vertices M(−4, 8), A(8, 8), T(−4, −12), and H(8, −12). Dilate the figure by $\frac{3}{4}$. Give the coordinates of the vertices of the image.

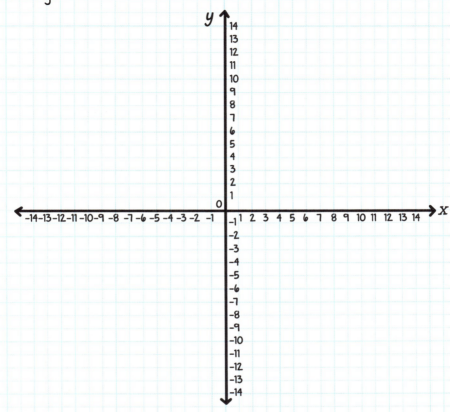

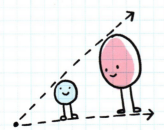

Chapter 27

SIMILAR FIGURES

Two figures are **SIMILAR** if they have the same shape but not necessarily the same size.

> Similar figures are dilations of each other, but they can also be rotated, translated, or reflected.

Similar figures have:

CORRESPONDING ANGLES

(angles that are in the same relative position on each figure) that are congruent.

CORRESPONDING SIDES

(sides that are in the same relative position on each figure) that are proportional in size.

Look at the polygons below. Since all corresponding angles are congruent *and* all corresponding side lengths are proportional, these two polygons are similar: ABCD ~ EFGH.

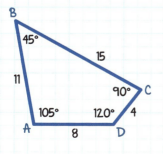

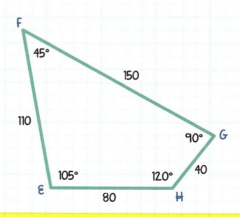

Corresponding angles are congruent	Corresponding sides are proportional
$\angle A \cong \angle E$ $\angle C \cong \angle G$ $\angle B \cong \angle F$ $\angle D \cong \angle H$	$\dfrac{AB}{EF} = \dfrac{11}{110} = \dfrac{1}{10}$ $\dfrac{CD}{GH} = \dfrac{4}{40} = \dfrac{1}{10}$ $\dfrac{BC}{FG} = \dfrac{15}{150} = \dfrac{1}{10}$ $\dfrac{DA}{HE} = \dfrac{8}{80} = \dfrac{1}{10}$

The **SCALE FACTOR** of two similar polygons is the ratio of the lengths of the corresponding sides.

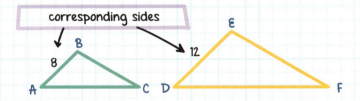

corresponding sides

If $\triangle ABC \sim \triangle DEF$, then the scale factor of $\triangle ABC$ to $\triangle DEF$ is $\dfrac{8}{12}$ or $\dfrac{2}{3}$.

The scale factor of $\triangle DEF$ to $\triangle ABC$ is $\dfrac{12}{8}$ or $\dfrac{3}{2}$.

THINK:
- If the ratios of the corresponding side lengths are not all equal, then the polygons are *not* similar.
- If it is known that two figures are similar, then their proportionality can be used to find unknown measurements.

EXAMPLE: Given △ABC ~ △DEC, find the value of x.

Because the triangles are similar,
the corresponding side lengths
are proportional:

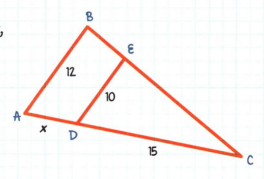

$$\frac{CA}{CD} = \frac{AB}{DE}$$

$$\frac{15 + x}{15} = \frac{12}{10}$$

$(15 + x)10 = 15 \cdot 12$ Cross multiply.

$150 + 10x = 180$

$150 - 150 + 10x = 180 - 150$ Subtraction Property of Equality

$10x = 30$

$10x \div 10 = 30 \div 10$ Division Property of Equality

$x = 3$

CHECK YOUR ANSWER: Substitute $x = 3$ into the proportion.

$$\frac{15 + 3}{15} = \frac{12}{10}$$

$18 \cdot 10 = 15 \cdot 12$

$180 = 180$ ✓

EXAMPLE: Determine if the given figures are similar. If they are similar, write a similarity statement and give the scale factor.

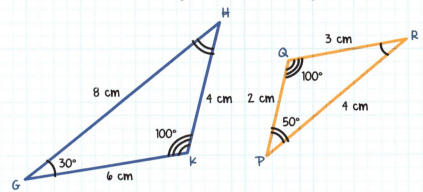

When the orientation of the shapes is different, compare proportions of the longest and shortest sides to help match up the correct corresponding sides.

Corresponding angles are congruent.

$$\angle G \cong \angle R \qquad\qquad \angle H \cong \angle P \qquad\qquad \angle K \cong \angle Q$$

$\angle H$ *must* be $50°$ since the sum of the angle measures of a triangle is $180°$: $30° + 50° + 100° = 180°$.

Corresponding sides are proportional.

$$\frac{GH}{RP} = \frac{8}{4} = 2 \qquad\qquad \frac{HK}{PQ} = \frac{4}{2} = 2 \qquad\qquad \frac{KG}{QR} = \frac{6}{3} = 2$$

The similarity statement is $\triangle GHK \sim \triangle RPQ$.
The scale factor, r, is 2.

USE WHAT YOU KNOW ABOUT SIMILAR FIGURES TO ANSWER THE QUESTIONS.

1. Explain why similar figures are dilations of each other but can also be rotated, translated, or reflected.

2. Write a similarity statement for the similar polygons.

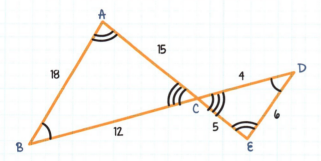

3. What is the scale factor of △BAC to △DEC in question 2?

4. Find the value of x.

   Given: ADCB ~ EHGF

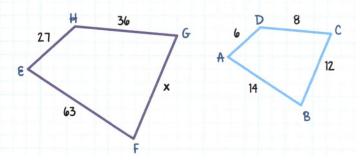

5. Find the values of x and y.

Given: $\triangle EDF \sim \triangle KLJ$

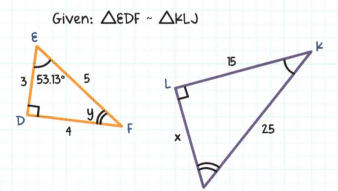

FOR QUESTIONS 6 THROUGH 9, DETERMINE IF THE POLYGONS ARE SIMILAR. IF SO, WRITE A SIMILARITY STATEMENT AND GIVE THE SCALE FACTOR.

6.

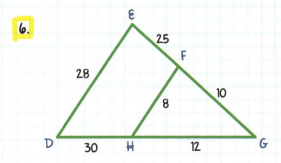

7.

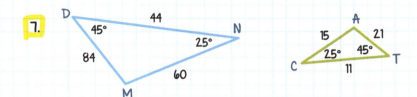

8.

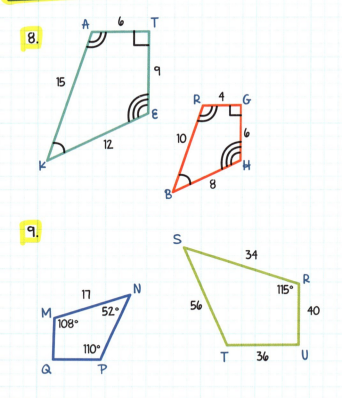

9.

10. Herman says that $\triangle DEF \sim \triangle DGF$ and $\triangle DEF \cong \triangle DGF$. Maddie says that is not correct. They are equal and congruent, but not similar. Which student is correct? Explain your reasoning.

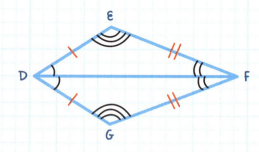

SIMILAR TRIANGLES

You can use a similarity postulate or theorem to determine or prove two triangles are similar.

ANGLE-ANGLE (AA) SIMILARITY POSTULATE

If two angles of one triangle are congruent to two angles of another triangle, then those two triangles are similar.

If $\angle B \cong \angle E$ and $\angle C \cong \angle F$,

then $\triangle ABC \sim \triangle DEF$.

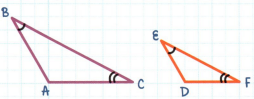

SIDE-ANGLE-SIDE (SAS) SIMILARITY THEOREM

If two corresponding sides of two triangles are proportional and the included angles of those sides are congruent, then the triangles are similar.

If $\angle A \cong \angle D$ and $\dfrac{AB}{DE} = \dfrac{AC}{DF}$,

then $\triangle ABC \sim \triangle DEF$.

SIDE-SIDE-SIDE (SSS) SIMILARITY THEOREM

If the corresponding sides of two triangles are proportional, then the triangles are similar.

If $\dfrac{AB}{DE} = \dfrac{BC}{EF} = \dfrac{AC}{DF}$,

then $\triangle ABC \sim \triangle DEF$.

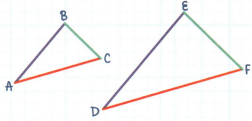

EXAMPLE: Determine if $\triangle CAS$ is similar to $\triangle RTS$.

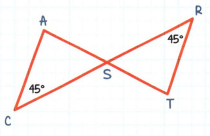

STATEMENTS	REASONS
1. $m\angle ACS = m\angle TRS$ $45° = 45°$	**1.** Given
2. $\angle ACS \cong \angle TRS$	**2.** Definition of congruence
3. $\angle CSA \cong \angle RST$	**3.** Vertical angles are congruent
4. $\triangle CAS \sim \triangle RTS$	**4.** Angle-Angle (AA) Similarity Postulate: If two angles of one triangle are congruent to two angles of another triangle, then those two triangles are similar.

FOR QUESTIONS 1 THROUGH 5, STATE THE SIMILARITY THEOREM OR POSTULATE YOU WOULD USE TO SHOW THAT THE TRIANGLES ARE SIMILAR.

1.

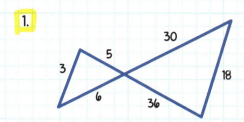

2.

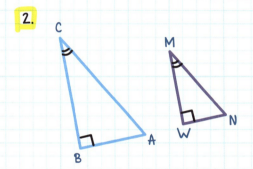

3.

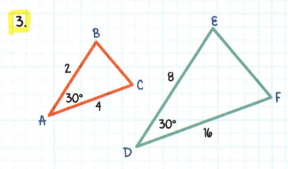

4.

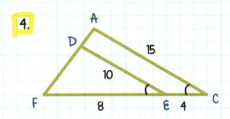

5.

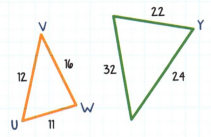

FOR QUESTIONS 6 THROUGH 10, DETERMINE IF THE TRIANGLES ARE SIMILAR. IF SO, WRITE A SIMILARITY STATEMENT.

6. △SRT and △PQT

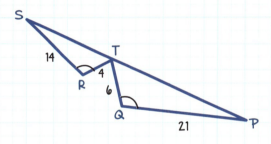

7. △ACD and △CBD

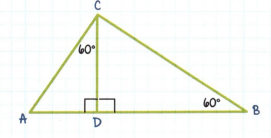

8. △RKN and △SKM

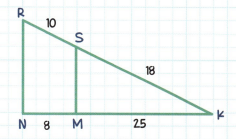

9. △QPR and △APB

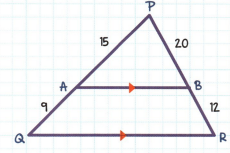

10. An engineer is constructing the two premade ramps illustrated below; however, the ramp labeled DEF is missing the height label. If the two ramps are similar, what is the height of the ramp labeled DEF?

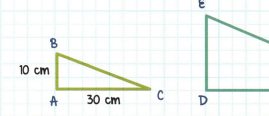

PROPORTIONS IN TRIANGLES

Proportions can be used to find measurements. The theorems and corollary given below can be helpful.

A **COROLLARY** is a statement that follows from a theorem or postulate and requires little or no proof (it is "self-evident").

TRIANGLE PROPORTIONALITY THEOREM

If a line is parallel to one side of a triangle and it intersects the other two sides, then it divides the two sides proportionally.

If $\overline{BD} \parallel \overline{AE}$, then $\dfrac{v}{w} = \dfrac{z}{x}$.

The converse is also true:
If $\dfrac{v}{w} = \dfrac{z}{x}$, then $\overline{BD} \parallel \overline{AE}$.

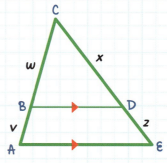

ANGLE BISECTOR THEOREM

If $\overline{AD}$ is a bisector of $\angle A$, then $\dfrac{c}{m} = \dfrac{b}{n}$.

The converse of this theorem
is also true.

If $\dfrac{c}{m} = \dfrac{b}{n}$, then $\overline{AD}$ is a bisector

of $\angle A$.

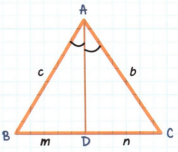

COROLLARY TO THE TRIANGLE PROPORTIONALITY THEOREM

If three or more parallel lines intersect two transversals,
then they divide the transversals proportionally.

If $\overline{PX} \parallel \overline{QY} \parallel \overline{RZ}$,

then $\dfrac{PQ}{QR} = \dfrac{XY}{YZ}$.

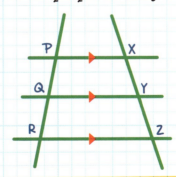

Find the value of x. Then state the length of $\overline{AT}$.

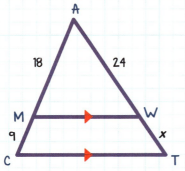

To find the value of x, use the Triangle Proportionality Theorem.

$\dfrac{CM}{MA} = \dfrac{TW}{WA}$ Proportion

THINK:
Since $\overline{MW} \parallel \overline{CT}$, and $\overline{MW}$ intersects the other two sides, $\overline{CA}$ and $\overline{AT}$, then $\overline{MW}$ divides the two sides of the triangle proportionally.

$\dfrac{9}{18} = \dfrac{x}{24}$

$9 \cdot 24 = 18x$ Cross multiply.

$216 = 18x$

$\dfrac{216}{18} = \dfrac{18x}{18}$ Division Property of Equality

$12 = x$

So, the value of x is 12.

The length of $\overline{AT}$ is $24 + x = 24 + 12 = 36$.

So, the length of $\overline{AT}$ is 36.

Find the value of **a** in the figure below.

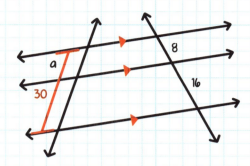

To find the value of **a**, use the Corollary to the Triangle Proportionality Theorem.

$$\frac{a}{30 - a} = \frac{8}{16}$$ Proportion

$16a = 8(30 - a)$ Cross multiply.

$16a = 240 - 8a$

$16a + 8a = 240 - 8a + 8a$ Addition Property of Equality

$24a = 240$

$$\frac{24a}{24} = \frac{240}{24}$$ Division Property of Equality

$a = 10$

So, the value of **a** is 10.

THINK: Since three parallel lines intersect two transversals, then the parallel lines divide the transversals proportionally.

EXAMPLE: Find the length of $\overline{AB}$.

To find the length of $\overline{AB}$, use the Angle Bisector Theorem.

Since $\overline{AD}$ is a bisector of $\angle A$, then $\dfrac{AB}{BD} = \dfrac{AC}{CD}$.

$\dfrac{4x + 1}{10} = \dfrac{45}{30}$ Proportion

$30(4x + 1) = 45 \cdot 10$ Cross multiply.

$120x + 30 = 450$

$120x + 30 - 30 = 450 - 30$ Subtraction Property of Equality

$120x = 420$

$\dfrac{120x}{120} = \dfrac{420}{120}$ Division Property of Equality

$x = 3.5$

Substitute $x = 3.5$ into the expression that represents the segment's length.

$AB = 4x + 1$
$AB = 4 \cdot 3.5 + 1$
$AB = 14 + 1$
$AB = 15$

So, the length of $\overline{AB}$ is 15.

USE WHAT YOU KNOW ABOUT PROPORTIONS TO ANSWER THE QUESTIONS.

1. Find the length of $\overline{RS}$.

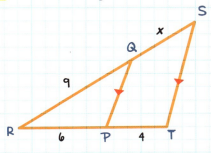

2. Given $\dfrac{SR}{CR} = \dfrac{TE}{CE}$, what can you conclude?

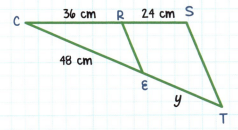

3. What is the length of $\overline{TE}$ in the figure above?

CHAPTER 29

4. Haley is constructing a miniature ramp for her train set. The ramp is supported by two perpendicular pillars, as shown in the diagram. Find the length of $\overline{BC}$ and $\overline{AB}$.

Note: All lengths are in inches.

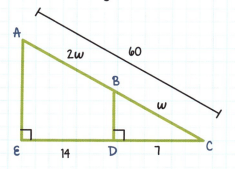

5. Find the value of a in the given figure.

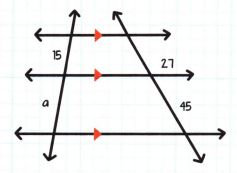

6. Find the value of b in the given figure.

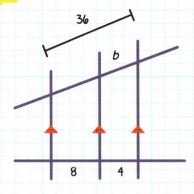

36

b

8   4

7. Find the length of $\overline{GH}$ and $\overline{HJ}$.

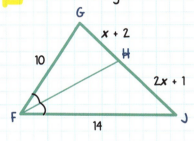

G

$x + 2$

H

10

$2x + 1$

F

14   J

8. Find the length of $\overline{XZ}$.

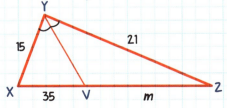

Y

15   21

X   35   V m Z

FOR QUESTIONS 9 AND 10, USE THE GIVEN FIGURE.

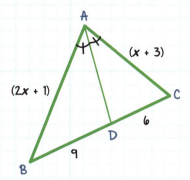

9. Find the value of x.

10. Find the length of $\overline{AB}$ and $\overline{AC}$.

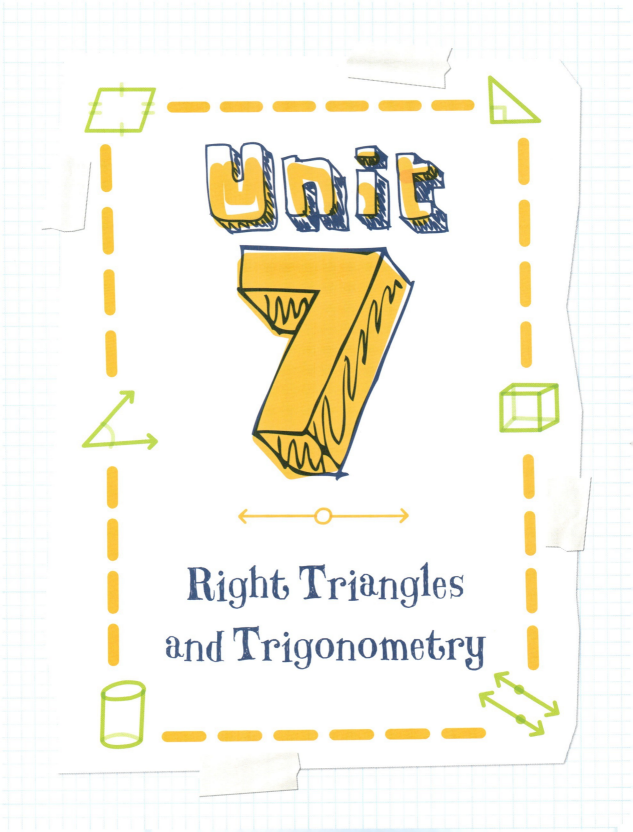

Unit 7

Right Triangles and Trigonometry

30 SLOPE AND LINEAR EQUATIONS

SLOPE is the ratio that describes the tilt of a line.

$$\text{Slope}\,(m) = \frac{\text{Rise}}{\text{Run}}$$

> how much a line goes up or down

> how much a line moves left or right

There are four types of slope.

Positive Slope

▶ rises from left to right

▶ rise and run are positive, so $\frac{\text{rise}}{\text{run}}$ = positive

Negative Slope

▶ falls from left to right

▶ rise is negative and run is positive or vice versa, so $\frac{\text{rise}}{\text{run}}$ = negative

Zero Slope

▶ is horizontal

▶ rise = 0, so $\frac{\text{rise}}{\text{run}} = \frac{0}{\text{run}} = 0$

Undefined Slope

▶ is vertical

▶ run = 0, so $\frac{\text{rise}}{\text{run}} = \frac{\text{rise}}{0}$, which is undefined.

> A number divided by zero is undefined.

There is more than one way to determine the slope of a line.

You can use the slope triangle to determine the slope of a line.

EXAMPLE: Determine the slope of the line that connects the points A(−5, −2) and B(0, 1).

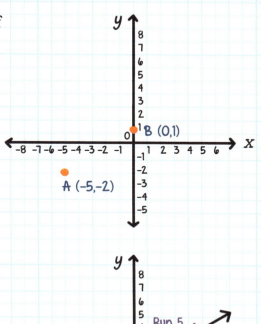

STEP 1: Plot the two points on a coordinate plane and draw a line that connects the points.

STEP 2: Starting with the point that is farthest to the left, draw a right triangle to get from A to B. Find the **rise** and the **run**.

rise = 3 (because we moved up 3 spaces)

run = 5 (because we moved right 5 spaces)

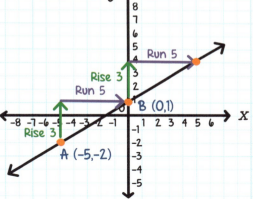

STEP 3: Insert these values into the ratio for slope.

Slope $(m) = \dfrac{\text{rise}}{\text{run}} = \dfrac{3}{5} = \dfrac{3}{5}$

So, the slope of the line that connects the points A(−5, −2) and B(0, 1) is $\dfrac{3}{5}$.

You can use the slope formula to determine the slope of a line.

$$m = \frac{y_2 - y_1}{x_2 - x_1}$$

EXAMPLE: Find the slope of the line that passes through the points $(-12, 3)$ and $(-6, 2)$.

STEP 1: Find the values of x_1, y_1, x_2, and y_2.

Label each given value as (x_1, y_1) and (x_2, y_2).

$x_1 = -12$ $x_2 = -6$

$y_1 = 3$ $y_2 = 2$

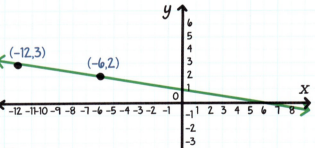

STEP 2: Substitute the values into the slope formula.

Slope $(m) = \dfrac{\text{the change in } y}{\text{the change in } x} = \dfrac{y_2 - y_1}{x_2 - x_1}$

Slope $(m) = \dfrac{2 - 3}{-6 - (-12)} = \dfrac{-1}{6}$

The answer appears correct because a line that falls from left to right has a negative slope.

So, the slope of the line that goes through $(-12, 3)$ and $(-6, 2)$ is $-\dfrac{1}{6}$.

A **RECIPROCAL** is a fraction in which the numerator and denominator are reversed.

$\frac{a}{b}$ and $\frac{b}{a}$ are reciprocals of each other.

$\frac{a}{b}$ and $-\frac{b}{a}$ are **NEGATIVE RECIPROCALS** of each other.

Slope: Parallel and Perpendicular Lines

Parallel lines have the same slope.

Perpendicular lines have slopes that are the NEGATIVE RECIPROCALS of each other.

$\frac{2}{1}$ and $-\frac{1}{2}$ are negative reciprocals.

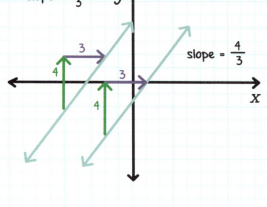

slope = $\frac{4}{3}$

3

4

slope = $\frac{4}{3}$

3

4

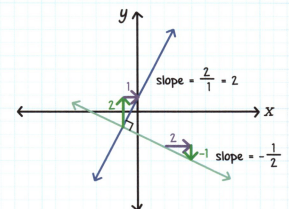

1

slope = $\frac{2}{1}$ = 2

2

2

-1 slope = $-\frac{1}{2}$

Slope: Horizontal and Vertical Lines

$x = a$ is a vertical line with x-intercept $(a, 0)$.

$y = b$ is a horizontal line with y-intercept $(0, b)$.

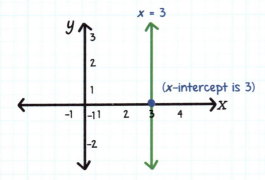

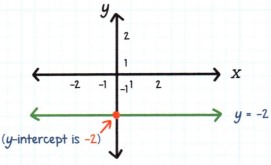

REMEMBER:
The slope of a vertical line is undefined.

REMEMBER:
The slope of a horizontal line is zero.

Graphing Linear Equations

The equation of a line is a **LINEAR EQUATION**.

Linear equations can take the form: $y = mx + b$

y = every y value in the line

m = slope ($\frac{rise}{run}$)

b = y-intercept [where the line crosses the y-axis-point $(0, b)$]

Linear equations can also be written as: $Ax + By = C$ (standard form)

A, B, and C are constants.

THINK:
If you know *both* the y-intercept and the slope of a line, you can graph the line.

FOR QUESTIONS 1 THROUGH 3, IDENTIFY THE SLOPE AND _y_-INTERCEPT FOR THE LINEAR EQUATIONS.

1. $y = -\dfrac{2}{5}x - 12$

2. $y = 3x + 5$

3. $y = 1\dfrac{1}{4}x$

4. Find the slope of the line that passes through the coordinates $(5, 8)$ and $(-6, 3)$.

5. Find the slope of the line that passes through the coordinates $(0, 2)$ and $(-4, 2)$.

FOR QUESTIONS 6 AND 7, FIND THE SLOPE OF THE LINE IN THE GRAPH.

6.

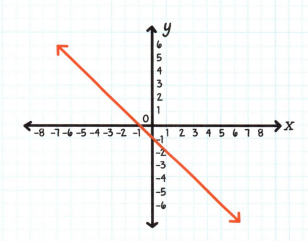

7.

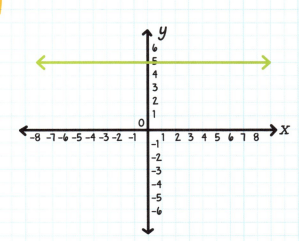

8. Line a has slope $-\dfrac{3}{4}$. What is the slope of a line that is parallel to line a?

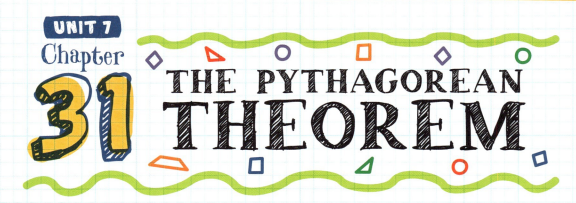

THE PYTHAGOREAN THEOREM

The **PYTHAGOREAN THEOREM** is used to find the length of a side of a right triangle.

PYTHAGOREAN THEOREM

In a right triangle, the sum of the squares of the lengths of the legs is equal to the square of the hypotenuse.

$$a^2 + b^2 = c^2$$

leg   leg   hypotenuse

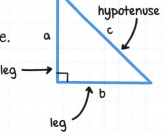

hypotenuse
c

a

leg →

b

leg

SQUARE ROOTS

The square root of a number is a number that when multiplied by itself gives the first number. It is shown by putting the number inside a radical sign, or $\sqrt{}$.

$$\sqrt{64} = \sqrt{8 \times 8} = 8 \text{ and } \sqrt{64} = \sqrt{-8 \times -8} = -8$$

A **PERFECT SQUARE** is the product of two equal integers.

If a number under the radical sign is *not* a perfect square, it is an
IRRATIONAL NUMBER.

> A **PYTHAGOREAN TRIPLE** is a sequence of three
> positive integers such that $a^2 + b^2 = c^2$.
>
> Geometrically, we can think of a Pythagorean triple as three side
> lengths that always form a right triangle.
>
> Examples of common triples:
>
> 3, 4, 5   ($3^2 + 4^2 = 5^2$)
>
> 5, 12, 13   ($5^2 + 12^2 = 13^2$)
>
> 8, 15, 17   ($8^2 + 15^2 = 17^2$)
>
> Multiples of Pythagorean triples are also Pythagorean triples.

RIGHT, ACUTE, AND OBTUSE TRIANGLE RULES

If $c^2 = a^2 + b^2$, then $\triangle ABC$ is
a right triangle.

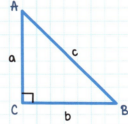

If $c^2 < a^2 + b^2$, then $\triangle ABC$ is
an acute triangle.

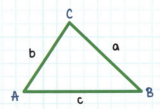

If $c^2 > a^2 + b^2$, then $\triangle ABC$ is
an obtuse triangle.

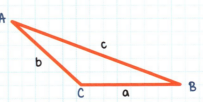

A rectangular dog park has a length of 24 feet and a width of 7 feet. The park has a straight walkway that connects two opposite corners. How long is the walkway?

To find the length of the walkway, use the Pythagorean Theorem.

$a^2 + b^2 = c^2$

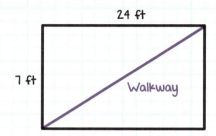

24 ft

7 ft

Walkway

Here, a and b are the legs (length and width) of the right triangle, and c is the hypotenuse or diagonal (walkway).

THINK:
The rectangular park is divided into two congruent right triangles.

Let $a = 24$, $b = 7$, and $c = ?$.

$a^2 + b^2 = c^2$ Pythagorean Theorem

$24^2 + 7^2 = c^2$ Substitute.

$576 + 49 = c^2$ Square each leg value.

$625 = c^2$ Find the sum of the addends.

$\sqrt{625} = \sqrt{c^2}$ Take the positive square root of each side of the equation.

$25 = c$ So, the length of the walkway in the dog park is 25 feet.

A carpenter is tiling a kitchen floor. To install the floor pattern correctly, the carpenter uses the Pythagorean Theorem but omits writing one leg's measure in the sketch. Find the missing leg measure.

Let $a = 10$, $b = ?$, and $c = 26$.

$a^2 + b^2 = c^2$ Pythagorean Theorem

$10^2 + b^2 = 26^2$ Substitute.

$100 + b^2 = 676$ Square the leg and the hypotenuse.

$100 - 100 + b^2 = 676 - 100$ Subtraction Property of Equality

$b^2 = 576$

$\sqrt{b^2} = \sqrt{576}$ Take the positive square root of each side of the equation.

$b = 24$

So, the missing leg measure is 24 feet.

10-24-26 is a multiple of Pythagorean Triple 5-12-13

USE THE PYTHAGOREAN THEOREM TO ANSWER THE QUESTIONS.

1. A firefighter leans a 29-foot ladder against a building to a window 21 feet off the ground. How far is the bottom of the ladder from the building? Find the value of x.

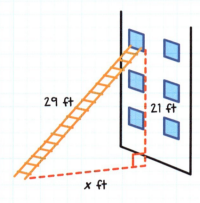

29 ft   21 ft x ft

2. Tarik drives his car south on Market Street and then west on Craig Street to visit his best friend, Kyle. He then drives home northeast on Jasper Street to get back home. A map of his commute is shown below. How many miles did Tarik drive to return home from Kyle's house?

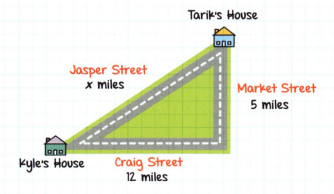

Tarik's House

Jasper Street
x miles

Market Street
5 miles

Kyle's House

Craig Street
12 miles

FOR QUESTIONS 3 AND 4, FIND THE MISSING SIDE LENGTH OF THE TRIANGLE. ROUND YOUR ANSWER TO THE NEAREST WHOLE NUMBER.

3.

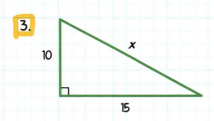

10

x

15

4.

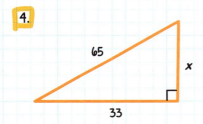

65

x

33

IN QUESTIONS 5 THROUGH 8, THE LENGTHS OF THE SIDES OF A TRIANGLE ARE GIVEN. DETERMINE IF THE TRIANGLE IS ACUTE, OBTUSE, OR RIGHT.

5. 44, 117, 125

6. 8, 12, 16

7. 9, 10, 13

8. 18, 20, 30

32 MIDPOINT AND DISTANCE FORMULAS

The midpoint of a line segment is the point on the segment that is halfway between the segment's endpoints.

The **MIDPOINT FORMULA** is used to find the coordinates of a line segment's midpoint on a number line or a coordinate plane.

MIDPOINT ON A NUMBER LINE

The midpoint of $\overline{AB}$ is:

$$\text{midpoint} = \frac{a + b}{2}$$

MIDPOINT ON A COORDINATE PLANE

The midpoint of $\overline{AB}$ is:

$$\text{midpoint} = \left(\frac{x_1 + x_2}{2}, \frac{y_1 + y_2}{2}\right)$$

(x_1, y_1) and (x_2, y_2) are the coordinates of the endpoints.

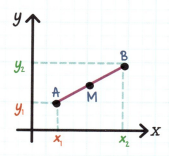

The **DISTANCE FORMULA** is used to find the distance between two points (or the length of a line segment) on a number line or coordinate plane.

DISTANCE ON A NUMBER LINE

The distance between A and B is:

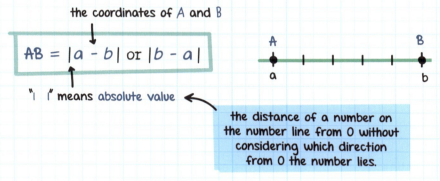

the coordinates of A and B

$$AB = |a - b| \text{ or } |b - a|$$

"| |" means absolute value

the distance of a number on the number line from 0 without considering which direction from 0 the number lies.

DISTANCE ON A COORDINATE PLANE

The distance between A and B is:

$$AB = \sqrt{(x_2 - x_1)^2 + (y_2 - y_1)^2}$$

the coordinates of A and B

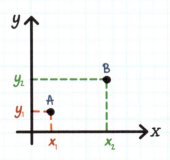

EXAMPLE: What is the midpoint of $\overline{MN}$?

Use the midpoint formula:

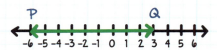

$\text{midpoint} = \dfrac{a + b}{2}$ a and b are the endpoints of $\overline{MN}$.

$a = -1$ and $b = 4$

$= \dfrac{-1 + 4}{2}$ Substitute.

$= \dfrac{3}{2}$ Add.

$= 1\dfrac{1}{2}$ or 1.5 Simplify.

So, the midpoint of $\overline{MN}$ is 1.5.

EXAMPLE: Find the length of $\overline{PQ}$.

Use the distance formula:

$PQ = |a - b|$ a and b are coordinates of P and Q on the number line.

$a = -6$ and $b = 3$

$= |-6 - 3|$ Substitute.

$= |-9|$ Subtract.

$= 9$ Find the absolute value.

So, the length of $\overline{PQ}$ is 9.

Given right triangle RST, find the length of the hypotenuse, $\overline{RS}$.

To find the length of the hypotenuse, $\overline{RS}$, use the distance formula.

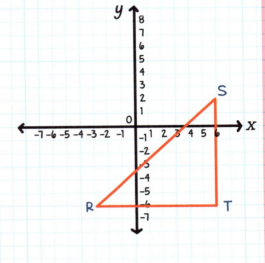

$$AB = \sqrt{(x_2 - x_1)^2 + (y_2 - y_1)^2}$$

Point R: $(x_1, y_1) = (-3, -6)$

Point S: $(x_2, y_2) = (6, 2)$

$$RS = \sqrt{(x_2 - x_1)^2 + (y_2 - y_1)^2}$$

$= \sqrt{(6 - (-3))^2 + (2 - (-6))^2}$ Substitute into the formula. Then solve.

$= \sqrt{9^2 + 8^2}$ Follow the order of operations: Subtract inside the parentheses.

$= \sqrt{81 + 64}$ Square each addend.

$= \sqrt{145}$ Add.

$= 12.04$ Take the positive square root of 145.

$RS = 12.04$

So, the length of the hypotenuse, $\overline{RS}$, is 12.04 units.

FOR QUESTIONS 1 THROUGH 3, FIND THE MIDPOINT OF $\overline{AB}$ ON THE NUMBER LINE.

1.

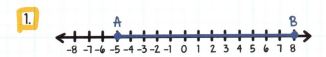

2.

3.

4. Find the midpoint of $\overline{RS}$ on the graph.

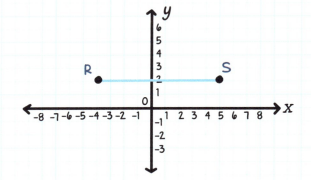

5. Find the midpoint of $\overline{DE}$ on the graph.

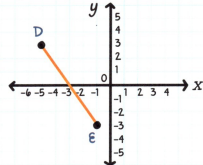

6. Find the midpoint of $\overline{GH}$ given G(4, 1) and H(10, 5).

7. Line segment $\overline{FP}$ has endpoint F(5, 2) and midpoint G(0, −2).
Find the coordinates of endpoint P.

8. What is the distance between A and C?

9. What is the distance between M(−3, −2) and K(5, 4)?

10. Given rectangle MATH,
find the length of the
diagonal $\overline{MT}$.

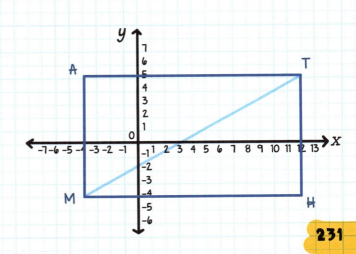

COORDINATE TRIANGLE PROOFS

A **COORDINATE PROOF** involves drawing figures on a coordinate plane.

Statements about the figure can be proven using the **DISTANCE** and **MIDPOINT FORMULAS**, **THEOREMS**, and **POSTULATES**.

Slope Formula	Distance Formula
$m = \dfrac{y_2 - y_1}{x_2 - x_1}$	$D = \sqrt{(x_2 - x_1)^2 + (y_2 - y_1)^2}$
Midpoint Formula	**Pythagorean Theorem**
midpoint = $\left(\dfrac{x_1 + x_2}{2}, \dfrac{y_1 + y_2}{2} \right)$	$a^2 + b^2 = c^2$

When writing a coordinate triangle proof, follow these steps:

1. Draw and label a coordinate graph.

2. Write the formulas you will use to construct the coordinate proof.

3. Make a plan and write the steps you will use to show that the given information leads to what you are proving.

4. Write a final statement that states what you have proven and why it must be true.

EXAMPLE: **Given:** △XYZ has vertices
X(20, -4), Y(-20, -4), and Z(-20, 5).

Prove: △XYZ is a right triangle.

There are two ways to prove a triangle is a right triangle:

Method 1: Use the slope formula.

STEP 1: Plot the points
on a coordinate plane
and connect them.
Label the points.

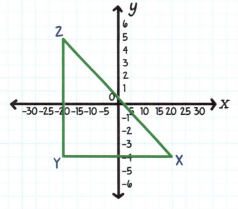

STEP 2: Write the formula you will
use to construct the coordinate proof.

Slope formula: $(m) = \dfrac{y_2 - y_1}{x_2 - x_1}$

STEP 3: Write the steps to show that the triangle has two sides
($\overline{XY}$ and $\overline{YZ}$) that are perpendicular or that m∠XYZ = 90°.

If two lines have slopes that are negative reciprocals of each other, then
the lines are perpendicular. Additionally, if one line has an *undefined
slope* and the other a *zero slope*, they are a vertical line and horizontal
line, respectively, and form a **90°** angle.

Slope of $\overline{ZY}$**:** undefined

Point Z: (x_1, y_1) = (-20, 5)
Point Y: (x_2, y_2) = (-20, -4)

$$m = \frac{-4 - 5}{-20 - (-20)}$$

$$m = \frac{-9}{0} = \text{undefined}$$

A line with undefined slope is a vertical line.

Slope of $\overline{YX}$: zero

Point Y: $(x_1, y_1) = (-20, -4)$
Point X: $(x_2, y_2) = (20, -4)$

$$m = \frac{-4 - (-4)}{20 - (-20)}$$

$$m = \frac{0}{40} = 0$$

A line with a slope of zero is a horizontal line.

Since $\overline{ZY}$ and $\overline{YX}$ are a vertical line and horizontal line, respectively, they are perpendicular, and m∠XYZ = 90°.

So, △XYZ is a right triangle because it contains one right angle.

Method 2: Use the Pythagorean Theorem and the distance formula.

Find the lengths a, b, and c of the sides of the triangle and then show that they satisfy $a^2 + b^2 = c^2$.

Use the distance formula to find the length of each side of the triangle.

The length of $\overline{XY}$: 40 units

Point X: $(x_1, y_1) = (20, -4)$
Point Y: $(x_2, y_2) = (-20, -4)$

$D = \sqrt{(x_2 - x_1)^2 + (y_2 - y_1)^2}$

$D = \sqrt{(-20 - 20)^2 + (-4 - (-4))^2}$

$D = \sqrt{(-40)^2 + 0^2}$

$D = \sqrt{1,600}$

$D = 40$

The length of $\overline{YZ}$: 9 units

Point Y: $(x_1, y_1) = (-20, -4)$
Point Z: $(x_2, y_2) = (-20, 5)$

$D = \sqrt{(x_2 - x_1)^2 + (y_2 - y_1)^2}$

$D = \sqrt{(-20 - (-20))^2 + (5 - (-4))^2}$

$D = \sqrt{0^2 + 9^2}$

$D = \sqrt{0 + 81}$

$D = \sqrt{81}$

$D = 9$

The length of $\overline{ZX}$: 41 units

Point Z: $(x_1, y_1) = (-20, 5)$
Point X: $(x_2, y_2) = (20, -4)$

$$D = \sqrt{(x_2 - x_1)^2 + (y_2 - y_1)^2}$$

$$D = \sqrt{(20 - (-20))^2 + (-4 - 5)^2}$$

$$D = \sqrt{40^2 + (-9)^2}$$

$$D = \sqrt{1{,}600 + 81}$$

$$D = \sqrt{1{,}681}$$

$$D = 41$$

Use the Pythagorean Theorem.

$$a^2 + b^2 = c^2$$

$$XY^2 + YZ^2 = ZX^2$$

$$40^2 + 9^2 = 41^2 \qquad \text{Substitute the side lengths.}$$

$$1{,}600 + 81 = 1{,}681$$

$$1{,}681 = 1{,}681 \ \checkmark$$

$\triangle XYZ$ is a right triangle because the lengths of its three sides satisfy the Pythagorean Theorem.

COMPLETE THE FOLLOWING PROOFS. USE WHAT YOU KNOW ABOUT COORDINATE TRIANGLE PROOFS.

1. **Given:** △LRP has vertices L(−6, −4), R(−3, 4), and P(5, 0).

   Prove: △LRP is scalene.

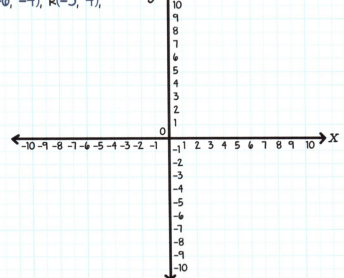

2. **Given:** △ABC has vertices A(2, −2), B(−2, 5), and C(−4, 2).

   Prove: △ABC is a right triangle.

   (Use the slope formula.)

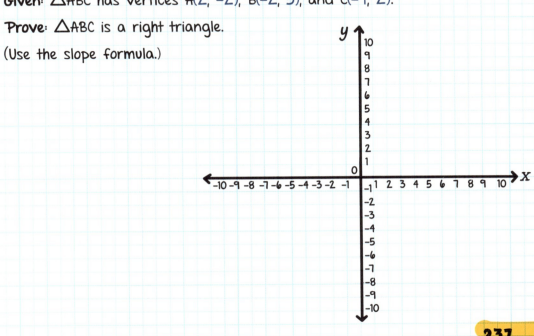

3. **Given:** △RST has vertices R(6, 7), S(4, 2), and T(8, 2).

   Prove: △RST is isosceles.

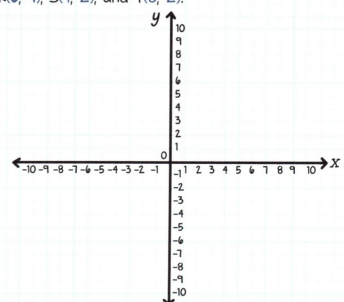

4. **Given:** △QVW has vertices Q(−5, 5), V(0, −5), and W(−1, 7).

   Prove: △QVW is a right triangle. (Use the Pythagorean Theorem.)

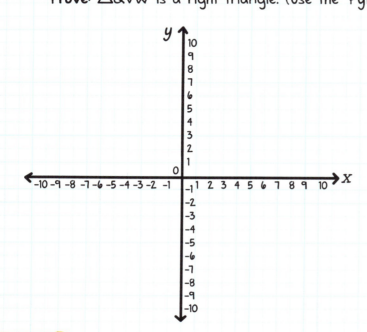

COORDINATE QUADRILATERAL PROOFS

Statements about a quadrilateral drawn on a coordinate plane can be proven using the distance and midpoint formulas.

When writing a coordinate quadrilateral proof, follow these steps:

1. Draw and label a coordinate graph.

2. Write the formulas you will use to construct the coordinate proof.

3. Make a plan and write the steps you will use to show that the given information leads to what you are proving.

4. Write a final statement that states what you have proven and why it must be true.

Methods to prove a quadrilateral is a parallelogram:

METHOD	FORMULA NEEDED
Show that both pairs of opposite sides are parallel.	**Slope:** $m = \dfrac{y_2 - y_1}{x_2 - x_1}$
Show that both pairs of opposite sides are congruent.	**Distance:** $D = \sqrt{(x_2 - x_1)^2 + (y_2 - y_1)^2}$

METHOD	FORMULA NEEDED
Show that the quadrilateral has one pair of parallel and congruent sides.	Slope: $m = \dfrac{y_2 - y_1}{x_2 - x_1}$ Distance: $D = \sqrt{(x_2 - x_1)^2 + (y_2 - y_1)^2}$

EXAMPLE: **Given:** Quadrilateral MNOP has vertices
M(-2, -2), N(-3, 4), O(2, 2), and P(3, -4).

Prove: Quadrilateral MNOP has one pair of parallel and congruent sides.

STEP 1: Draw and label a coordinate graph.

STEP 2: Write the formulas you will use to construct the coordinate proof.

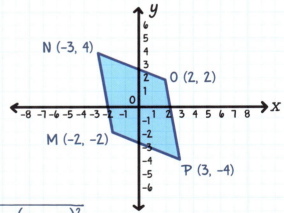

Slope formula: $m = \dfrac{y_2 - y_1}{x_2 - x_1}$

Distance formula: $D = \sqrt{(x_2 - x_1)^2 + (y_2 - y_1)^2}$

STEP 3: Make a plan and write the steps you will use to show that the given information leads to what you are proving.

If one pair of opposite line segments has the same slope, then those segments are parallel. So, first determine the slope of $\overline{ON}$ and $\overline{PM}$.

Slope of $\overline{ON}$:

Point O: $(x_1, y_1) = (2, 2)$

Point N: $(x_2, y_2) = (-3, 4)$

$m = \dfrac{4 - 2}{-3 - 2}$

$m = \dfrac{2}{-5} = -\dfrac{2}{5}$

Slope of $\overline{PM}$:

Point P: $(x_1, y_1) = (3, -4)$

Point M: $(x_2, y_2) = (-2, -2)$

$m = \dfrac{-2 - (-4)}{-2 - 3}$

$m = \dfrac{2}{-5} = -\dfrac{2}{5}$

So, $\overline{ON}$ and $\overline{PM}$ have the same slope, and therefore they are parallel.

Now, to determine if $\overline{ON}$ and $\overline{PM}$ are congruent, determine the line segment lengths. Use the distance formula.

Length of $\overline{ON}$:

Point O: $(x_1, y_1) = (2, 2)$

Point N: $(x_2, y_2) = (-3, 4)$

$D = \sqrt{(x_2 - x_1)^2 + (y_2 - y_1)^2}$

$D = \sqrt{(-3 - 2)^2 + (4 - 2)^2}$

$D = \sqrt{(-5)^2 + 2^2}$

$D = \sqrt{25 + 4}$

$D = \sqrt{29}$

Length of $\overline{PM}$:

Point P: $(x_1, y_1) = (3, -4)$

Point M: $(x_2, y_2) = (-2, -2)$

$D = \sqrt{(x_2 - x_1)^2 + (y_2 - y_1)^2}$

$D = \sqrt{(-2 - 3)^2 + (-2 - (-4))^2}$

$D = \sqrt{(-5)^2 + 2^2}$

$D = \sqrt{25 + 4}$

$D = \sqrt{29}$

So, $\overline{ON}$ and $\overline{PM}$ have the same length, and therefore they are congruent.

STEP 4: Write a final statement.

Quadrilateral MNOP is a parallelogram since it has one pair of parallel and congruent sides.

COMPLETE THE FOLLOWING PROOFS. USE WHAT YOU KNOW ABOUT COORDINATE QUADRILATERAL PROOFS.

1. **Given**: Quadrilateral FGHK has vertices F(−4, 5), G(−1, −2), H(6, −4), and K(3, 3).

   Prove: Quadrilateral FGHK is a parallelogram.

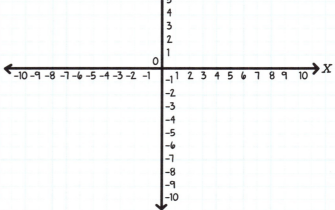

2. **Given**: Quadrilateral ABCD has vertices A(−1, 2), B(1, 5), C(2, 0), and D(4, 3).

   Prove: Quadrilateral ABCD has one pair of opposite sides that are parallel and congruent.

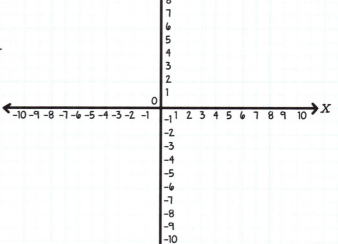

3. **Given:** Quadrilateral WXYZ has vertices W (–4, 1), X(–3, 4), Y(2, 2), and Z(1, –1).

   Prove: Quadrilateral WXYZ is a parallelogram.

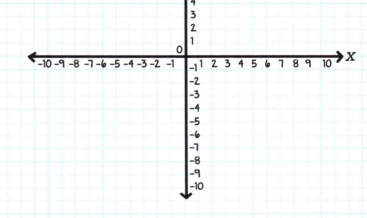

4. **Given:** Quadrilateral MATH has vertices M(–5, 1), A(5, 1), T(1, –4), and H(3, –4).

   Prove: Quadrilateral MATH is a trapezoid.

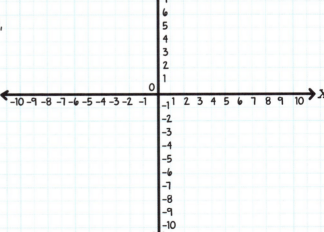

CHAPTER 34

5. **Given:** Quadrilateral RSTV has vertices R(–9, 1), S(0, 10), T(0, 4), and V(–3, 1).

Prove: Quadrilateral RSTV is a trapezoid.

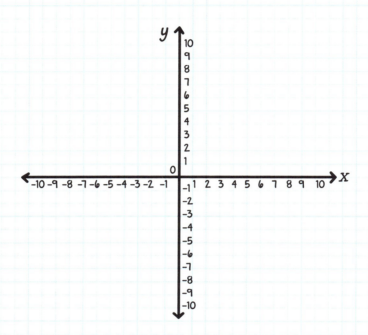

Chapter 35 TRIGONOMETRIC RATIOS

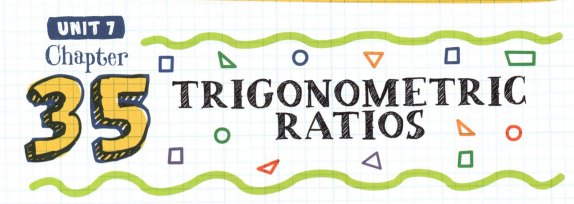

TRIGONOMETRY is used to find measures in triangles.

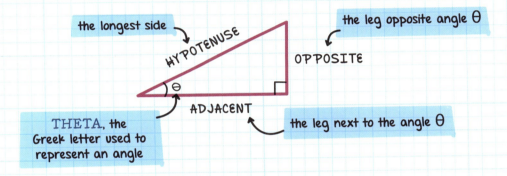

the longest side → HYPOTENUSE

the leg opposite angle θ → OPPOSITE

ADJACENT

THETA, the Greek letter used to represent an angle

the leg next to the angle θ

The trigonometric functions **SINE (SIN)**, **COSINE (COS)**, and **TANGENT (TAN)** are each a ratio of side lengths of a right triangle. They are often used to find unknown angle measures or side lengths of a right triangle.

Sine:

$$\sin \theta = \frac{\text{opposite}}{\text{hypotenuse}}$$

Cosine:

$$\cos \theta = \frac{\text{adjacent}}{\text{hypotenuse}}$$

Tangent:

$$\tan \theta = \frac{\text{opposite}}{\text{adjacent}}$$

A **special right triangle** is a triangle with a feature (angle or side length) that makes calculations of its side lengths or angle measures easier or for which formulas exist.

The two most common special right triangles are:

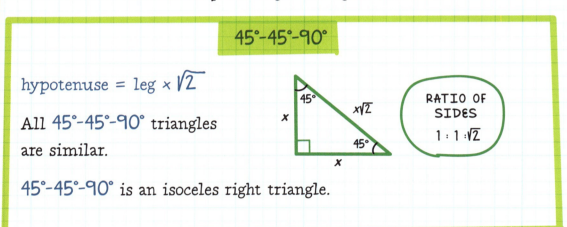

45°-45°-90°

hypotenuse = leg × $\sqrt{2}$

All 45°-45°-90° triangles are similar.

45°-45°-90° is an isoceles right triangle.

RATIO OF SIDES

1 : 1 : $\sqrt{2}$

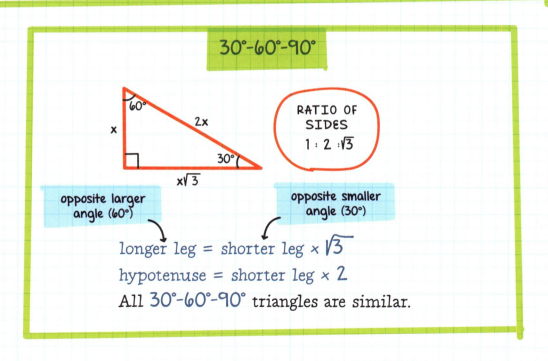

30°-60°-90°

RATIO OF SIDES

1 : 2 : $\sqrt{3}$

opposite larger angle (60°)

opposite smaller angle (30°)

longer leg = shorter leg × $\sqrt{3}$

hypotenuse = shorter leg × 2

All 30°-60°-90° triangles are similar.

EXAMPLE: Find the values of h and w.

Given:

Shorter leg = h

Hypotenuse = 20

Angles = 30°, 60°, 90°

Using the ratio of a 30°-60°-90° triangle:

hypotenuse = shorter leg × 2

$20 = h \times 2$

$\dfrac{20}{2} = h \cdot \dfrac{2}{2}$ Division Property of Equality

$10 = h$

THINK: Now that you know the value of the shorter leg, you can find the value of the longer leg.

Given:

The longer leg = w

The shorter leg = 10

Angles = 30°, 60°, 90°

Using the ratio of a 30°-60°-90° triangle:

longer leg = shorter leg × $\sqrt{3}$

$w = 10 \times \sqrt{3}$

$w = 10\sqrt{3}$

So, the value of h is 10, and the value of w is $10\sqrt{3}$.

EXAMPLE: Find sin 61° and tan 29°.

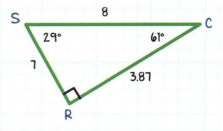

$\sin 61° = \dfrac{\text{leg opposite } \angle C}{\text{hypotenuse}} = \dfrac{7}{8}$

$\tan 29° = \dfrac{\text{leg opposite } \angle S}{\text{leg adjacent } \angle S} = \dfrac{3.87}{7}$

USE WHAT YOU KNOW ABOUT TRIGONOMETRIC RATIOS TO ANSWER THE QUESTION.

1. Find sin 32°, cos 32°, and tan 32°.

   (Theta = 32°)

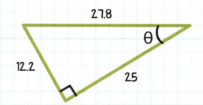

FOR QUESTIONS 2 THROUGH 6, FIND SIN x, COS x, AND TAN x.

2.

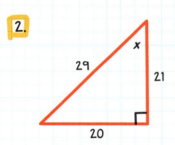

3.

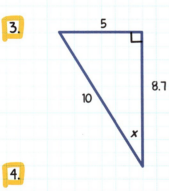

4.

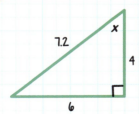

5.

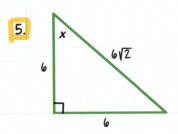

6.

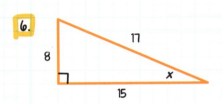

FOR QUESTIONS 7 THROUGH 9, FIND THE VALUE OF *a*.

7.

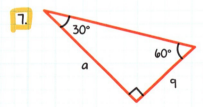

8.

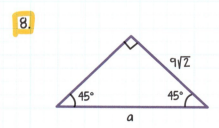

9.

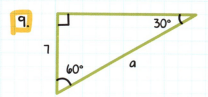

10. Find the values of x and y.

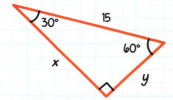

11. Ms. Niles shows $\triangle DRP$. Adeet says that the equation $\sin R = \cos P$ is true. Reardon says that the equation $\sin P = \cos R$ is true. Which student is correct? Explain your reasoning.

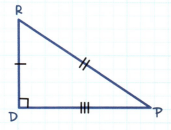

LAWS OF SINES AND COSINES

The **LAWS OF SINES AND COSINES** can be used to help find a triangle's unknown angle measures and side lengths.

The **LAW OF SINES** relates the side lengths of an arbitrary triangle to its angles using the sine function.

LAW OF SINES

$$\frac{\sin A}{a} = \frac{\sin B}{b} = \frac{\sin C}{c}$$

∠A, ∠B, and ∠C are opposite a, b, and c.

When we know the lengths of two sides of a triangle and the measure of the included angle, we can find the length of the third side using the **LAW OF COSINES**.

LAW OF COSINES

$$c^2 = a^2 + b^2 - 2ab \cos C$$

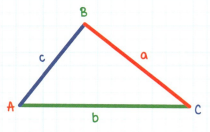

c (the side length)
is opposite angle C.

Sometimes a problem requires us to find an unknown angle in a trigonometric function like $(\sin \theta = \frac{1}{2})$. To do this, we use **INVERSE TRIGONOMETRIC FUNCTIONS**.

INVERSE TRIGONOMETRIC FUNCTIONS do the *opposite* of regular trigonometric functions. They are represented as $\sin^{-1}$, $\cos^{-1}$, and $\tan^{-1}$.

The –1 is not an exponent. It just indicates "opposite of."

If $\sin \theta = \frac{a}{c}$, the inverse sine function is $\sin^{-1}(\frac{a}{c}) = \theta$.

If $\cos \theta = \frac{b}{c}$, the inverse cosine function is $\cos^{-1}(\frac{b}{c}) = \theta$.

If $\tan \theta = \frac{a}{b}$, the inverse tangent function is $\tan^{-1}(\frac{a}{b}) = \theta$.

If you know the trigonometric ratio but not the angle, you can use the inverse function to find the angle.

So, if $\sin 30° = \frac{1}{2}$, then $\sin^{-1}(\frac{1}{2}) = 30°$.

EXAMPLE:

Find the value of x to the nearest degree.

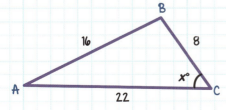

Use the Law of Cosines with $m\angle C = x°$, $c = 16$, $a = 8$, and $b = 22$.

$c^2 = a^2 + b^2 - 2ab \cos C$ Law of Cosines

$16^2 = 8^2 + 22^2 - 2 \cdot 8 \cdot 22 \cos x°$ Substitute.

$256 = 64 + 484 - 352 \cos x°$ Order of operations

$256 = 548 - 352 \cos x°$

$256 - 548 = 548 - 548 - 352 \cos x°$ Subtraction Property
of Equality

$-292 = -352 \cos x°$

$\dfrac{-292}{-352} = \dfrac{-352 \cos x°}{-352}$ Division Property of Equality

$\dfrac{292}{352} = \cos x°$

$x = \cos^{-1} \dfrac{292}{352}$ Use the inverse cosine function.

$x \approx 34$

So, the value of x is approximately $34°$.

FOR QUESTIONS 1 THROUGH 4, USE THE LAW OF SINES TO APPROXIMATE THE VALUE OF _x_. ROUND YOUR ANSWER TO THE NEAREST TENTH.

1.

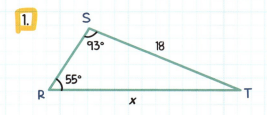

2.

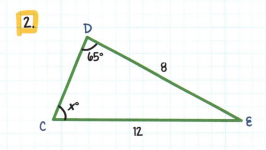

3.

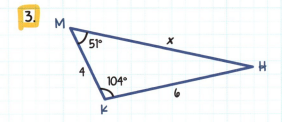

4.

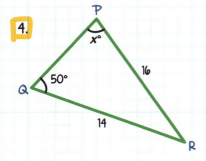

FOR QUESTIONS 5 THROUGH 8, USE THE LAW OF COSINES TO FIND THE VALUE OF x. ROUND YOUR ANSWER TO THE NEAREST TENTH.

5.

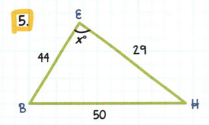

6.

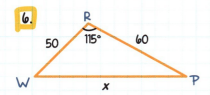

7.

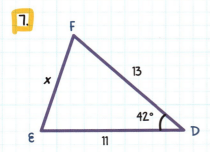

8.

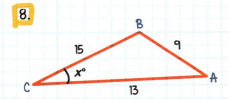

WORK SPACE

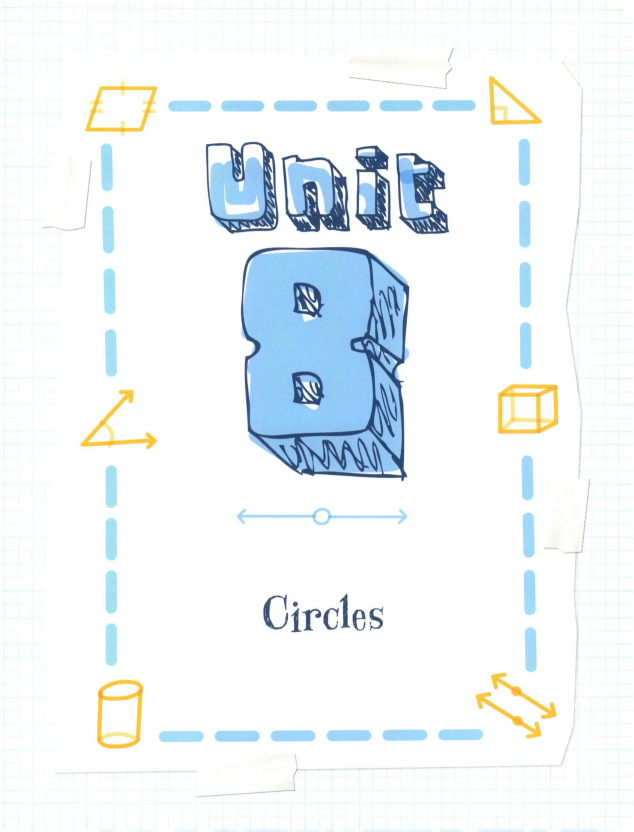

Unit 8

Circles

CIRCLE FUNDAMENTALS

A **CIRCLE** is the set of all points on a plane that are an equal distance from a point called the **CENTER**.

We name a circle using the center point.

PARTS OF A CIRCLE

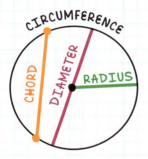

FORMULAS

diameter (d): $d = 2r$

radius (r): $r = \frac{1}{2}d$

Pi (π): The ratio of a circle's circumference to its diameter:

Formula: $\pi = \dfrac{\text{circumference}}{\text{diameter}}$ or $\pi = \dfrac{C}{d}$

Because π is an irrational number, it cannot be expressed as a fraction, a terminating decimal, or a repeating decimal. Therefore, we may sometimes approximate π with 3.14 or $\frac{22}{7}$.

CIRCUMFERENCE

> The circumference, C, of a circle is π times the diameter.
>
> Circumference = π × diameter ⟶ C = πd

Because the diameter is twice the length of the radius, you can also find the circumference with this formula:

$C = 2πr$

CONCENTRIC CIRCLES are circles with the same center.

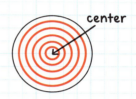

center

EXAMPLE: Find the circumference of the given circle. Use 3.14 for π and round your answer to the nearest hundredth.

Formula: $C = 2πr$

Given: radius = $8\frac{1}{2}$ m

$C = 2π(8\frac{1}{2})$ Substitute.

$C = 17π$ Multiply.

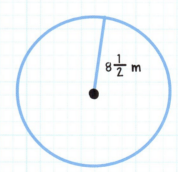

$8\frac{1}{2}$ m

Since π is approximately 3.14,
$17π ≈ 17(3.14) = 53.38$ m.

So, the circumference of the circle is $17π$ or approximately 53.38 m.

EXAMPLE: The circumference of circle D is 24π, AB = 8, and CD = 5. Find the circumference of circle A.

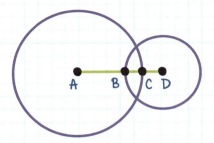

To find the circumference of circle A, we need to know AC, the radius, which means we need to first find BC.

We can find BC using circle D (since we know its circumference).

STEP 1: Find BD, using circle D.

$C = 2\pi r$

$C = 24\pi$

$24\pi = 2\pi \times BD$

$\dfrac{24\pi}{2\pi} = \dfrac{2\pi \times BD}{2\pi}$ Division Property of Equality

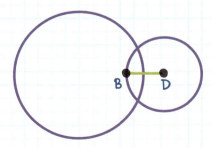

$12 = BD$

REMEMBER:
BD is the radius of circle D.

STEP 2: Find BC.

BD = BC + CD

12 = BC + 5

12 − 5 = BC + 5 − 5

7 = BC

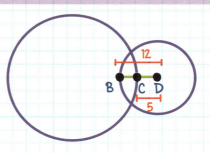

STEP 3: Find the circumference of circle A.

The radius of circle A is:

AB + BC = radius of circle A

8 + 7 = 15

The circumference of circle A is:

C = 2πr

C = 2π(15)

C = 30π

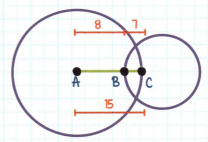

So, the circumference of circle A is 30π.

USE WHAT YOU KNOW ABOUT CIRCLES TO ANSWER THE FOLLOWING QUESTIONS.

1. Find the radius and diameter of a circle with circumference 64π.

2. Find the approximate circumference of a circle with diameter 18.75. Use 3.14 for π and round your answer to the nearest hundredth.

3. Bart walks around a circular track four times. The track has a radius of 185 yards. Approximately how many yards did Bart walk? Use 3.14 as an approximation for π.

4. Find the circumference of the given circle. Use 3.14 as an approximation for π and round your answer to the nearest hundredth.

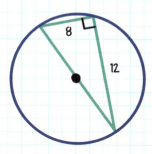

5. The circumference of circle P is 36π, QS = 3, and TP = 10. Find the circumference of circle Q.

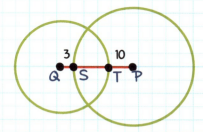

6. In the concentric circles below, the circumference of the larger circle is 72π. Find the circumference of the smaller circle. Use 3.14 as an approximation for π.

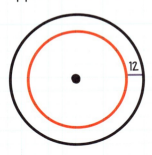

7. Naima is building a circular model table. The current blueprint shows only the radius of the table and the radius of a mounted circular design Naima will construct on the interior portion of the table. To complete the blueprint, Naima needs to calculate the difference between the circumference of the mounted inner circular design and the circumference of the table. Use what you know about circles to calculate that measure. Use 3.14 as an approximation for π.

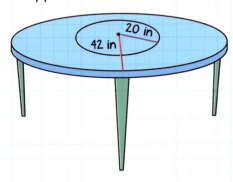

Chapter 38

CENTRAL ANGLES AND ARCS

A **CENTRAL ANGLE** is an angle that has its vertex on the center of a circle. The segments forming the central angle are radii of the circle.

An **ARC** is a part of the circumference. We name an arc by its two endpoints under a ⌢ symbol: $\overset{\frown}{AB}$.

A **SECTOR** is a "slice" of the circle.

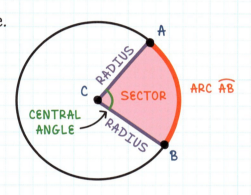

The **MEASURE OF AN ARC** is equal to the measure of its central angle.

In an entire circle, the measure of the central angle is 360 degrees and the measure of the arc is 360 degrees.

An arc that is 180 degrees is a **SEMICIRCLE**. ← half a circle

A **MAJOR ARC** is larger than a semicircle (greater than 180 degrees).

The major arc is $\overset{\frown}{ADB}$. ← Always use three letters when naming a major arc.

A **MINOR ARC** is smaller than a semicircle (less than 180 degrees).

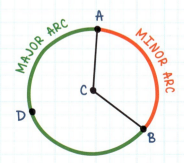

Since the measure of a circle is 360 degrees:

▶ The sum of all the central angles in a circle equals 360 degrees.

▶ In a circle whose circumference is divided into a minor arc and major arc, the sum of the two arcs is 360 degrees.

ADJACENT ARCS are next to each other. They share one endpoint.

ARC ADDITION POSTULATE

The sum of two adjacent arcs equals the total arc.

$$m\overarc{AD} = m\overarc{AB} + m\overarc{BD}$$

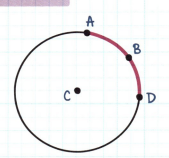

ARC LENGTH is the length of an arc (the distance from endpoint to endpoint).

Arc measure is equal to the measure of the central angle.

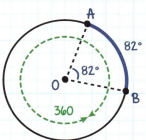

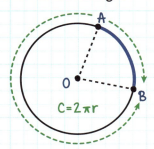

Arc length is a fraction of the circumference.

CONGRUENT ARCS are arcs that have the same measure and are in the same circle or congruent circles.

Two circles are congruent if they have the same radius.

ARC LENGTH FORMULA

To calculate the arc length (ℓ) of a sector with central angle $x°$:

$$\ell = \frac{x}{360} \times 2\pi r$$

EXAMPLE: $\overline{NM}$ is a diameter of circle P. Find $m\widehat{NQ}$, $m\widehat{QM}$, and $m\widehat{NSM}$.

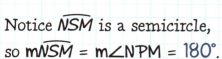

Since the measure of an arc is equal to the measure of its central angle, $m\widehat{NQ} = m\angle NPQ = 78°$.

Notice $\widehat{NSM}$ is a semicircle, so $m\widehat{NSM} = m\angle NPM = 180°$.

$\widehat{NQM}$ is also a semicircle and equal to $180°$.

By the Arc Addition Postulate:

$m\widehat{NQ} + m\widehat{QM} = m\widehat{NQM}$
$78° + m\widehat{QM} = 180°$
$78° - 78° + m\widehat{QM} = 180° - 78°$
$m\widehat{QM} = 102°$

So, the measures are: $m\widehat{NQ} = 78°$, $m\widehat{QM} = 102°$, and $m\widehat{NSM} = 180°$.

FOR QUESTIONS 1 THROUGH 8, USE CIRCLE P. NOTE THAT $\overline{FW}$ IS A DIAMETER.

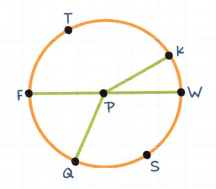

1. Name a major arc.

2. Name a minor arc.

3. Name a semicircle.

4. Name a sector.

5. Name a diameter.

6. Name a radius.

7. If $m\overarc{FQ} = 53°$, find $m\overarc{QSW}$.

8. If $m\overarc{KW} = 27°$, find $m\overarc{FTK}$.

9. Use circle F to answer the following questions.

A. Find x.

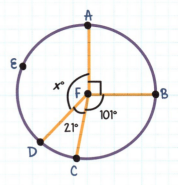

B. If the radius of circle F is 12 inches, what is the length of $\overarc{CB}$? Use $\pi = 3.14$. Round your answer to the nearest tenth.

10. Find the length of $\overset{\frown}{LN}$. Use π = 3.14. Round your answer to the nearest tenth.

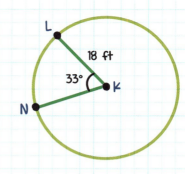

11. Find the length of $\overset{\frown}{RSW}$. Use π = 3.14. Round your answer to the nearest tenth. Note that $\overline{RW}$ is a diameter of the circle.

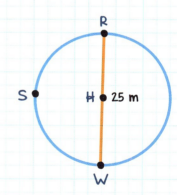

Chapter 39 RADIANS

One **RADIAN (RAD)** is the measure of a central angle that has an arc length that is equal to the radius.

arc length = radius (r)

$m\angle\theta = 1$ radian

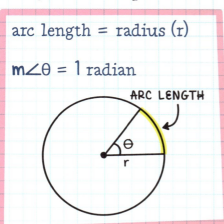

ARC LENGTH

THINK:

Since $C = 2\pi r$, we know that there are 2π radii in the circumference of a circle.

2π radians = 360°

π radians = 180°

1 radian = $\frac{180°}{\pi} \approx 57.3°$

COMMON RADIAN MEASURES

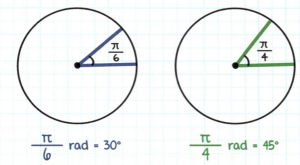

$\frac{\pi}{6}$ rad = 30°

$\frac{\pi}{4}$ rad = 45°

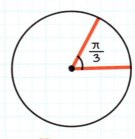

$\frac{\pi}{3}$ rad = 60°

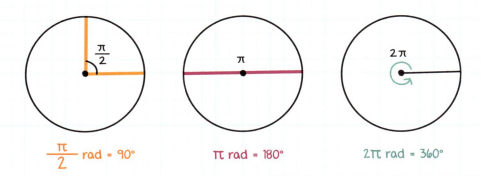

$\dfrac{\pi}{2}$ rad = 90°   π rad = 180°   2π rad = 360°

Converting Degrees to Radians *or* Radians to Degrees

To convert degrees to radians, multiply by $\dfrac{\pi}{180°}$.

To convert radians to degrees, multiply by $\dfrac{180°}{\pi}$.

EXAMPLE: Convert the following to radians:

A. 74°   **B.** 105°

Multiply each degree measure by $\dfrac{\pi}{180}$.

$74° \times \dfrac{\pi}{180}$

$\dfrac{74\pi}{180} = \dfrac{37\pi}{90}$

So, $74° = \dfrac{37\pi}{90}$ rad.

$105° \times \dfrac{\pi}{180}$

$\dfrac{105\pi}{180} = \dfrac{7\pi}{12}$

So, $105° = \dfrac{7\pi}{12}$ rad.

FOR QUESTIONS 1 THROUGH 5, CONVERT THE DEGREE MEASURES TO RADIANS.

1. 90°

2. 350°

3. 58°

4. 32°

5. 145°

FOR QUESTIONS 6 THROUGH 10, CONVERT THE RADIAN MEASURES TO DEGREES.

6. $\frac{\pi}{8}$ rad

7. $\frac{2\pi}{5}$ rad

8. $\frac{9\pi}{4}$ rad

9. $2\frac{3}{4}\pi$ rad

10. $\frac{\pi}{14}$ rad

Chapter

40 ARCS AND CHORDS

A **CHORD** divides a circle into major and minor arcs (unless the chord is a diameter).

The minor arc is called the **ARC OF THE CHORD**.

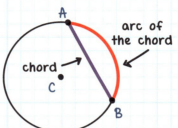

arc of the chord

chord

Chord $\overline{AB}$ has arc $\overarc{AB}$.

IN A CIRCLE OR IN CONGRUENT CIRCLES, CONGRUENT CHORDS HAVE CONGRUENT ARCS.

If $\overline{PQ} \cong \overline{RS}$, then $\overarc{PQ} \cong \overarc{RS}$.

The converse is also true:
If $\overarc{PQ} \cong \overarc{RS}$, then $\overline{PQ} \cong \overline{RS}$.

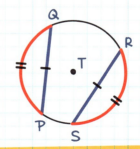

IN A CIRCLE OR IN CONGRUENT CIRCLES, CONGRUENT CHORDS ARE EQUIDISTANT FROM THE CENTER.

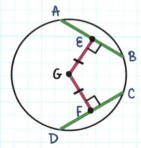

If $\overline{AB} \cong \overline{CD}$, then EG = FG.

The converse is also true:
If EG = FG, then $\overline{AB} \cong \overline{CD}$.

IF A DIAMETER IS PERPENDICULAR TO A CHORD, THEN IT BISECTS THE CHORD AND ITS ARC.

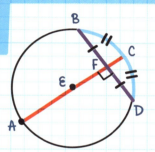

If $\overline{AC} \perp \overline{BD}$, then $\overline{BF} \cong \overline{FD}$
and $\overarc{BC} \cong \overarc{CD}$.

THE PERPENDICULAR BISECTOR OF A CHORD IS A DIAMETER.

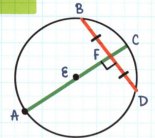

If $\overline{AC}$ is a perpendicular
bisector of $\overline{BD}$, then $\overline{AC}$ is
a diameter of ⊙E.

Find the lengths of $\overline{OQ}$ and $\overline{QP}$ if OP = 54.

Then find the degree measures of $\overarc{ON}$ and $\overarc{NP}$ if $\overarc{OP}$ = 56°.

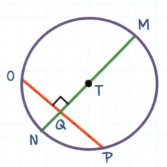

Since $\overline{MN} \perp \overline{OP}$, $\overline{OQ} \cong \overline{OP}$ and $\overarc{ON} \cong \overarc{NP}$.

Since OP = 54, OQ = 54 ÷ 2 = 27 units and QP = 54 ÷ 2 = 27 units.

Since $\overarc{OP}$ = 56°, $\overarc{ON}$ = 56 ÷ 2 = 28° and $\overarc{NP}$ = 56 ÷ 2 = 28°.

So, OQ = QP = 27 units, and $\overarc{ON}$ = $\overarc{NP}$ = 28°.

Find the value of x in circle D.

Since we know $m\overarc{AE} = m\angle ADE$, then $m\overarc{AE} = 64°$, which means $\overarc{AE}$ and $\overarc{FH}$ are congruent.

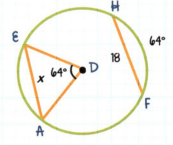

Since congruent arcs have congruent chords,

$\overline{AE} \cong \overline{FH}$

AE = FH

x = 18

USE WHAT YOU KNOW ABOUT ARCS AND CHORDS TO ANSWER THE FOLLOWING QUESTIONS.

1. Find the value of x.

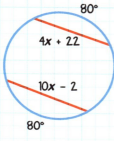

80°

$4x + 22$

$10x - 2$

80°

2. Given $\overline{AC} \cong \overline{DE}$, find the value of y.

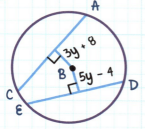

A

$3y + 8$

B $5y - 4$

C

E   D

3. Find m∠QRS. Point R is the center of the circle.

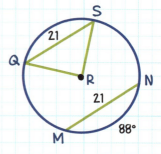

S

21

Q

R   N

21

M   88°

4. Find m$\overarc{WZ}$ and m$\overarc{XV}$.

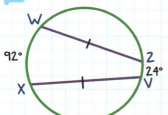

W

92°

Z

24°

X   V

CHAPTER 40

5. Find the value of x.

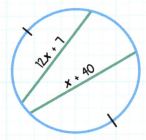

6. Find the length of $\overline{KJ}$.

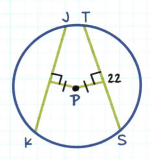

7. Find the lengths of $\overline{DB}$ and $\overline{BE}$ if $\overline{DE} = 29$.
Note that $\overline{AC}$ is a diameter of the circle.

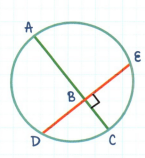

8. Find m∠MHT. Point H is the center of the circle.

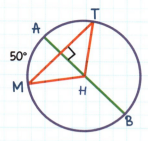

9. Find the value of y.

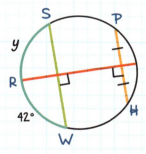

10. Find the lengths of $\overline{MT}$ and $\overline{CU}$ in circle P.

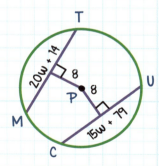

INSCRIBED ANGLES

An **INSCRIBED ANGLE** is formed by two intersecting chords with the point of intersection (called a vertex) on the circle.

The **INTERCEPTED ARC** is the part of the circle that is in the interior of the inscribed angle.

The measure of an inscribed angle is half the measure of its intercepted arc.

$$m\angle A = \frac{1}{2} m\overarc{BC}$$

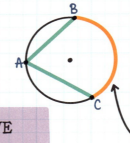

inscribed angle

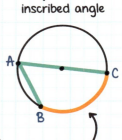

intercepted arc

IF TWO INSCRIBED ANGLES HAVE THE SAME INTERCEPTED ARC, THEN THOSE ANGLES ARE CONGRUENT.

$$m\angle A = \frac{1}{2} m\angle \overarc{BC}$$

$$m\angle D = \frac{1}{2} m\angle \overarc{BC}$$

$$m\angle A = m\angle D$$

$$\angle A \cong \angle D$$

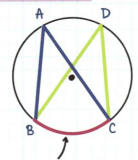

same intercepted arc

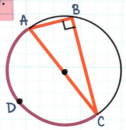

$$m\angle B = \frac{1}{2} m\overset{\frown}{ADC}$$

$$= \frac{1}{2}(180°)$$

$$= 90°$$

An **INSCRIBED SHAPE** is inside another shape, just touching the sides.

IF A QUADRILATERAL IS INSCRIBED IN A CIRCLE, THEN ITS OPPOSITE ANGLES ARE SUPPLEMENTARY.

∠A and ∠C are supplementary.

∠B and ∠D are supplementary.

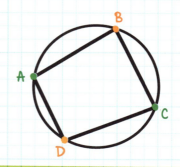

"INTERCEPT" MEANS TO "INTERRUPT" OR "STOP."

EXAMPLE: Find the value of y, m∠ABC, and m∠ADC.

Since the two inscribed angles, ∠ABC and ∠ADC, have the same intercepted arc, $\overarc{AC}$, those angles are congruent: ∠ABC ≅ ∠ADC.

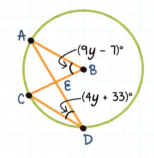

Therefore, set the two expressions equal to each other and solve for y.

m∠ABC = m∠ADC

$9y - 7 = 4y + 33$

$9y - 4y - 7 = 4y - 4y + 33$

$5y - 7 = 33$

$5y + 7 - 7 = 33 + 7$

$5y = 40$

$5y \div 5 = 40 \div 5$

$y = 8$

Substitute $y = 8$ into each expression.

THINK: Since m∠ABC = m∠ADC, this calculation is most likely correct.

m∠ABC = $(9y - 7)° = (9[8] - 7)° = 65°$

m∠ADC = $(4y + 33)° = (4[8] + 33)° = 65°$

So, the value of y is 8, and the m∠ABC and m∠ADC is 65°.

USE WHAT YOU KNOW ABOUT INSCRIBED ANGLES TO ANSWER THE FOLLOWING QUESTIONS.

1. Find m$\overarc{XZY}$.

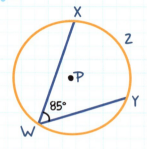

2. Find the value of x, m∠ABC, and m∠ADC.

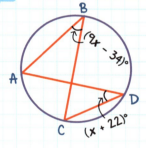

3. Find m∠QRS.

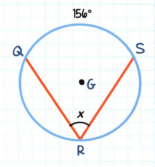

CHAPTER 41

4. Find the value of y.

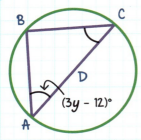

(3y – 12)°

5. Find m∠BDC.

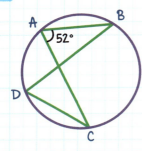

52°

6. Find m$\overarc{VZW}$, m$\overarc{WU}$, and m$\overarc{UV}$.

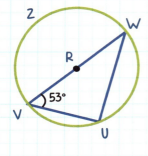

53°

7. Find the value of x.

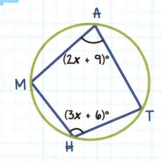

8. Find m∠J, m∠H, m∠B, and m∠G.

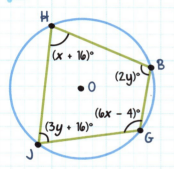

9. Find m∠SRU, m∠S, m∠STU, m∠U, m$\overarc{RST}$, and m$\overarc{TUR}$.

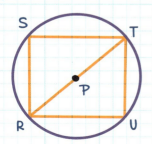

42 TANGENTS

A **TANGENT** is a line, segment, or ray that intersects a circle in exactly one point, called the **POINT OF TANGENCY**.

$\overleftrightarrow{AC}$, $\overrightarrow{DE}$, and $\overline{FH}$ are tangent to circle P.

B, D, and G are the corresponding points of tangency.

Two circles have a **COMMON TANGENT** if a line, line segment, or ray is tangent to both circles.

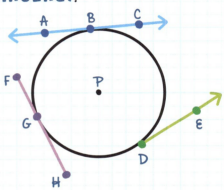

A LINE IS TANGENT TO A CIRCLE IF AND ONLY IF IT IS PERPENDICULAR TO THE RADIUS DRAWN TO THE POINT OF TANGENCY.

$\overleftrightarrow{AC}$ is tangent to $\odot O$ if and only if (iff) $\overline{OB} \perp \overleftrightarrow{AC}$.

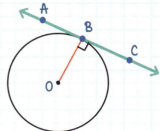

If $\overline{AB}$ and $\overline{AC}$ are tangent
to ⊙O at points B and C,
then $\overline{AB} \cong \overline{AC}$.

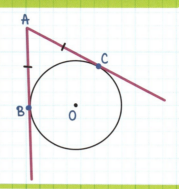

EXAMPLE: Determine if $\overline{AB}$ is a tangent to circle C.

If $\overline{AB} \perp \overline{BC}$, then $\overline{AB}$ is a tangent.

Use the converse of the **Pythagorean Theorem**
to check if △ABC is a right triangle.

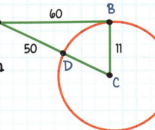

STEP 1: Find the length of $\overline{AC}$.

DC = 11, since it is a radius of the circle.

AC = AD + DC
AC = 50 + 11
AC = 61

THINK:
All radii of a circle
are congruent.
BC = 11, so DC = 11.

STEP 2: Check if △ABC is a right triangle.

$a^2 + b^2 \overset{?}{=} c^2$

$AB^2 + BC^2 \overset{?}{=} AC^2$

$60^2 + 11^2 \overset{?}{=} 61^2$

$3{,}600 + 121 \overset{?}{=} 3{,}721$

$3{,}721 = 3{,}721$ ✓

Since $AB^2 + BC^2 = AC^2$, $\triangle ABC$ is a right triangle and $\overline{AB} \perp \overline{BC}$.

Therefore, $\overline{AB}$ is a tangent to circle C.

EXAMPLE: Find the values of x and y given that $\overline{AQ}$ and $\overline{QF}$ are tangent to circle T and $m\angle Q = 78°$.

STEP 1: Find the value of x.

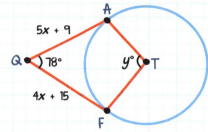

Since $\overline{AQ}$ and $\overline{QF}$ are tangent to circle T, they are congruent.

$AQ = QF$

$5x + 9 = 4x + 15$

$5x - 4x + 9 = 4x - 4x + 15$

$x + 9 = 15$

$x + 9 - 9 = 15 - 9$

$x = 6$

THINK:
The lengths of $\overline{AQ}$ and $\overline{QF}$ are both 39 units.

$5x + 9 = 5(6) + 9 = 39$
$4x + 15 = 4(6) + 15 = 39$

STEP 2: Find the value of *y.*

Since $\overline{AQ}$ and $\overline{QF}$ are tangent to circle T, $\overline{TA} \perp \overline{AQ}$ and $\overline{TF} \perp \overline{FQ}$.

Therefore, m∠A = 90° and m∠F = 90°.

Since the sum of the measures of a quadrilateral is equal to 360°,

m∠T + m∠F + m∠A + m∠Q = 360°

y + 90 + 90 + 78 = 360

y + 258 = 360

y + 258 − 258 = 360 − 258

y = 102

THINK:
The measure of ∠T is 102°.

So, the value of *x* is 6, and the value of *y* is 102.

FOR QUESTIONS 1 THROUGH 3, INDICATE WHETHER THE STATEMENT IS *TRUE* OR *FALSE*.

1. Two or more circles cannot have more than one common tangent.

2. A tangent can only be a ray that intersects a circle at exactly one point.

3. The points of tangency on circle H are points S, Y, and M.

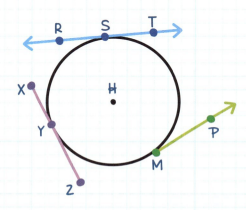

FOR QUESTIONS 4 AND 5, DETERMINE WHETHER $\overline{CD}$ IS TANGENT TO CIRCLE A.

4.

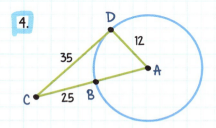

5.

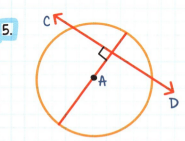

FOR QUESTIONS 6 THROUGH 10, FIND THE VALUE OF x. ASSUME THAT SEGMENTS THAT APPEAR TANGENT ARE TANGENT.

6.

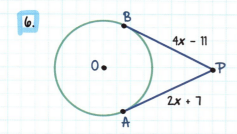

$4x - 11$

$2x + 7$

7.

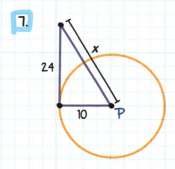

x

24

10

P

8.

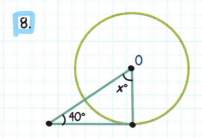

$x°$

$40°$

O

9.

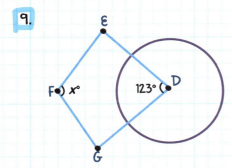

10.

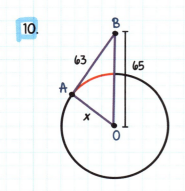

Chapter 43

SECANTS

A **SECANT** is a line, segment, or ray that intersects a circle at two points.

When two secants intersect **inside a circle:**

The measure of the angle that is formed is equal to one-half the sum of the intercepted arcs.

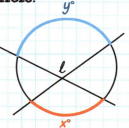

$$\ell = \frac{1}{2}(x° + y°)$$

When two secants intersect **outside a circle:**

The measure of the angle that is formed is equal to one-half the difference of the far arc less the near arc.

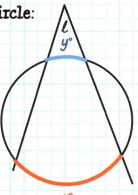

$$\frac{1}{2}(x° - y°)$$

This also applies to one secant and one tangent.

When secants and tangents intersect, their segment lengths have special properties.

Secants intersecting within a circle	Secants intersecting outside a circle	Tangent and secant intersecting
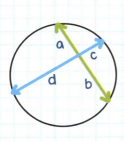	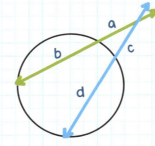	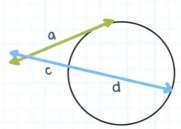
$a \times b = c \times d$	$a \times (a + b) = c \times (c + d)$	$a^2 = c \times (c + d)$

EXAMPLE: Find the value of x.

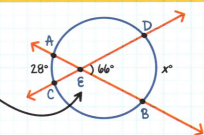

Two secants intersect *inside* circle E.

Therefore, $m\angle DEB = \frac{1}{2}(m\overset{\frown}{DB} + m\overset{\frown}{AC})$.

$66 = \frac{1}{2}(x + 28)$ Substitute.

$66 = \frac{1}{2}x + 14$ Distributive Property

THINK: $\overset{\frown}{DB}$ and $\overset{\frown}{AC}$ are the intercepted arcs.

$66 - 14 = \frac{1}{2}x + 14 - 14$ Subtraction Property of Equality

$52 \cdot 2 = \frac{1}{2}x \cdot 2$ Multiplication Property of Equality

$104 = x$

So, the value of x is 104.

EXAMPLE: Find m∠R.

Therefore, $m\angle R = \frac{1}{2}(m\overset{\frown}{SQ} - m\overset{\frown}{TS})$.

THINK:
The measure of $\overset{\frown}{SQ}$ is not given. Find that measure using what you know about a circle.

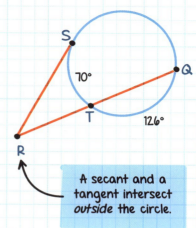

A secant and a tangent intersect *outside* the circle.

$m\overset{\frown}{SQ} + m\overset{\frown}{QT} + m\overset{\frown}{TS} = 360°$ Arc Addition Postulate

$m\overset{\frown}{SQ} + 126 + 70 = 360$ Substitute.

$m\overset{\frown}{SQ} + 196 = 360$ Add.

$m\overset{\frown}{SQ} + 196 - 196 = 360 - 196$ Subtraction Property of Equality

$m\overset{\frown}{SQ} = 164°$

$m\angle R = \frac{1}{2}(m\overset{\frown}{SQ} - m\overset{\frown}{TS})$

$m\angle R = \frac{1}{2}(164 - 70)$ Substitute.

$m\angle R = \frac{1}{2}(94)$ Subtract.

$m\angle R = 47°$ Multiply.

So, the measure of ∠R is 47°.

FOR QUESTIONS 1 THROUGH 6, FIND THE VALUE OF *x*. ASSUME THAT SEGMENTS THAT APPEAR TANGENT ARE TANGENT.

1.

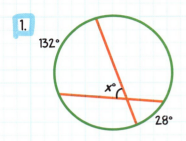

2.

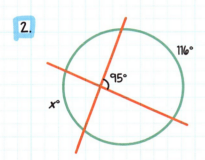

3.

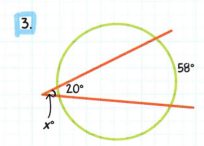

4.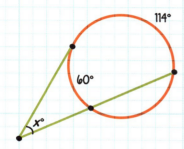

114°

60°

_x_°

5.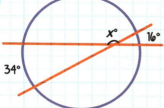

_x_°

16°

34°

6.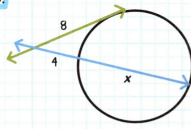

8

4

_x_

Chapter 44 ◇ EQUATIONS OF CIRCLES ◇

A circle can be graphed on a coordinate plane using its radius and the coordinates of its center.

The equation of a circle with its center at the origin $(0, 0)$ and radius r is: $x^2 + y^2 = r^2$.

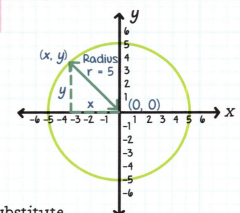

EXAMPLE: Find the equation of the circle.

Center: $(0, 0)$

Radius: 5

Equation of circle: $x^2 + y^2 = r^2$

$x^2 + y^2 = 5^2$ Substitute.

$x^2 + y^2 = 25$

 THINK:

This equation can be reached using the Pythagorean Theorem.

For any point (x, y) on the circle, $x^2 + y^2 = r^2$ (Pythagorean Theorem).

The circle is the shape formed by all points (x, y) where $x^2 + y^2 = r^2$ is true.

For a circle with a center (h, k) that is *not at the origin*, use the standard form equation: $(x - h)^2 + (y - k)^2 = r^2$

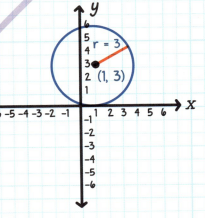

EXAMPLE: Find the equation of the circle.

Center: $(h, k) = (1, 3)$
Radius: 3
Equation of circle: $(x - h)^2 + (y - k)^2 = r^2$
$(x - 1)^2 + (y - 3)^2 = 3^2$ Substitute.
$(x - 1)^2 + (y - 3)^2 = 9$

If an equation of a circle is not given in standard form, we can use the process of **COMPLETING THE SQUARE** to rewrite the given equation in standard form. Then we can find the center and radius more easily.

Steps for completing the square:

1. Rearrange the quadratic equation, if necessary, so that the constants appear on one side of the expression.

2. Add $(\frac{b}{2})^2$ to each side of the equation.

3. Factor and solve for x.

How to draw circle graphs on the coordinate plane

Graph the circle $(x - 3)^2 + (y + 1)^2 = 25$.

STEP 1: Identify the center of the circle and the radius.

Equation of a circle: $(x - h)^2 + (y - k)^2 = r^2$
Center: (h, k)
Radius: r

Equation for our circle: $(x - 3)^2 + (y + 1)^2 = 25$
Center: $(3, -1)$
Radius: 5

STEP 2: Graph the center point of the circle, and then use the radius to graph four points on the circle.

The radius is 5, so count 5 units up from the center. Plot point $(3, 4)$. Repeat, counting 5 units down from the center $(3, -6)$, then right from the center $(8, -1)$, and left from the center $(-2, -1)$.

STEP 3: Use a compass to connect the points. Label the graph with the circle's equation.

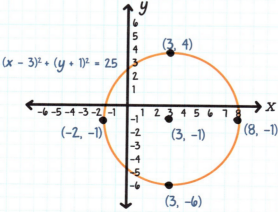

FOR QUESTIONS 1 AND 2, FIND THE CENTER AND RADIUS OF THE GIVEN CIRCLE. THEN DRAW THE GRAPH.

1. $(x - 3)^2 + (y + 2)^2 = 49$

2. $x^2 + y^2 = 64$

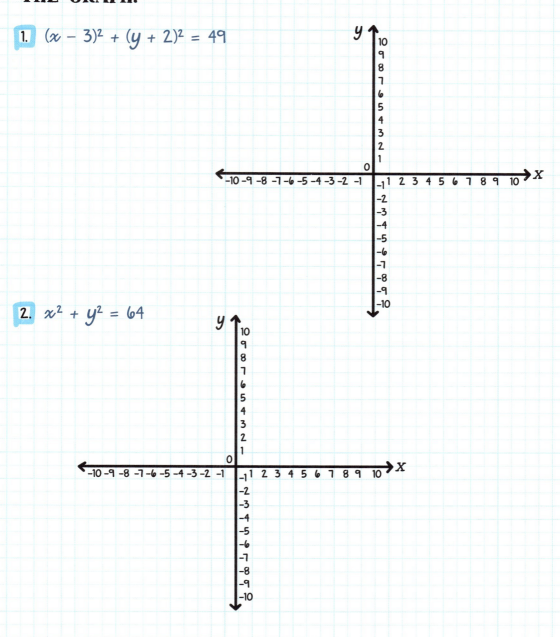

FOR QUESTIONS 3 THROUGH 5, WRITE THE EQUATION OF A CIRCLE WITH THE GIVEN INFORMATION OR GRAPH.

3. Center: at the origin, radius 12

4. Center (–8, 6), radius 10

5.

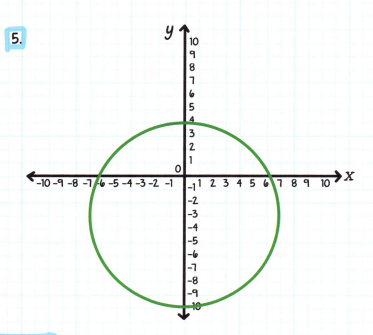

FOR QUESTIONS 6 AND 7, WRITE THE EQUATION OF THE CIRCLE IN STANDARD FORM. THEN FIND THE CENTER AND RADIUS AND DRAW THE GRAPH.

6. $x^2 + y^2 - 4x + 10y + 13 = 0$

7. $x^2 + y^2 + 6x - 8y - 11 = 0$

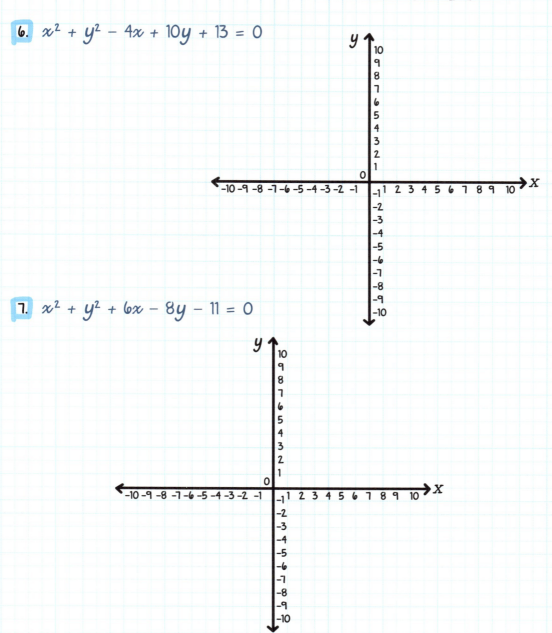

WORK SPACE

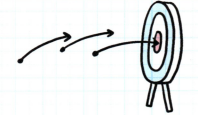

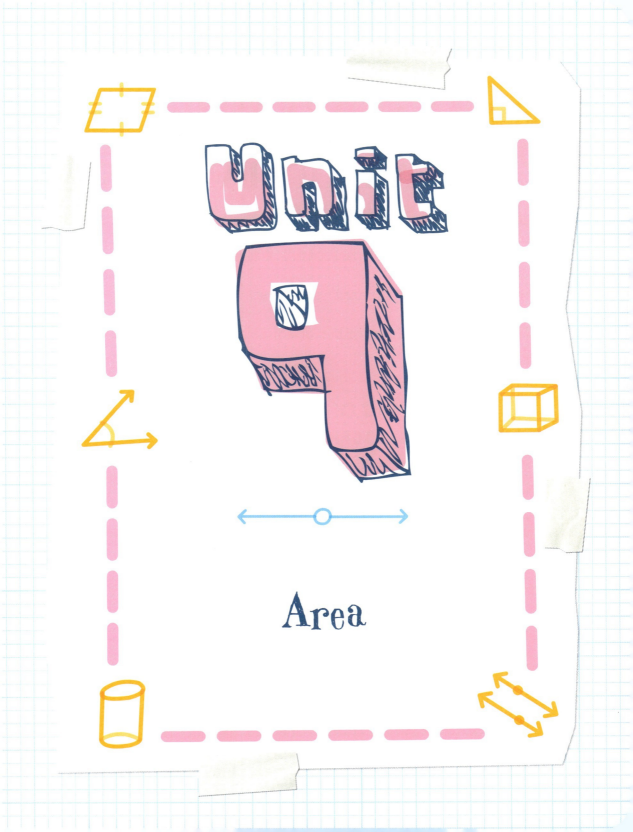

Unit 9

Area

UNIT 9
Chapter
45 AREAS OF PARALLELOGRAMS AND TRIANGLES

AREA (A) is the amount of space inside a two-dimensional object.

Area is written in "units squared" or units².

AREA OF A FIGURE is the number of equal-sized squares that the figure encloses.

AREA OF PARALLELOGRAMS

The **AREA OF A PARALLELOGRAM** is the length of the base *times* the height.

> This formula applies to rectangles, rhombuses, and squares too.

The formula for the area of a parallelogram is the *same* as the formula for the area of a rectangle because it is made up of the same parts. If we translate the shaded triangle in the parallelogram below, the parallelogram becomes a rectangle.

The base (b) of the parallelogram is the length of the rectangle, and the height (h) of the parallelogram is the width of the rectangle.

The formula to find the area of the rectangle is: $A = \ell w = bh$

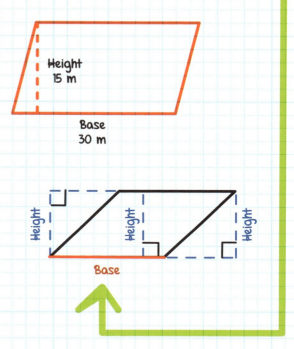

$A = bh = 30 \times 15 = 450 \text{ m}^2$

You can find the height of a parallelogram by drawing a perpendicular line from the line that contains the base to the line that contains the opposite side.

Note: This line can be *inside* or *outside* the parallelogram.

AREA OF TRIANGLES

The **AREA OF A TRIANGLE** is $\frac{1}{2}$ the length of the base *times* the height.

Formula: $A = \frac{1}{2} \times \text{base} \times \text{height}$ or $A = \frac{bh}{2}$

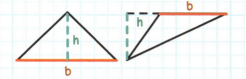

The height is the length of the perpendicular line drawn from a vertex to the base.

Note: This line can be *inside* or *outside* the triangle.

EXAMPLE: Find the area of △MAT.

Area of a triangle $= \frac{1}{2}$ base × height

Given: Base of △MAT
$= 3 + 16 = 19$ units

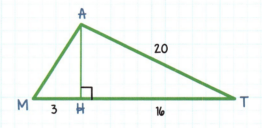

Since the measure of the height is *not* given, find the height using the Pythagorean Theorem.

Given: In △ATH, hypotenuse AT $= 20$, leg TH $= 16$, and leg HA $= b$

$a^2 + b^2 = c^2$
$16^2 + b^2 = 20^2$
$256 + b^2 = 400$
$256 - 256 + b^2 = 400 - 256$
$b^2 = 144$

$\sqrt{b^2} = \sqrt{144}$

$b = 12$

So, the height of △MAT is 12 units.

Area of △MAT $= \frac{1}{2}$ bh

$= \frac{1}{2}(19 \times 12)$

$= \frac{1}{2} \times 228$

$= 114$

Therefore, the area of △MAT is 114 square units.

FOR QUESTIONS 1 THROUGH 3, FIND THE AREA OF THE PARALLELOGRAMS.

1.

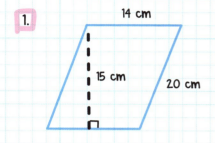

14 cm
15 cm
20 cm

2.

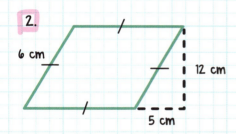

6 cm
12 cm
5 cm

3.

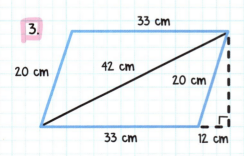

33 cm
20 cm
42 cm
20 cm
33 cm
12 cm

FOR QUESTIONS 4 AND 5, FIND THE HEIGHT, H, OF THE PARALLELOGRAMS. THEN CALCULATE THE PARALLELOGRAM'S AREA.

4.

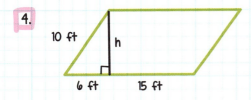

10 ft   h

6 ft   15 ft

5.

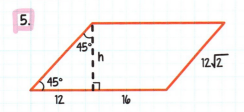

45°   h $12\sqrt{2}$

45°

12   16

FOR QUESTIONS 6 THROUGH 8, FIND THE AREA OF THE TRIANGLES.

6.

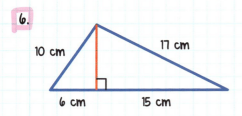

10 cm   17 cm

6 cm   15 cm

7.

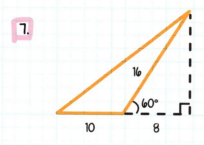

16

10   )60°

8

8.

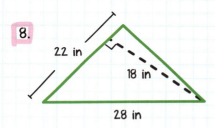

22 in

18 in

28 in

9. The area of the given triangle is **147 mm²** and the measure of its base is **14 mm**. Can you find the height of this triangle? If not, explain your reasoning. If yes, explain how and calculate the measure of the height.

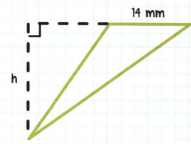

14 mm

h

Chapter

46 AREAS OF OTHER POLYGONS

AREAS OF TRAPEZOIDS

To calculate the area of a trapezoid, use the formula:

$$A = \frac{1}{2}h(b_1 + b_2)$$

h = height (the distance between the two bases)

b_1 and b_2 are the lengths of the two bases (the parallel sides) in any order.

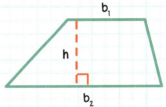

AREAS OF RHOMBUSES AND KITES

To calculate the area of a rhombus or kite, use the formula:

$$A = \frac{1}{2}d_1d_2$$

d_1 and d_2 are the lengths of the two diagonals (in any order)

AREA OF A RHOMBUS

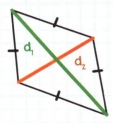

AREA OF A KITE

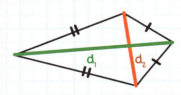

AREAS OF REGULAR POLYGONS

To calculate the area of a regular polygon, use the formula:

$$A = \frac{1}{2}aP$$

a = length of the **APOTHEM**, the perpendicular distance from the center to a side

P = perimeter, the sum of the lengths of all the sides

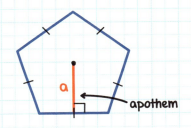

apothem

EXAMPLE: Find the area of the trapezoid.

Area of a trapezoid = $\frac{1}{2}h(b_1 + b_2)$

STEP 1: Find the height, DE.

Use $\triangle DEF$ and the Pythagorean Theorem (or Pythagorean triples) to find the height, DE.

$$a^2 + b^2 = c^2$$

$$DE^2 + EA^2 = AD^2$$

$$h^2 + 5^2 = 13^2$$

$$h^2 + 25 - 25 = 169 - 25$$

THINK:
You could also use $\triangle CFB$ to find the trapezoid's height.
$$a^2 + b^2 = c^2$$
$$CF^2 + BF^2 = BC^2$$
$$12^2 + 16^2 = 20^2$$

$h^2 = 144$

$\sqrt{h^2} = \sqrt{144}$

$h = 12$

STEP 2: Find the length of the bases.

Since EDCF is a rectangle, and opposite sides in a rectangle are equal in length, DC = EF, and therefore DC = 51.

Base 1 (b_1) = 51

Base 2 = AE + EF + FB
Base 2 = 5 + 51 + 16
Base 2 (b_2) = 72

STEP 3: Find the area.

Area = $\frac{1}{2}h(b_1 + b_2)$

$= \frac{1}{2} \times 12(51 + 72)$ Substitute.

$= \frac{1}{2} \times 12(123)$ Order of operations. Add inside the ( ).

$= 738$ Multiply.

Therefore, the area of the trapezoid is 738 square units.

EXAMPLE: Find the area of the kite.

Area of a kite = $\frac{1}{2}d_1d_2$

$d_1 = 8 + 8 = 16$

$d_2 = 11 + 23 = 34$

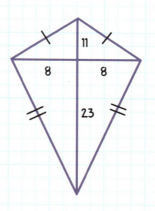

Area = $\frac{1}{2} \times 16 \times 34$ Substitute.

= 272   Multiply.

So, the area of the kite is 272 square units.

EXAMPLE: Find the area of the regular octagon.

A regular octagon has 8 congruent sides.

Area of regular octagon = $\frac{1}{2}aP$

apothem (a) = 14.6 cm

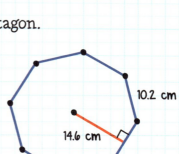

perimeter (P) = 10.2 × 8 *or*
10.2 + 10.2 + 10.2 + 10.2 + 10.2 + 10.2 + 10.2 + 10.2

= 81.6 cm

Area = $\frac{1}{2} \times 14.6 \times 81.6$ Substitute.

= 595.68   Multiply.

So, the area of the regular octagon is 595.68 cm².

USE WHAT YOU KNOW ABOUT AREAS OF POLYGONS TO ANSWER THE FOLLOWING QUESTIONS.

1. Find the area of the trapezoid.

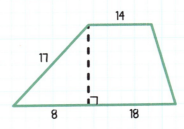

2. Harbor Health Fitness wants to install mirrors on a wall in the shape of a trapezoid. The blueprint of the wall is shown below. The mirrors cost $16 per square foot. Approximately how much will the mirrors cost?

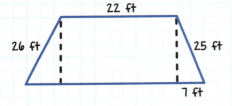

3. Find the area of the rhombus.

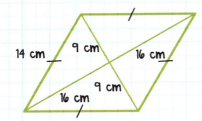

4. Find the area of the kite.

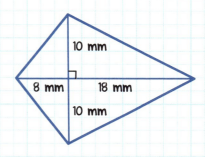

5. An environmental science class is constructing a garden on the school grounds. The completed garden will have the shape of a rhombus. What is the area of the garden if the length of one side is 26 feet and the length of one diagonal is 48 feet?

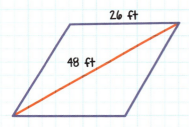

6. Find the area of the regular polygon.

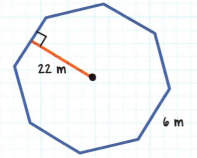

7. Harvey is designing a stone embellishment for the grounds of a park. An image of the regular polygon design and its measures are shown below. The design will be repeated 15 times throughout the park. Approximately how many square feet of the park will contain this stone embellishment? Round the answer to the nearest hundredth.

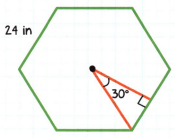

24 in

30°

8. Adeet states that the area of a fitness mat in the shape of a regular pentagon is 172.5 m², and the perimeter is 50 m. What is the length of the apothem?

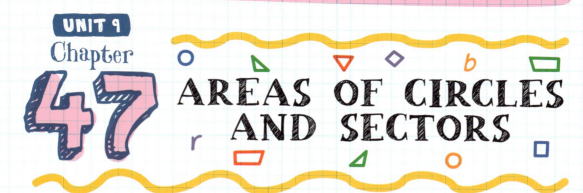

AREAS OF CIRCLES AND SECTORS

AREA OF A CIRCLE

To calculate the area of a circle, use the formula: $A = \pi r^2$

EXAMPLE: Find the area of a circle with a circumference of 28π centimeters. Round to the nearest tenth.

Use the circumference formula to find the radius.

$C = 2\pi r$ Circumference formula

$28\pi = 2\pi r$ Substitute.

$28\pi \div 2\pi = 2\pi r \div 2\pi$ Division Property of Equality

$14 = r$

Now use the area formula: $A = \pi r^2$

$= \pi(14)^2$ Substitute.

$= 196\pi$ Square the radius, 14.

≈ 615.4

So, the area of the circle is 196π cm^2 or approximately 615.4 cm^2.

AREA OF A SECTOR

The area of a sector (slice) can be found using a proportion that compares the sector to the whole circle.

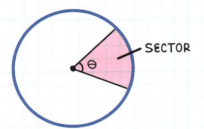

SECTOR

Formula for area of a sector:

$$A = \frac{\theta}{360°} \times \pi r^2$$

θ = measure of the sector's angle

EXAMPLE: Find the area of the shaded sector.

Given: The measure of the sector's angle is 140°.

The measure of the circle's radius is 16 ft.

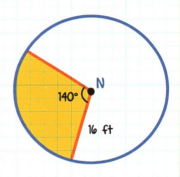

140° N

16 ft

$A = \dfrac{\theta}{360°} \times \pi r^2$ Area of a sector formula

$= \dfrac{140°}{360°} \times \pi(16)^2$ Substitute.

$= \dfrac{7}{18} \times 256\pi$ Simplify.

$= \dfrac{896}{9}\pi$

$\approx 99.56\pi$ or 312.6

So, the area of the shaded sector is about 99.56π or 312.6 ft².

FOR QUESTIONS 1 AND 2, FIND THE AREA OF THE CIRCLE. ROUND TO THE NEAREST TENTH.

1.

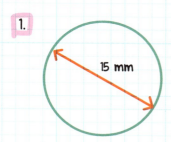

15 mm

2.

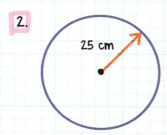

25 cm

3. Find the radius of a circle with area 126π mm².

4. Find the diameter of a circle with area 68π ft².

5. Find the area of a circle with circumference 76π cm². Round to the nearest tenth.

FOR QUESTIONS 6 THROUGH 9, FIND THE AREA OF THE SHADED PORTION OF THE CIRCLE. ROUND TO THE NEAREST TENTH.

6.
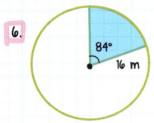
84°
16 m

7.
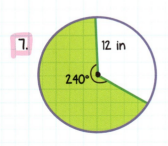
12 in
240°

8.

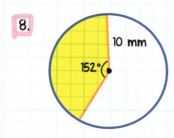

9.

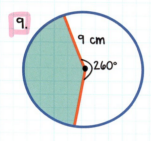

10. Stagehand workers are constructing a circular table. One carpenter is trying to determine if there is enough paint to accentuate the color of the shaded area shown in the design below. If the supply closet has a can of paint containing enough paint to color 130 square feet of space, is there enough paint? Explain your reasoning.

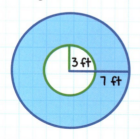

AREAS OF COMPOSITE FIGURES

A **COMPOSITE FIGURE** is a shape made up of two or more basic geometric shapes.

To find the area of a composite figure, follow these steps:

STEP 1: Break the composite figure into its basic shapes. Choose a way that requires the fewest or simplest calculations.

STEP 2: Find the area of each shape.

STEP 3: Add all the areas together (and subtract any missing parts if necessary) to find the area of the entire composite figure.

Formulas needed to calculate the areas of composite figures:

RECTANGLE	PARALLELOGRAM	TRIANGLE
$A = \ell w$	$A = bh$	$A = \dfrac{bh}{2}$
TRAPEZOID	RHOMBUS	KITE
$A = \dfrac{1}{2}h(b_1 + b_2)$	$A = \dfrac{1}{2}d_1 d_2$	$A = \dfrac{1}{2}d_1 d_2$
REGULAR POLYGON	CIRCLE	SECTOR
$A = \dfrac{1}{2}aP$	$A = \pi r^2$	$A = \dfrac{\theta}{360°} \times \pi r^2$

EXAMPLE: Find the approximate area of the shaded region. Round to the nearest whole number.

Since the area forms a composite figure, follow these three steps:

STEP 1: Break the composite figure into its basic shapes.

This composite figure can be broken down into a circle, a sector of that circle, and a regular hexagon (6-sided figure).

STEP 2: Find the area of each shape.

A. Regular hexagon area = $\frac{1}{2}aP$

apothem (a) = 6 yd

perimeter (P) = 10 yd × 6 sides = 60 yd

= $\frac{1}{2}$ × 6 × 60   Substitute: a = 6 and P = 60.

= 180 yd²   Simplify.

B. Circle area = πr^2

radius (r) = 6 yd

= $\pi(6)^2$ Substitute: r = 6.

= 36π

≈ 113 yd²   Simplify: Use $\pi = 3.14$. Round to the nearest whole number.

C. Sector area $= \dfrac{\theta}{360°} \times \pi r^2$

radius (r) = 6 yd

$\theta = 70°$

$= \dfrac{70°}{360°} \times \pi (6)^2$ Substitute: r = 6 and $\theta = 70°$.

$= 0.19\overline{4} \times 36\pi$

$= 7\pi$

≅ 22 yd²   Simplify: Use $\pi = 3.14$. Round to the nearest whole number.

STEP 3: Add all the areas together (and subtract any non-shaded area) to find the approximate area of the entire composite figure.

Regular hexagon area = 180 yd²

Circle area ≈ 113 yd²

Sector area ≅ 22 yd²

180 yd² + 22 yd² − 113 yd² = 89 yd²

THINK:
The shaded region does not include the entire circle's area, only a sector of its area. So, subtract the area of the circle from the combined area of the regular hexagon and the sector.

So, the area of the shaded region is approximately 89 square yards.

FOR QUESTIONS 1 THROUGH 8, FIND THE AREA OF THE SHADED FIGURES. ASSUME THAT ALL ANGLES THAT APPEAR TO BE RIGHT ARE RIGHT. ROUND TO THE NEAREST TENTH.

1.

2.

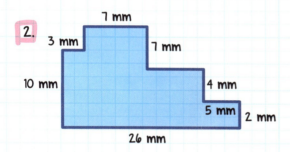

3.

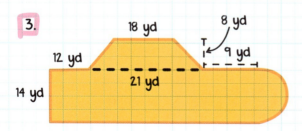

4.

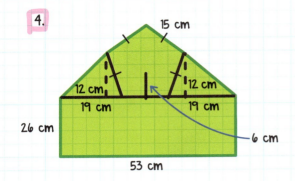

15 cm

12 cm

12 cm

19 cm

19 cm

26 cm

6 cm

53 cm

5.

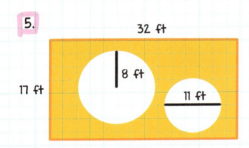

32 ft

8 ft

11 ft

17 ft

6.

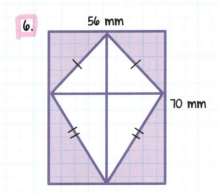

56 mm

70 mm

7.

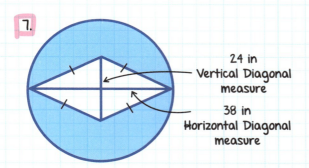

24 in
Vertical Diagonal
measure

38 in
Horizontal Diagonal
measure

8.

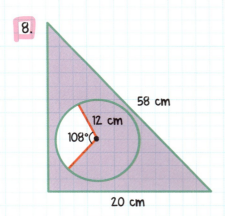

58 cm

12 cm

108°

20 cm

WORK SPACE

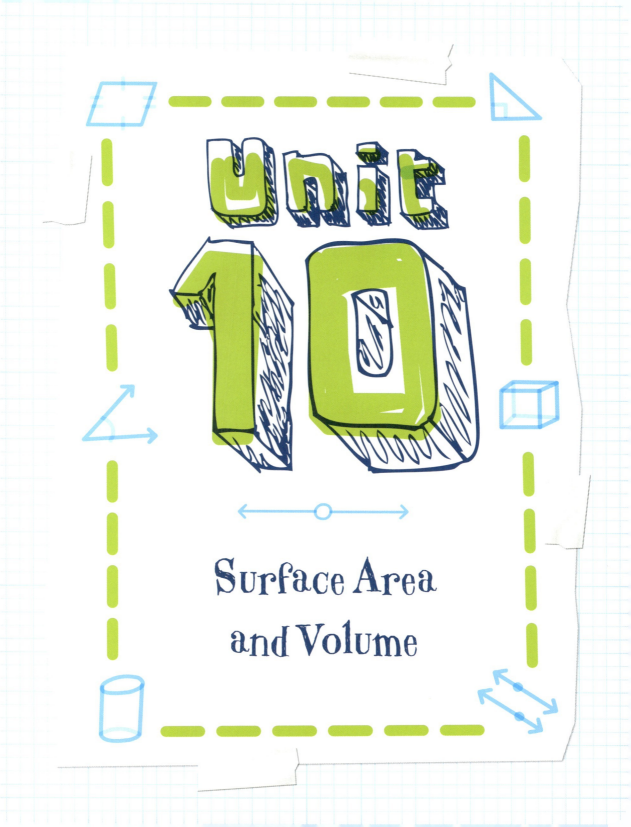

Unit 10

Surface Area and Volume

SURFACE AREAS OF PRISMS AND CYLINDERS

THREE-DIMENSIONAL (3-D) figures are shapes that have length, width, and height. They are also called **SPACE FIGURES** or **SOLIDS**.

A **POLYHEDRON** is a 3-D figure made up of polygons.

PRISMS are a type of polyhedron made up of two parallel and congruent polygon faces that are called **BASES**. The remaining faces are parallelograms and are called **LATERAL FACES**.

Prisms are categorized by the type of bases they have.

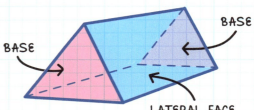

BASE

BASE

LATERAL FACE

A **RECTANGULAR PRISM** has all right angles, the bases are parallel rectangles, and the lateral faces are parallelograms.

A **TRIANGULAR PRISM** has bases that are parallel triangles and lateral faces that are parallelograms.

SURFACE AREA (SA) is the area of a shape's surfaces.

The surface area of a polyhedron is the sum of the area of its faces. We can calculate the surface area of a polyhedron by adding together the areas of each base and each lateral face.

The **LATERAL AREA (LA)** is the total area of the lateral faces.

The surface area of a prism can be calculated by unfolding the prism and looking at the **NET**, the two-dimensional representation of the prism's faces.

Lateral Area of a Prism	Surface Area of a Prism	
$LA = Ph$	$SA = 2B + Ph$	B = area of the base P = perimeter of the base h = height of the prism

EXAMPLE: A clothing boutique offers gift wrapping with any purchase. The manager purchases 50 rectangular prism-shaped boxes. How many square feet of wrapping paper will the store need to wrap the 50 boxes? Round your answer to the nearest square foot.

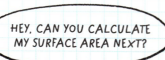

Hint: To find how many square feet of wrapping paper the store will need to wrap 50 boxes, find the surface area of one box, then multiply that number by 50.

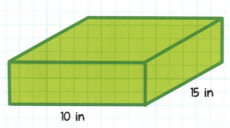

5 in

15 in

10 in

HEY, CAN YOU CALCULATE MY SURFACE AREA NEXT?

Method 1: Total Area of the Net

STEP 1: Draw a net of the prism.

STEP 2: Determine the area of each face. Since each face is rectangular, use the formula **area = length × width**.

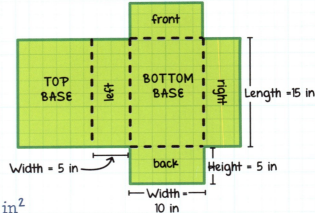

Top base: $A = 15$ in $\times$ 10 in $= 150$ in^2

Bottom base: $A = 15$ in $\times$ 10 in $= 150$ in^2

Left side: $A = 15$ in $\times$ 5 in $= 75$ in^2

Right side: $A = 15$ in $\times$ 5 in $= 75$ in^2

Front: $A = 10$ in $\times$ 5 in $= 50$ in^2

Back: $A = 10$ in $\times$ 5 in $= 50$ in^2

STEP 3: Find the sum of all the areas.

150 in^2 + 150 in^2 + 75 in^2 + 75 in^2 + 50 in^2 + 50 in^2
$= 550$ in^2

So, the surface area of the rectangular prism box is 550 square inches.

Method 2: Surface Area Formula

Use the formula for the surface area of a prism: $SA = 2B + Ph$.

B = area of the base = 150 in^2

P = perimeter of the base = $15 + 10 + 15 + 10 = 50$ in

h = height of the prism = 5 in

$$SA = 2B + Ph$$
$$SA = 2(150) + 50(5) \quad \text{Substitute.}$$
$$= 300 + 250$$
$$= 550 \text{ in}^2 \quad \text{Simplify. Notice: This is the } \textit{same} \text{ result determined in Method 1. Our answer checks!}$$

Last, calculate the *total square feet* of wrapping paper the store will need.

$$50 \text{ boxes} \times 550 \text{ in}^2 \text{ of wrapping paper} = 27,500 \text{ in}^2$$

That is the total amount of wrapping paper needed in square inches.

Now convert square inches to square feet: 12 inches $= 1$ foot.

$$27,500 \div 144 \approx 191 \text{ ft}^2$$

So, the clothing boutique will need approximately 191 square feet of wrapping paper.

EXAMPLE: Find the surface area of the triangular prism.

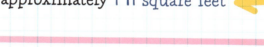

STEP 1: Draw a net.

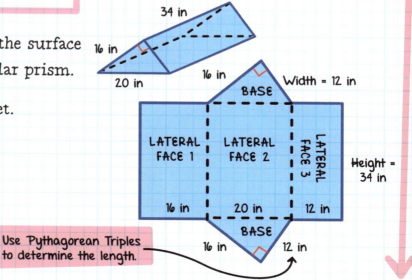

Use Pythagorean Triples to determine the length.

STEP 2: Use the formula for the surface area of a prism:
SA = 2B + Ph.

B = area of the base (a triangle) = $\frac{1}{2}$bh = $\frac{1}{2}$ × 12 × 16 = 96 in²

P = perimeter of the base = 16 + 20 + 12 = 48 in

h = height of the prism = 34 in

SA = 2B + Ph

SA = 2(96) + 48(34)   Substitute.

= 192 + 1,632

= 1,824 in²   Simplify.

So, the surface area of the triangular prism is 1,824 square inches.

A **CYLINDER** is a 3-D shape that has two parallel circular bases connected by a curved surface.

To find the surface area of a cylinder, look at the net.

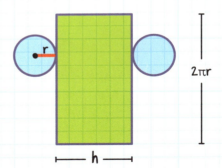

When you unfold a cylinder, the lateral area is shaped like a rectangle. The bases are shaped like circles.

Add the area of the two circle bases and the rectangle (lateral area) to get the total surface area.

Notice: The length of the rectangle *is the same as* the circumference of the circle.

Lateral Area of a Cylinder	Surface Area of a Cylinder	r = radius of the base
		h = height of the cylinder
LA = $2\pi rh$	SA = $2\pi r^2 + 2\pi rh$	

EXAMPLE: Find the surface area of the cylinder. Let $\pi = 3.14$.

STEP 1: Draw a net.

STEP 2: Use the formula for the surface area of a cylinder:
SA = $2\pi r^2 + 2\pi rh$.

r = radius of the base: 10 m

h = height of the cylinder = 25 m

SA = $2\pi r^2 + 2\pi rh$

SA ≈ $2(3.14)(10)^2 + 2(3.14)(10)(25)$ Substitute.

≈ 628 + 1,570

≈ 2,198 m²   Simplify.

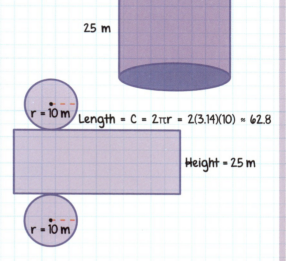

10 m

25 m

r = 10 m   Length = C = $2\pi r$ = 2(3.14)(10) ≈ 62.8

Height = 25 m

r = 10 m

So, the surface area of the cylinder is approximately 2,198 square meters.

FOR QUESTIONS 1 THROUGH 5, FIND THE SURFACE
AREA OF EACH PRISM. ROUND THE ANSWER TO THE
NEAREST TENTH, IF NECESSARY.

1.

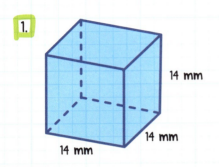

14 mm

14 mm

14 mm

2.

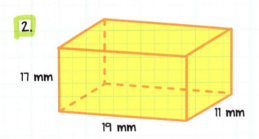

17 mm

19 mm

11 mm

3.

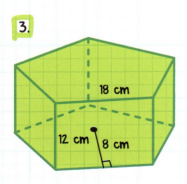

18 cm

12 cm

8 cm

4.

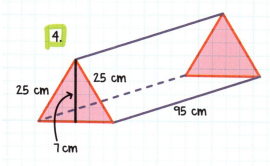

25 cm

25 cm

25 cm

95 cm

7 cm

5.

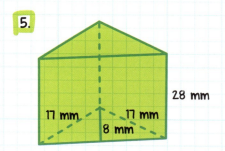

28 mm

17 mm   17 mm

8 mm

6. Ms. Santos wants to renovate an outdoor rectangular prism compost bin by painting its surface. If the compost bin has a height of 5 feet, width of 4 feet, and length of 8 feet, how many square feet of paint will the bin require?

FOR QUESTIONS 7 THROUGH 9, FIND THE SURFACE AREA OF EACH CYLINDER. LET π = 3.14, AND ROUND THE ANSWER TO THE NEAREST TENTH.

7.

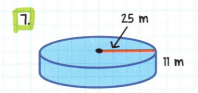

25 m

11 m

8. 8.6 cm

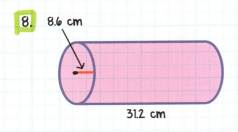

31.2 cm

9.

9 ft

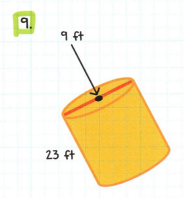

23 ft

10. A canned soup company is designing a new label for their tomato soup cans. Each label will completely wrap around the can without overlapping. How much paper will the company need to make 2,000 labels for cans that have a diameter of 3 inches and a height of 6 inches? Let $\pi = 3.14$, and round the answer to the nearest tenth.

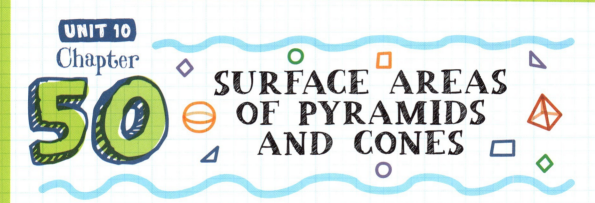

SURFACE AREAS OF PYRAMIDS AND CONES

A **PYRAMID** is a polyhedron in which the base is a polygon and the lateral faces are triangles.

A **REGULAR PYRAMID** has congruent lateral faces and a regular polygon for its base.

The faces of a pyramid meet at one point, called the **VERTEX** or **APEX**.

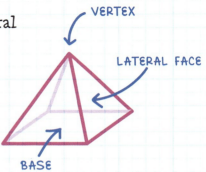

The **SLANT HEIGHT** (ℓ) of a regular pyramid is the height of a triangular lateral face.

The **HEIGHT OF THE PYRAMID** (h) is the length of the perpendicular line drawn from the vertex to the base.

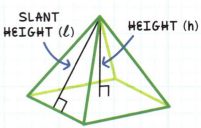

Pyramids are named by the shape of their base.

To calculate the surface area of a pyramid, add the area of all the faces. To calculate the surface area of a *regular pyramid*, use the following formulas:

Lateral Area of a Regular Pyramid

$LA = \frac{1}{2}Pl$

Surface Area of a Regular Pyramid

$SA = B + \frac{1}{2}Pl$

P = perimeter of base
l = slant height
B = area of base

EXAMPLE: Find the surface area of the square pyramid.

STEP 1: Draw a net.

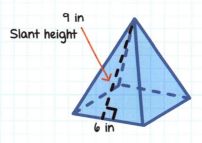

9 in
Slant height

6 in

STEP 2: Add the area of all the faces *or* use the formulas.

Method 1:

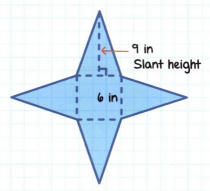

9 in
Slant height

6 in

Area of square base = side^2

$= 6^2 = 36$ in^2

Area of one triangular face = $\frac{1}{2}bh$

$= \frac{1}{2} \times 6 \times 9$

$= 27$ in^2

surface area = sum of all faces

$$= 27 + 27 + 27 + 27 + 36$$
$$= 144 \text{ in}^2$$

Method 2:

Lateral area $= \frac{1}{2} P\ell$

$$= \frac{1}{2} \times (6 + 6 + 6 + 6) \times 9$$

$$= 108 \text{ in}^2$$

Now substitute the **lateral area** into the surface area formula.

Surface area $= B + \frac{1}{2} P\ell$

$$= 6^2 + 108$$

$$= 144 \text{ in}^2$$

So, the surface area of the square pyramid is 144 square inches.

A **CONE** is a solid with a circular base and one vertex.

Note: A cone is *not* a polyhedron, unlike a pyramid. A polyhedron has *no* curved surfaces.

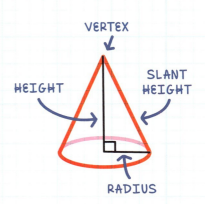

To calculate the surface area of a cone, use the following formulas:

Lateral Area of a Cone	Surface Area of a Cone	ℓ = slant height
$LA = \pi r \ell$	$SA = \pi r^2 + \pi r \ell$	r = radius of base

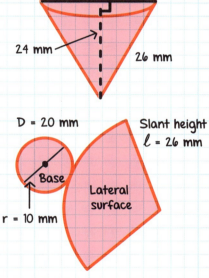

EXAMPLE: Find the surface area of the cone. Let $\pi = 3.14$, and round the answer to the nearest tenth.

STEP 1: Draw a net.

Notice the diameter is 20 mm. Therefore, the radius is 10 mm (half the diameter).

D = 20 mm

Slant height
ℓ = 26 mm

Base

r = 10 mm

Lateral surface

STEP 2: Use the formula $SA = \pi r^2 + \pi r \ell$.

$= \pi(10)^2 + \pi(10)(26)$

$= 100\pi + 260\pi = 360\pi$

$\approx 360(3.14) = 1{,}130.4$ mm^2

So, the surface area of the cone is 360π mm^2 or approximately 1,130.4 mm^2.

FIND THE LATERAL AREA OF EACH REGULAR PYRAMID.

1.

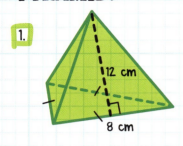

12 cm

8 cm

2.

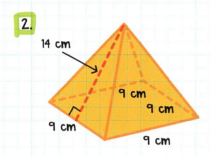

14 cm

9 cm
9 cm
9 cm
9 cm

FOR QUESTIONS 3 THROUGH 5, FIND THE SURFACE AREA OF EACH REGULAR PYRAMID.

3.

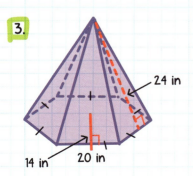

24 in

14 in   20 in

4.

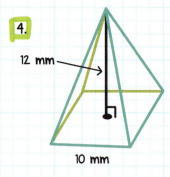

12 mm

10 mm

5.

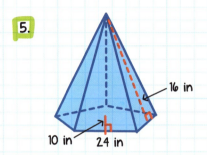

16 in

10 in   24 in

6. Find the lateral area of the cone. Let π = 3.14, and round the answer to the nearest tenth.

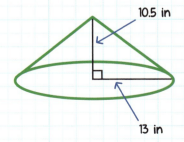

10.5 in

13 in

FOR QUESTIONS 7 AND 8, FIND THE SURFACE AREA OF EACH CONE. LEAVE YOUR ANSWER IN TERMS OF π.

7.

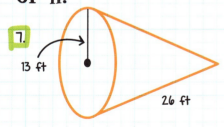

13 ft

26 ft

8.

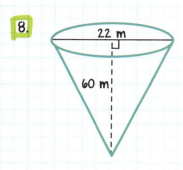

22 m

60 m

9. The roof on a farm's storage shed is in the shape of a cone. The facility manager is replacing the roof at a cost of $40 per square foot. If the slant height of the cone-shaped roof is 58 feet and the diameter is 28 feet, approximately how much will the new roof cost? Let π = 3.14, and round the answer to the nearest tenth.

10. Carlton is designing a square pyramid sculpture using flexible poles and multicolored fabric. If Carlton uses 5,775 square feet of fabric and the side length of the base is 35 feet, what is the measure of the pyramid's slant height?

11. Reardon accidentally substituted the height of a triangular pyramid into the surface area formula instead of its slant height. He says that the surface area he calculated is less than the actual surface area. Is Reardon correct? Explain your reasoning.

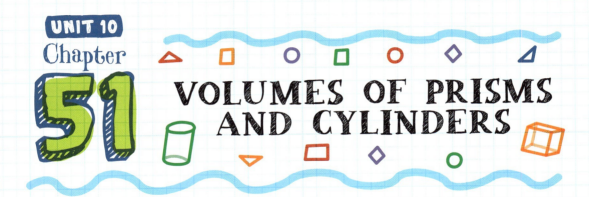

VOLUMES OF PRISMS AND CYLINDERS

The **VOLUME (V)** of a 3-D figure refers to the amount of space the solid encloses.

Volume is expressed in **CUBIC UNITS**—the number of cubes with an edge length of 1 unit that fit inside the solid.

To find the volume of most prisms, use the formula:

volume = area of the base × height of the prism

or

> Use a capital B to show that it's the area of the base.

V = Bh

> cubic units

The answer is given in units^3.

To find the **VOLUME OF A RECTANGULAR PRISM**, use the formula:

V = Bh

> area of the base
>
> height

or

V = lwh (length × width × height)

To find the **VOLUME OF A TRIANGULAR PRISM,** use the formula:

$V = Bh$

or

$V = \frac{1}{2} \times$ base $\times$ height $\times$ length $(V = \frac{1}{2} bhl)$

height of triangle

length of prism

To find the **VOLUME OF A CYLINDER,** use the formula:

$V = Bh$ — area of the base

$= \pi r^2 h$ — radius of the base

 **THINK:**

Since the base of a cylinder is a circle, we use the formula for the area of a circle ($A = \pi r^2$) to find the area of the base.

EXAMPLE: Find the volume of the rectangular prism.

Method 1	Method 2
$B = lw$	$V = lwh$
$= 14 \times 10$	$= 14 \times 10 \times 18$
$= 140$	$= 2,520$
$V = Bh$	
$= 140 \times 18$	
$= 2,520$	

18 in

14 in

10 in

So, the volume of the rectangular prism is 2,520 cubic inches.

Oblique Prisms and Cylinders

The volume of an oblique prism is taken from the volume of a regular (right angle) prism.

To find the volume of an oblique prism, which is the same as that of a right prism with the same base and height, use the formula $V = Bh$.

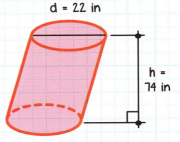

OBLIQUE means slanted, *not* parallel or perpendicular.

EXAMPLE: Find the volume of the oblique cylinder. Let $\pi = 3.14$, and round the answer to the nearest tenth.

d = 22 in

h = 74 in

$V = \pi r^2 h$ Formula

The diameter = 22 in, so the radius = 11 in.

$= \pi \times (11)^2 \times 74$ Substitute.

$= 8,954\pi$ in³

$\approx 28,115.6$ in³

So, the volume of the oblique cylinder is $8,954\pi$ cubic inches or about 28,115.6 cubic inches.

FOR QUESTIONS 1 THROUGH 8, FIND THE VOLUME OF THE PRISM OR CYLINDER. ROUND THE ANSWER TO THE NEAREST TENTH.

1.

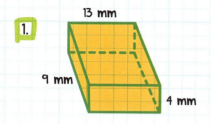

13 mm

9 mm

4 mm

2.

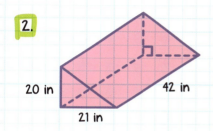

20 in

42 in

21 in

3.

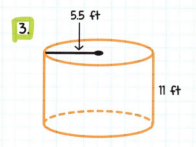

5.5 ft

11 ft

4.

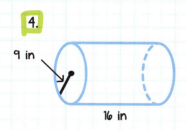

9 in

16 in

5.

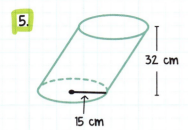

32 cm

15 cm

6.

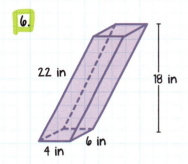

22 in

18 in

4 in

6 in

7.

16 ft

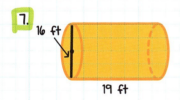

19 ft

8.

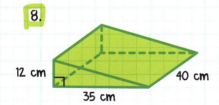

12 cm

40 cm

35 cm

9. A fish tank is 6 feet long, 3 feet wide, and 4 feet tall. If the aquarist fills the tank with 45 cubic feet of water, what is the height of the water level in the tank?

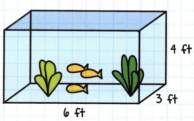

4 ft

3 ft

6 ft

10. A farm stores its grain in the two cylinder-shaped grain bins shown below. Approximately how much more grain can be stored in the larger grain bin? Round the answer to the nearest hundredth.

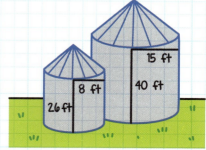

15 ft

8 ft

40 ft

26 ft

VOLUMES OF PYRAMIDS AND CONES

To calculate the volume of a pyramid, use the formula:

$V = \dfrac{1}{3} \times$ area of base $\times$ height

or

$V = \dfrac{1}{3} Bh$

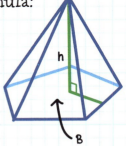

To calculate the volume of a cone, use the formula:

$V = \dfrac{1}{3} \times$ area of base $\times$ height

or

$V = \dfrac{1}{3} Bh$

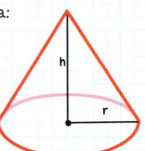

Since the base of a cone is a circle with area πr^2, this formula becomes:

Volume $= \dfrac{1}{3} \times \pi \times$ radius$^2 \times$ height

$V = \dfrac{1}{3} \pi r^2 h$

A **FRUSTUM** is the part of a pyramid or cone that is left when its top is cut off by a plane parallel to its base.

volume of frustum = volume of entire solid −
volume of missing part

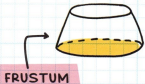

FRUSTUM

EXAMPLE: Find the volume of the hexagonal pyramid.

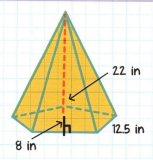

22 in

12.5 in

h

8 in

STEP 1: Find the area of the base.

Since the base is a regular hexagon, use the formula:

area of the base $(B) = \frac{1}{2}aP$

apothem $(a) = 8$ in   perimeter $(P) = 12.5 \times 6 = 75$ in²

$B = \frac{1}{2} \times 8 \times 75$ Substitute.

$= 300$ in²

STEP 2: Use this value and the height, given as 22 in. in the diagram above, in the formula for the volume of a pyramid.

$V = \frac{1}{3} \times$ area of base $\times$ height

$V = \frac{1}{3} \times 300 \times 22$ Substitute.

$= 2,200$ in³

So, the volume of the hexagonal pyramid is 2,200 cubic inches.

EXAMPLE: Find the volume of the cone.

STEP 1: Find the radius and the height of the cone.

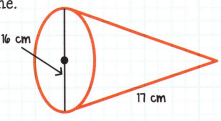

radius = $\frac{1}{2}$ diameter = $\frac{1}{2}$(16) = 8

To find the height, use the Pythagorean Theorem.

$a^2 + b^2 = c^2$

$a^2 + 8^2 = 17^2$ Substitute.

$a^2 + 64 = 289$

$a^2 = 225$

$a = 15$ The height of the cone is 15 cm.

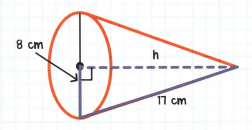

STEP 2: Use these values in the formula for the volume of a cone.

Volume = $\frac{1}{3}$ × area of base × height

Volume = $\frac{1}{3}$ × πr^2 × height

$V = \frac{1}{3} \times \pi \times 8^2 \times 15$ Substitute.

$= 320\pi$

$\approx 1{,}004.8$ cm³

So, the volume of the cone is 320π cubic centimeters or approximately 1,004.8 cubic centimeters.

EXAMPLE:

Find the volume of the frustum.

STEP 1: Determine the radius of the larger cone and the radius of the smaller cone (the top portion being cut off).

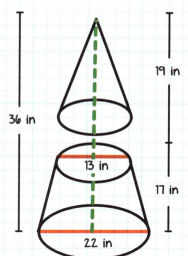

Larger cone:

radius = $\frac{1}{2}$ diameter = $\frac{1}{2}$(22) = 11 in.

Smaller cone (top portion):

radius = $\frac{1}{2}$ diameter = $\frac{1}{2}$(13) = 6.5 in.

STEP 2: Now use the formula for the volume of a frustum.

To distinguish between the formulas for both portions of the figure use R (for radius) and H (for height) in the formula for the larger portion, and r (for radius) and h (for height) in the smaller portion.

Volume = $(\frac{1}{3} \pi R^2 H) - (\frac{1}{3} \pi r^2 h)$

$= (\frac{1}{3} \times \pi \times 11^2 \times 36) - (\frac{1}{3} \times \pi \times 6.5^2 \times 19)$

$= 1,452\pi - 267.58\overline{3}\pi$

$\approx 1,184.42\pi$

$\approx 3,719.07$ in.^{3}

So, the volume of the frustum is about 1,184.42π cubic inches or about 3,719.07 cubic inches.

FOR QUESTIONS 1 AND 2, FIND THE VOLUME OF EACH REGULAR PYRAMID. ROUND TO THE NEAREST TENTH IF NECESSARY.

1.

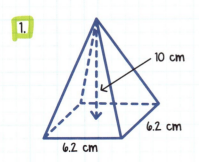

10 cm

6.2 cm

6.2 cm

2.

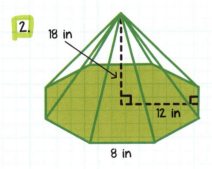

18 in

12 in

8 in

FOR QUESTIONS 3 AND 4, FIND THE VOLUME OF THE PYRAMIDS. ROUND TO THE NEAREST TENTH IF NECESSARY.

3.

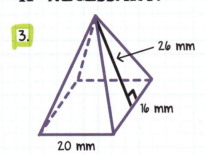

26 mm

16 mm

20 mm

4.

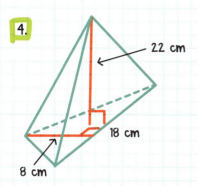

22 cm

18 cm

8 cm

FOR QUESTIONS 5 THROUGH 7, FIND THE VOLUME OF THE CONE. ROUND TO THE NEAREST TENTH.

5.

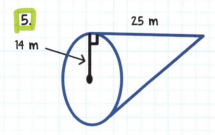

25 m

14 m

6.

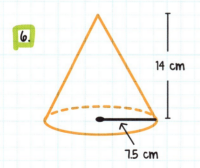

14 cm

7.5 cm

7.

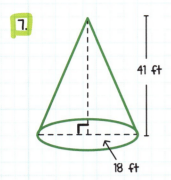

41 ft

18 ft

FOR QUESTIONS 8 AND 9, FIND THE VOLUME OF THE FRUSTUM. ROUND TO THE NEAREST TENTH.

8.

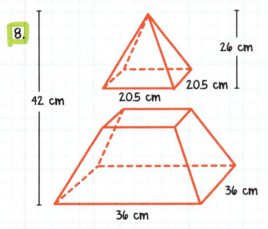

26 cm

20.5 cm

20.5 cm

42 cm

36 cm

36 cm

9.

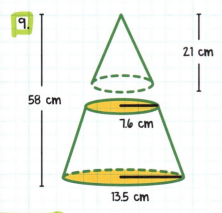

21 cm

58 cm

7.6 cm

13.5 cm

10. The volume of a cone-shaped water tank is 2,034.72 cubic feet. Its height is 24 feet. What is the radius of the water tank's base? Use 3.14 as an approximation of π.

11. Find the height of a rectangular pyramid with a volume of 1,320 cubic centimeters and a base area of 180 square centimeters.

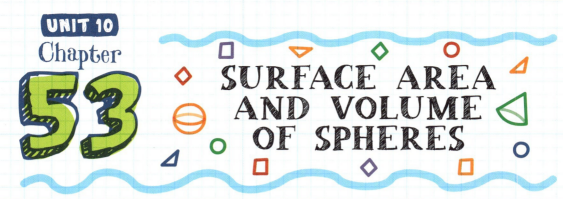

Chapter 53 SURFACE AREA AND VOLUME OF SPHERES

A **SPHERE** is a set of points in a space that are equidistant from a **CENTER** point, like a basketball.

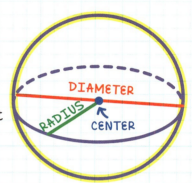

A **DIAMETER OF A SPHERE** is a line segment that passes through the center with both endpoints on the sphere.

A **RADIUS OF A SPHERE** is a line segment from the center to a point on the sphere.

To calculate the **surface area of a sphere**, use the formula:

$$SA = 4\pi r^2$$

To calculate the **volume of a sphere**, use the formula:

$$V = \frac{4}{3}\pi r^3$$

A **HEMISPHERE** is half of a sphere.

A circle that divides a sphere into two hemispheres is called a **GREAT CIRCLE**.

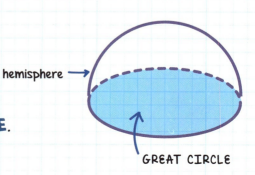

hemisphere →

GREAT CIRCLE

To calculate the **surface area of a hemisphere,** use the formula:

$$SA = \frac{1}{2}(4\pi r^2) + \pi r^2$$

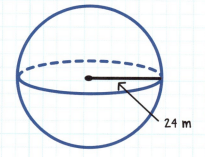

SA OF HEMISPHERE $\qquad$ $\frac{1}{2}$ SA OF HEMISPHERE $\qquad$ AREA OF GREAT CIRCLE

$\qquad\qquad\qquad$ ($\frac{1}{2}$ $4\pi r^2$) $\qquad\qquad$ (πr^2)

To calculate the **volume of a hemisphere,** use the formula:

$$V = \frac{1}{2} \times \frac{4}{3}\pi r^3 \quad \longleftarrow$$ The volume of a hemisphere is one-half the volume of a sphere.

EXAMPLE: Find the surface area of the sphere.

$SA = 4\pi r^2$ $\quad$ Formula

$= 4\pi(24)^2$ $\quad$ Substitute.

$= 2,304\pi$

$\approx 7,234.56$

24 m

So, the surface area of the sphere is $2,304\pi$ square meters or approximately $7,234.56$ square meters.

EXAMPLE: Find the volume of the sphere.

STEP 1: Determine the radius of the sphere.

radius = $\frac{1}{2}$ diameter = $\frac{1}{2}(30)$ = 15 yd

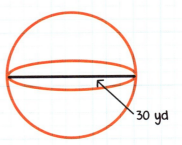

30 yd

STEP 2: Now use the formula for the volume of a sphere.

$V = \frac{4}{3}\pi r^3$ Formula

$= \frac{4}{3}\pi(15)^3$ Substitute.

$= 4{,}500\pi$

$\approx 14{,}130$

So, the volume of the sphere is $4{,}500\pi$ cubic yards or approximately 14,130 cubic yards.

EXAMPLE: Find the surface area of the hemisphere.

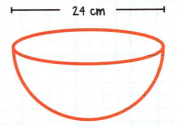

|← 24 cm →|

STEP 1: Determine the radius of the hemisphere.

radius = $\frac{1}{2}$ diameter = $\frac{1}{2}(24)$ = 12 cm

Use the formula for the surface area of a hemisphere.

$SA = \frac{1}{2}(4\pi r^2) + \pi r^2$ Formula

$= \frac{1}{2}(4\pi[12]^2) + \pi(12)^2$ Substitute.

$= 288\pi + 144\pi$

$= 432\pi$

$\approx 1{,}356.48$

So, the surface area of the hemisphere is 432π square centimeters or approximately $1{,}356.48$ square centimeters.

EXAMPLE: Find the volume of the hemisphere.

$V = \frac{1}{2} \times \frac{4}{3}\pi r^3$ Formula

$= \frac{1}{2} \times \frac{4}{3}\pi(10)^3$ Substitute.

$= 666.\overline{6}\pi$

$\approx 2{,}093.3$

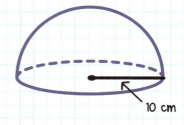

10 cm

So, the volume of the hemisphere is $666.\overline{6}\pi$ cubic centimeters or approximately $2{,}093.3$ cubic centimeters.

FOR QUESTIONS 1 THROUGH 3, FIND THE SURFACE AREA OF EACH SPHERE OR HEMISPHERE. LEAVE ANSWERS IN TERMS OF π.

1.

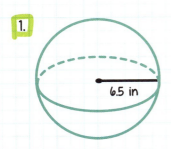

6.5 in

2.

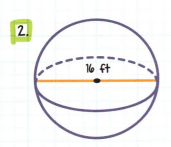

16 ft

3.

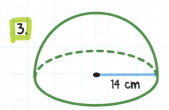

14 cm

4. Find the surface area of a sphere if the circumference of the great circle is 21.5π centimeters. Use 3.14 as an approximation for π and round the answer to the nearest tenth.

5. Find the surface area of a hemisphere if the area of the great circle is 25π square inches. Leave your answer in terms of π.

6. Find the volume of a sphere if the surface area is 144π cubic yards. Use 3.14 as an approximation for π and round the answer to the nearest tenth.

FOR QUESTIONS 7 THROUGH 9, FIND THE VOLUME OF EACH SPHERE OR HEMISPHERE. LEAVE ANSWERS IN TERMS OF π.

7.

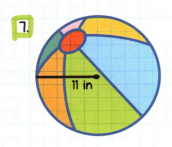

11 in

8.

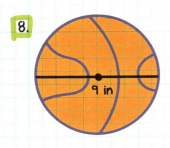

9 in

9.

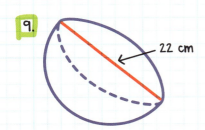

22 cm

10. Find the volume of a hemisphere if the circumference of the great circle is 60 yards. Use 3.14 as an approximation for π and round the answer to the nearest tenth.

11. A sphere-shaped balloon is leaking helium at 28 cubic feet per minute. If the diameter of the balloon is 16 feet, how long will it take for the balloon to fully empty and collapse? Use 3.14 as an approximation for π and round the answer to the nearest minute.

12. A physical therapist is using a piece of equipment that is hollow and in the shape of a hemisphere. The base of the object has an area of 56.25π square inches. What is the surface area of this hemisphere-shaped equipment? Use 3.14 as an approximation for π and round the answer to the nearest tenth.

UNIT 10
Chapter
54
VOLUMES OF COMPOSITE FIGURES

A **3-D COMPOSITE FIGURE** is a shape made up of two or more basic geometric solids.

We can split a composite figure into its basic geometric solids to make calculations.

Surface Area of Composite Figures

▶ The surface area of a composite figure is the area that covers the entire outside of the solid.

▶ To find the surface area, add up the areas of the outside faces, including any curved surfaces.

Volume of Composite Figures

▶ To find the volume of a composite figure, separate the shape into its basic solids. Then find the volume of each solid, using the appropriate volume formulas. Finally, add all the volumes together.

SOLID	LATERAL AREA	SURFACE AREA	VOLUME
Cone	$\pi r l$	$B + \pi r l$ or $\pi r^2 + \pi r l$	$\frac{1}{3} Bh$ or $\frac{1}{3} \pi r^2 h$
Cylinder	$2\pi rh$	$2B + 2\pi rh$ or $2\pi r^2 + 2\pi rh$	Bh or $\pi r^2 h$
Hemisphere		$\frac{1}{2}(4\pi r^2) + \pi r^2$	$\frac{1}{2}(\frac{4}{3}\pi r^3)$
Prism	Ph	$2B + Ph$	Bh
Pyramid	$\frac{1}{2} Pl$	$B + \frac{1}{2} Pl$	$\frac{1}{3} Bh$
Sphere		$4\pi r^2$	$\frac{4}{3}\pi r^3$

REMEMBER:
P = perimeter of the base
B = area of the base
r = radius of the base
h = height
l = slant height

EXAMPLE: Find the surface area and volume of the composite figure.

STEP 1: Calculate the surface area.

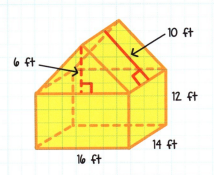

THINK:

The composite figure is made up of a *triangular prism* and a *rectangular prism*.

The parts on the surface are the lateral area of the triangular prism, the lateral area of the rectangular prism, and the bottom of the composite figure, which is the base of the prism.

To find the surface area of the composite figure, use the equation:

Total surface area of prism = lateral area of triangular prism + lateral area of rectangular prism + area of one of the prism bases.

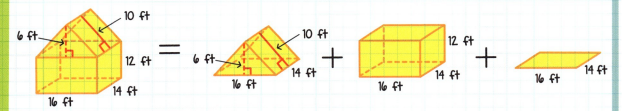

= Ph + Ph + lw

= (16 + 16 + 14 + 14)(10) + (16 + 16 + 14 + 14)(12) + 16 × 14

= 600 + 720 + 224

= 1,544 ft²

So, the surface area of the composite figure is 1,544 ft².

STEP 2: Calculate the volume.

To find the volume of the composite figure, use the equation:

Total Volume = Volume of the Triangular Prism +
             Volume of the Rectangular Prism

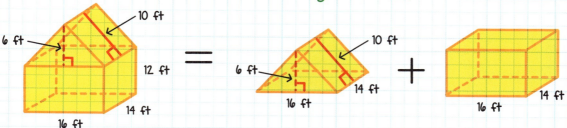

$= Bh + Bh$

$= (\frac{1}{2} \times 14 \times 16 \times 6) + (14 \times 16 \times 12)$

$= 672 + 2{,}688$

$= 3{,}360 \text{ ft}^3$

So, the volume of the composite figure is $3{,}360 \text{ ft}^3$.

EXAMPLE: Find the volume of the composite figure. Round the answer to the nearest tenth.

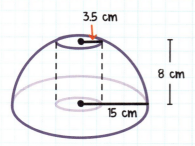

THINK:

The composite figure is made up of a hemisphere and a cylinder, which takes up space inside the hemisphere. If we subtract the volume of the cylinder from the volume of the hemisphere, we end up with the volume of the remaining solid.

To find the volume of the composite figure, use the equation:

Total Volume = **Volume of the Hemisphere** − **Volume of the Cylinder**

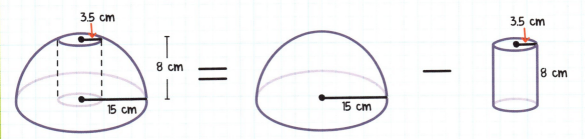

$= \dfrac{1}{2}(\dfrac{4}{3}\pi r^3) - \pi r^2 h$

$= \dfrac{1}{2}(\dfrac{4}{3}\pi [15]^3) - \pi(3.5)^2(8)$

$= 2{,}250\pi - 98\pi$

$= 2{,}152\pi \ \text{cm}^3$

$\approx 6{,}757.28 \ \text{cm}^3$

So, the volume of the composite figure is $2{,}152\pi \ \text{cm}^3$ or about $6{,}757.3 \ \text{cm}^3$.

FOR QUESTIONS 1 THROUGH 3, FIND THE SURFACE AREA OF EACH COMPOSITE FIGURE. USE 3.14 AS AN APPROXIMATION FOR π AND ROUND THE ANSWER TO THE NEAREST TENTH IF NECESSARY.

1.

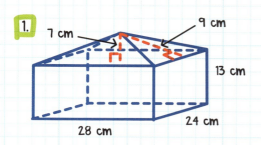

2.

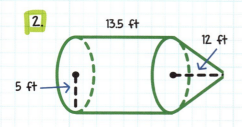

3.

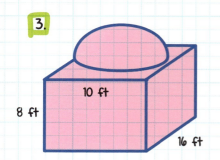

FOR QUESTIONS 4 THROUGH 6, FIND THE VOLUME OF THE COMPOSITE FIGURES. USE 3.14 AS AN APPROXIMATION FOR π AND ROUND THE ANSWER TO THE NEAREST TENTH.

4.

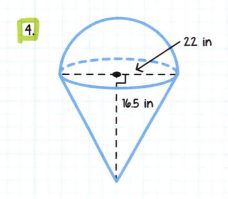

22 in

16.5 in

5.

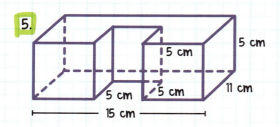

5 cm

5 cm

11 cm

5 cm   5 cm

15 cm

6.

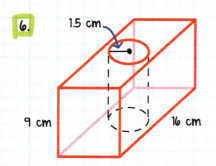

1.5 cm

9 cm   16 cm

SOLIDS OF REVOLUTION

A **SOLID OF REVOLUTION** is the solid formed when a two-dimensional object is rotated about a line, called the **axis**.

Examples of a solid of revolution:

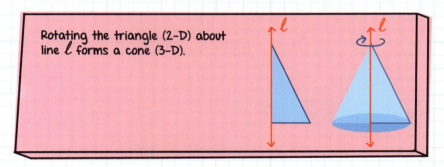

Rotating the triangle (2-D) about line l forms a cone (3-D).

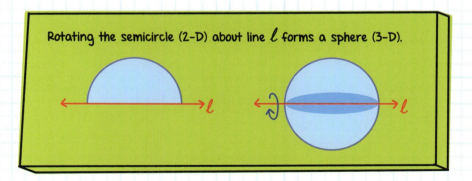

Rotating the semicircle (2-D) about line l forms a sphere (3-D).

EXAMPLE: Find the volume of the solid formed when the triangle is rotated about line ℓ.

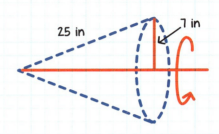

25 in

7 in

ℓ

STEP 1: Identify the solid formed by the rotation.

The solid formed is a cone. The hypotenuse of the triangle becomes the slant height of the cone, so $\ell = 25$ in. The 7-in. leg of the triangle becomes the radius of the base of the cone, so $r = 7$ in.

25 in

7 in

STEP 2: Calculate the volume of the solid. Use the formula for the volume of a cone:

$$V = \frac{1}{3}\pi r^2 h$$

To use the formula for the volume of a cone, first find the height, h, of the cone. Use the Pythagorean Theorem.

$a^2 + b^2 = c^2$ Pythagorean Theorem

$height^2 + radius^2 = slant\ height^2$

$h^2 + 7^2 = 25^2$ Substitute.

$h^2 + 49 = 625$

$h^2 = 576$

$h = 24$ The height of the cone is 24 in.

$V = \frac{1}{3}\pi r^2 h$ Formula

$= \frac{1}{3}\pi(7)^2(24)$ Substitute.

$= 392\pi$

$\approx 1{,}230.88$

So, the volume of the solid formed when the triangle is rotated about line ℓ is 392π in³ or approximately $1{,}230.88$ in³.

SOLIDS OF REVOLUTION ON A COORDINATE PLANE

A two-dimensional figure rotated around the x- or y-axis (or another line in the plane) also forms a three-dimensional object.

EXAMPLE: Find the volume of the solid formed by rotating the shaded figure around the y-axis.

STEP 1: Identify the solid formed by the rotation.

The shaded figure is formed of two semicircles. The solid formed by each semicircle is a sphere. The portion between the spheres (the shaded part) is the volume we need to find.

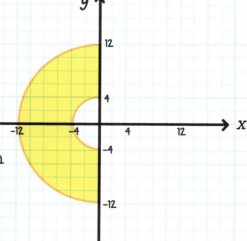

STEP 2: Calculate the volume of the solid. Use the formula for the volume of a sphere and the equation.

$$V = \frac{4}{3}\pi r^3$$

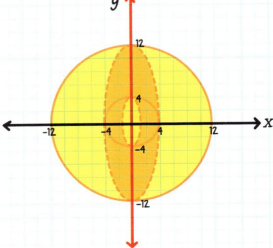

$$\begin{array}{ccc} \text{Volume of} & & \text{Volume of} \\ \text{shaded portion} & = & \text{larger sphere} \end{array} - \begin{array}{c} \text{Volume of} \\ \text{smaller sphere} \end{array}$$

$$V = \frac{4}{3}\pi r^3 - \frac{4}{3}\pi r^3$$

$$= \frac{4}{3}\pi(12)^3 - \frac{4}{3}\pi(4)^3 \qquad \text{Substitute.}$$

Radius of larger sphere = 12.

Radius of smaller sphere = 4.

$$= 2{,}304\pi - 85.\overline{3}\pi$$

$$\approx 2{,}218.67\pi \text{ units}^3 \approx 6{,}966.61 \text{ units}^3$$

So, the volume of the shaded portion is approximately 2,218.67π units³ or 6,966.61 units³.

FOR QUESTIONS 1 THROUGH 3, NAME THE SOLID
FORMED WHEN THE SHADED FIGURE IS ROTATED
ABOUT LINE l.

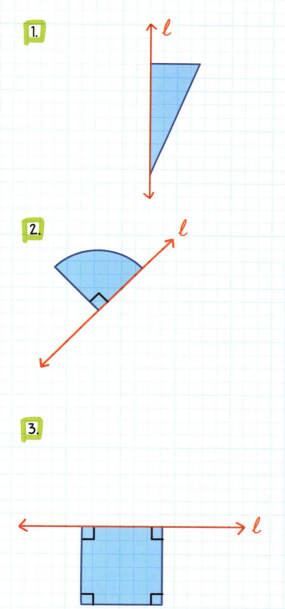

1.

2.

3.

FOR QUESTIONS 4 THROUGH 6, FIND THE VOLUME OF THE SOLID FORMED WHEN THE SHADED FIGURE IS ROTATED ABOUT LINE l. USE 3.14 AS AN APPROXIMATION FOR π AND ROUND YOUR ANSWER TO THE NEAREST TENTH.

4.

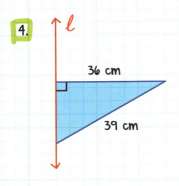

36 cm

39 cm

5.

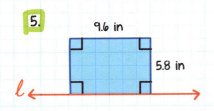

9.6 in

5.8 in

6.

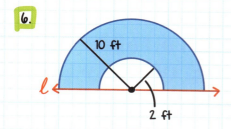

7. Find the surface area of the solid formed when the rectangle is rotated about line ℓ. Leave the answer in terms of π.

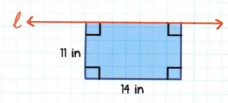

8. Find the volume of the solid formed when the figure is rotated about the x-axis. Leave the answer in terms of π.

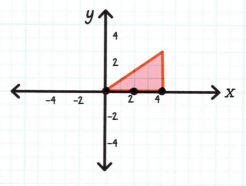

FOR QUESTIONS 9 AND 10, FIND THE VOLUME OF THE SOLID FORMED WHEN THE SHADED FIGURE IS ROTATED ABOUT THE *y*-AXIS. LEAVE THE ANSWERS IN TERMS OF π.

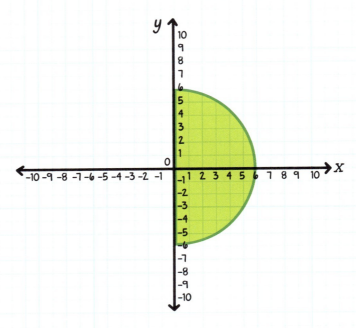

10.

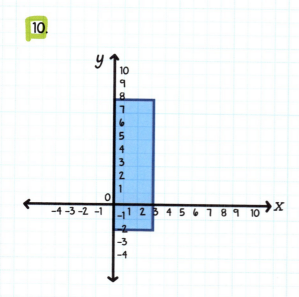

WORK SPACE

SOLUTIONS

Answer Key

UNIT 1

Basics of Geometry
(Chapters 1-6)

CHAPTER 1

POINTS, LINES, AND PLANES

1. The other six names for plane A are KVP, VPK, PKV, KPV, VKP, and PVK.

2. Points K, V, and P are coplanar.

3. The intersection of line $\overleftrightarrow{NM}$ and plane A is point V.

4. Three collinear points are N, V, and M.

5. There are **six** planes shown in the figure.

6. The intersection of plane EFG and plane EAD is $\overline{EH}$.

7. If H is a point on segment $\overline{GI}$, then $GH + HI = GI$.

8. Use the Segment Addition Postulate.
   $AB + BC = AC$
   $25 + 43 = 68$

9. Use the Segment Addition Postulate.

   $HJ + JV = HV$
   $24 + 6x = 78$
   $\underline{-24 \qquad = -24}$
   $6x = 54$
   $\dfrac{6x}{6} = \dfrac{54}{6}$
   $x = 9$

10. Parallel lines are illustrated in A, F, and G. The lines are parallel because they are always the same distance apart and never meet.

11. Perpendicular lines are illustrated in B, D, and G. The lines are perpendicular because they intersect to form four right angles (angles that measure 90°).

12. $\overrightarrow{AB}$ bisects $\overline{DF}$ at point E, and plane M bisects $\overline{DF}$ at point E. A segment bisector is a line, ray, or plane that passes through a segment at its midpoint, bisecting it.

13. $\overline{AD} \cong \overline{BC}$, $\overline{BA} \cong \overline{CD}$, $\overline{AC} \cong \overline{AC}$

14. Jonathan is incorrect because a theorem is a statement that has to be proven to be true using other theorems, definitions, or postulates.

CHAPTER 2

ANGLES

1. $\angle LGK$, $\angle KGL$, $\angle 1$

2. $\angle MAT$ is an acute angle because its measure is greater than 0° but less than 90°.

3. $\angle RSN$ is an obtuse angle because its measure is greater than 90° but less than 180°.

4. $\angle HBP$ is a right angle because it measures exactly 90°.

5. $\angle W$ is a straight angle because it measures exactly 180°.

6. Use the Angle Addition Postulate.
$$m\angle CAE = m\angle CAD + m\angle DAE$$
$$102° = (x - 3)° + (2x)°$$
$$3 + 102 = 3x - 3 + 3$$
$$\frac{105}{3} = \frac{3x}{3}$$
$$x = 35$$

7. First, use the Angle Addition Postulate to find the value of x.
$$m\angle NSP = m\angle NSH + m\angle HST + m\angle TSP$$
$$180° = (4x - 24)° + x° + (2x - 13)°$$
$$180 + 37 = 7x - 37 + 37$$
$$\frac{217}{7} = \frac{7x}{7}$$
$$x = 31$$

Then substitute that value for x in the measure of $\angle NSH$
$$m\angle NSH = (4x - 24)°$$
$$= 4(31) - 24$$
$$= 124 - 24$$
$$= 100$$

Therefore, $m\angle NSH$ equals 100°.

8. $\angle EDC$

9. $\angle BCA$

10. $\angle CED$

11. $\angle ECB$

CHAPTER 3

ANGLE PAIRS

1. $\angle EFD$ and $\angle BFA$ are vertical angles because they are nonadjacent and opposite each other.

2. $\angle BFC$ and $\angle BFA$ are complementary angles because the sum of their measures is 90°.

3. $\angle CFD$ and $\angle CFA$ are supplementary angles because the sum of their measures is 180°.

4 ∠DFE and ∠AFE form a linear pair because these two angles are adjacent and supplementary.

5 ∠AFE and ∠BFD are vertical angles because they are nonadjacent and opposite each other.

6 m∠FOD = m∠COE because they are vertical angles.

$$8x - 4 = 60$$
$$8x - 4 + 4 = 60 + 4$$
$$\frac{8x}{8} = \frac{64}{8}$$
$$x = 8$$
$$m\angle AOB = 180°$$
$$m\angle AOB = m\angle AOC + m\angle COE + m\angle EOB$$
So, m∠AOC + m∠COE + m∠EOB = 180

$$5y + 60 + 5y = 180$$
$$10y + 60 - 60 = 180 - 60$$
$$\frac{10y}{10} = \frac{120}{10}$$
$$y = 12$$
So, the value of x is 8 and the value of y is 12.

7 If ∠1 and ∠2 form a linear pair, they are supplementary. So, the sum of their measures is 180°.
$$m\angle 1 + m\angle 2 = 180°$$
$$118° + m\angle 2 = 180°$$
$$118 - 118 + m\angle 2 = 180 - 118$$
$$m\angle 2 = 62°$$

8 If two angles are complementary, the sum of their measures is 90°.

If we assume that m∠1 ≥ m∠2, then we know the following:
$$m\angle 1 + m\angle 2 = 90°$$
$$m\angle 1 - m\angle 2 = 32°$$

Adding these two equations gives us the following:
$$2(m\angle 1) = 122°$$

Divide both sides of the equation by 2:
$$\frac{2(m\angle 1)}{2} = \frac{122°}{2}$$
$$m\angle 1 = 61°$$

Now we can substitute that value in our original equation:
$$m\angle 1 + m\angle 2 = 90°$$
$$61 + m\angle 2 = 90$$
$$61 - 61 + m\angle 2 = 90 - 61$$
$$m\angle 2 = 29$$
So, m∠1 = 61° and m∠2 = 29°.

9 If ray $\overrightarrow{DB}$ is an angle bisector of ∠ADC, then ∠ADB ≅ ∠BDC (or equivalently, m∠ADB = m∠BDC).

10 Because it is a perpendicular bisector, m forms four right angles with $\overline{ST}$.

m∠PRT = 90°

$7x + 6 = 90$
$7x + 6 - 6 = 90 - 6$
$\dfrac{7x}{7} = \dfrac{84}{7}$
$x = 12$

SR = RT
$8y - 14 = 3y - 4$
$8y - 14 + 14 = 3y - 4 + 14$
$8y - 3y = 3y - 3y + 10$
$\dfrac{5y}{5} = \dfrac{10}{5}$
$y = 2$

CHAPTER 4

CONSTRUCTIONS

1

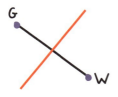

2

S

T

3

Q

m

4

n

W

5

b

H

6

M

7

Q

8

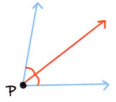

P

9

D

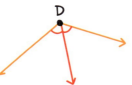

10

k

B •———————• A

CHAPTER 5

LOGIC AND REASONING

1 The example indicates deductive reasoning. It is the type of reasoning that uses given facts and statements to reach a conclusion logically. Mateo used information indicated in the chart to reach his conclusion that the sum of the two odd positive natural numbers in each row is even.

2 Counterexamples will vary. As just one counterexample, the sum of $\frac{1}{4} + \frac{1}{4}$ is $\frac{2}{4} = \frac{1}{2}$, which is a fraction, not a whole number. This example shows that the sum of two fractions is not always a whole number and proves that the conjecture is false.

3 If a pair of lines is perpendicular, then those lines form right angles.

4 The converse of the conditional statement is: If two angles form a straight line, then the two angles are supplementary. This statement is true.

5 Converse statement:
If a polygon has three sides, then it is a triangle.

Biconditional statement:
A polygon has three sides if and only if it is a triangle.

6 The Law of Detachment states:
If statements p → q and p are true, then the statement q is true.

If ∠C and ∠D are complementary angles, then the sum of their measures equals 90°.

∠C and ∠D are complementary angles.

Therefore, the sum of their measures equals 90°.

7 The Law of Syllogism states:
If the statements p → q and q → r are both true, then the statement p → r is also true.

If the school marching band raises $2,000, then the band will purchase new instruments.

If the school marching band purchases new instruments, then the band will perform at the annual homecoming parade.

Therefore, if the school marching band raises $2,000, then the band will perform at the annual homecoming parade.

CHAPTER 6

GEOMETRIC PROOFS

1

Statements	Reasons
1. $m\angle 1 = m\angle 3$ $m\angle 2 = m\angle 4$	1. Given
2. $m\angle 1 + m\angle 2$ $= m\angle 3 + m\angle 2$	2. Addition Property of Equality
3. $m\angle 1 + m\angle 2$ $= m\angle 3 + m\angle 4$	3. Substitution Property of Equality
4. $m\angle 1 + m\angle 2$ $= m\angle ABC$ $m\angle 3 + m\angle 4$ $= m\angle DEF$	4. Angle Addition Postulate
5. $m\angle ABC$ $= m\angle DEF$	5. Substitution Property of Equality

2 Sample proof (proofs may vary)

Statements	Reasons
1. Points A, B, and C $\overline{AB} \cong \overline{BC}$ $AB = 6x - 8$ $BC = 7x - 12$ $AC = 32$	1. Given
2. $AB = BC$	2. Definition of Congruent Line Segments
3. $6x - 8 = 7x - 12$	3. Substitution Property of Equality
4. $6x - 6x - 8$ $= 7x - 6x - 12$ $-8 = x - 12$	4. Subtraction Property of Equality
5. $-8 + 12$ $= x - 12 + 12$ $x = 4$	5. Addition Property of Equality
6. $AB = 16$ $BC = 16$	6. $AB = 6x - 8$ $6(4) - 8$ $24 - 8$ $= 16$ $BC = 7x - 12$ $7(4) - 12$ $28 - 12$ $= 16$ Substitution Property
7. $AB + BC = AC$	7. $16 + 16 = 32$ Substitution Property of Equality

3

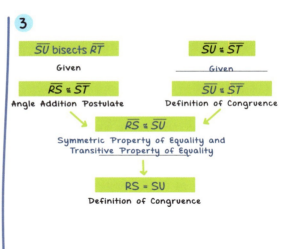

UNIT 2
Parallel Lines
(Chapters 7–9)

CHAPTER 7

PARALLEL LINES AND TRANSVERSALS

1 Answers may vary. As an example, plane QTS ∥ plane MPO. Parallel planes are two planes that never intersect.

2 Answers may vary. As an example, two skew segments are $\overline{QR}$ and $\overline{SO}$.

Skew segments are two segments that are not parallel and do not intersect.

3 Answers may vary. As an example, two segments parallel to $\overline{TS}$ are $\overline{QR}$ and $\overline{PO}$. Parallel segments are segments on the same plane that will never meet no matter how far they are extended.

4 Answers may vary. As an example, two segments parallel to $\overline{QM}$ are $\overline{RN}$ and $\overline{TP}$. Parallel segments are segments on the same plane that will never meet no matter how far they are extended.

5 Alternate interior angle pairs
∠B and ∠H
∠C and ∠E

6 Same-side interior angle pairs
∠B and ∠E
∠C and ∠H

7 Alternate exterior angle pairs
∠A and ∠G
∠D and ∠F

8 Corresponding angle pairs
∠A and ∠E
∠B and ∠F
∠D and ∠H
∠C and ∠G

9 Same-side interior angles
∠12 and ∠15
∠9 and ∠14
Transversal A connects each pair.

Same-side interior angles
∠8 and ∠3
∠5 and ∠2
Transversal B connects each pair.

Same-side interior angles
∠10 and ∠7
∠9 and ∠8
Transversal C connects each pair.

Same-side interior angles
∠14 and ∠3
∠13 and ∠4
Transversal D connects each pair.

10 Alternate interior angles
∠12 and ∠14
∠9 and ∠15
Transversal A connects each pair.

Alternate interior angles
∠8 and ∠2
∠5 and ∠3
Transversal B connects each pair.

Alternate interior angles
∠10 and ∠8
∠9 and ∠7
Transversal C connects each pair.

Alternate interior angles
∠14 and ∠4
∠13 and ∠3
Transversal D connects each pair.

11 Alternate exterior angles
∠11 and ∠13
∠10 and ∠16
Transversal A connects each pair.

Alternate exterior angles
∠7 and ∠1
∠6 and ∠4
Transversal B connects each pair.

Alternate exterior angles
∠11 and ∠5
∠12 and ∠6
Transversal C connects each pair.

Alternate exterior angles
∠15 and ∠1
∠16 and ∠2
Transversal D connects each pair.

12 Corresponding angles
∠11 and ∠15
∠12 and ∠16
∠10 and ∠14
∠9 and ∠13
Transversal A connects each pair.

Corresponding angles
∠7 and ∠3
∠8 and ∠4
∠6 and ∠2
∠5 and ∠1
Transversal B connects each pair.

Corresponding angles
∠11 and ∠7
∠10 and ∠6
∠12 and ∠8
∠9 and ∠5
Transversal C connects each pair.

Corresponding angles
∠15 and ∠3
∠14 and ∠2
∠16 and ∠4
∠13 and ∠1
Transversal D connects each pair.

CHAPTER 8

PROVING SPECIAL ANGLE PAIRS

1 $m\angle 1 = 50°$
$m\angle 5 = m\angle 1 = 50°$

Use the Corresponding
Angles Postulate.

2 $m\angle 3 = 50°$
$m\angle 3 + m\angle 6 = 180°$
$m\angle 6 = 180° - m\angle 3$
$M\angle 6 = 180° - 50° = 130°$

Use the Same-Side Interior
Angles Theorem.

3 $m\angle 2 = 130°$
$m\angle 8 = m\angle 2 = 130°$

Use the Alternate Exterior Angles Theorem.

4 $m\angle 3 = 50°$
$m\angle 7 = m\angle 3 = 50°$

Use the Corresponding Angles Postulate.

5 $m\angle 6 = 130°$
$m\angle 4 = m\angle 6 = 130°$

Use the Alternate Interior Angles Theorem.

6 Use the Alternate Exterior Angles Theorem.

$m\angle XYB = m\angle CZW$
$3x + 38 = 8x - 77$
$3x - 3x + 38 = 8x - 3x - 77$
$38 = 5x - 77$
$38 + 77 = 5x - 77 + 77$
$115 = 5x$
$\dfrac{115}{5} = \dfrac{5x}{5}$
$x = 23$

7 Use the Same-Side Interior Angles Theorem.

$m\angle BYZ + m\angle DZY = 180°$
$(9y - 33)° + (5y + 3)° = 180°$
$14y - 30 = 180$
$14y - 30 + 30 = 180 + 30$
$14y = 210$

$\dfrac{14y}{14} = \dfrac{210}{14}$
$y = 15$

8 $m\angle AYX = m\angle CZY$ because they are corresponding angles (the Corresponding Angles Postulate).

$\angle CZY$ and $\angle DZY$ form a linear pair, and therefore they are supplementary (the sum of their measures is 180°).

$(5z + 75)° + (13z - 21)° = 180°$
$18z + 54 = 180$
$18z + 54 - 54 = 180 - 54$
$18z = 126$
$\dfrac{18z}{18} = \dfrac{126}{18}$
$z = 7$

9 $\angle CZW$ and $\angle DZW$ form a linear pair, and therefore they are supplementary.

$m\angle CZW + m\angle DZW = 180°$
$(8k - 24)° + (5k + 35)° = 180°$
$13k + 11 = 180$
$13k + 11 - 11 = 180 - 11$
$13k = 169$
$\dfrac{13k}{13} = \dfrac{169}{13}$
$k = 13$

CHAPTER 9

PROVING LINES PARALLEL

1. Line v and line z are parallel using the Converse of Corresponding Angles Postulate, which states: If corresponding angles are congruent, then the lines are parallel.

2. Line w and line v are parallel using the Converse of Alternate Exterior Angles Theorem, which states: If alternate exterior angles are congruent, then the lines are parallel.

3. Line v and line z are parallel using the Converse of Alternate Interior Angles Theorem, which states: If alternate interior angles are congruent, then the lines are parallel.

4. Line w and line v are parallel using the Converse of Alternate Interior Angles Theorem, which states: If alternate interior angles are congruent, then the lines are parallel.

5. Line v and line z are parallel using the Converse of Same-Side Interior Angles Theorem, which states: If same-side interior angles are supplementary, then the lines are parallel.

6. Line w and line v are parallel using the Converse of Same-Side Interior Angles Theorem, which states: If same-side interior angles are supplementary, then the lines are parallel.

7. Line v and line z are parallel using the Converse of Alternate Exterior Angles Theorem, which states: If alternate exterior angles are congruent, then the lines are parallel. Note that $m\angle 7 = m\angle 5$ is superfluous to this proof, as $\angle 7$ and $\angle 5$ are vertical angles.

8. Line n is parallel to line o. Because of vertical angles, we can say that $65° + 115° = 180°$ and then we can use the Converse of the Same-Side Interior Angles Theorem, which states: If same-side interior angles are supplementary, then the lines are parallel.

9.

Statements	Reasons
1. $\angle 1 \cong \angle 2$	1. Given
2. $m\angle 1 = m\angle 2$	2. Definition of Congruent Angles

Statements	Reasons
3. $\angle 1 \cong \angle 3$	3. Vertical Angles Are Congruent
4. $m\angle 1 = m\angle 3$	4. Definition of Congruent Angles
5. $m\angle 2 = m\angle 3$	5. Symmetric and Transitive Properties of Equality
6. $\angle 2 \cong \angle 3$	6. Definition of Congruent Angles
7. line ℓ ‖ line m	7. Converse of Corresponding Angles Postulate
8. $m\angle 4 + m\angle 2 = 180°$	8. Same-Side Interior Angles Theorem

10 We are given that $m\angle 2 + m\angle 5 = 180°$. Since vertical angles have equal measure, $m\angle 2 = m\angle 4$. Substituting into the given equation, $m\angle 4 + m\angle 5 = 180°$, and then by the Converse of Same-Side Interior Angles Theorem, ℓ ‖ m.

11 Line e is parallel to line f. The supplementary angle to the angle that measures 62° is 118°, which is the corresponding angle to the angle labeled 118°. We know that 62° + 118° = 180°; therefore, by the Converse of Corresponding Angles Postulate, the lines are parallel.

UNIT 3
Triangles and Congruence (Chapters 10–15)

CHAPTER 10
TYPES OF TRIANGLES

1 Scalene triangle: 0 congruent sides and 0 congruent angles

2 Equilateral equiangular triangle: 3 congruent sides and 3 congruent angles

3 Scalene triangle: 0 congruent sides and 0 congruent angles

4 Isosceles right triangle: 2 congruent sides, 2 congruent angles, and 1 right (90°) angle

5 Triangle CDE has two congruent base angles: $\angle C$ and $\angle E$. Therefore, legs $\overline{CD}$ and $\overline{DE}$ are congruent, making it an isosceles triangle.

$CD = DE$
$4z + 3 = 6z - 7$
$4z + 3 - 3 = 6z - 7 - 3$
$4z = 6z - 10$
$4z - 6z = 6z - 6z - 10$
$\dfrac{-2z}{-2} = \dfrac{-10}{-2}$
$z = 5$

CD = 4z + 3   DE = 6z − 7
= 4(5) + 3   = 6(5) − 7
= 23   = 23

6 $\overline{CA} \cong \overline{BA}$ $\overline{CD} \cong \overline{DB}$

6w − 1 = 2   1 = x

6w − 1 + 1 = 2 + 1

$\frac{6w}{6} = \frac{3}{6}$

$w = \frac{1}{2}$

$\overline{AD}$ bisects ∠CAB, making
m∠CAD = m∠BAD, so y = 30.

7 Marti is incorrect. An equilateral triangle is an equiangular triangle and therefore has three congruent angles. Since the sum of the measures of the interior angles of a triangle is 180°, each angle in an equilateral triangle measures 60°. No interior angle of this triangle measures 90°.

CHAPTER 11

INTERIOR AND EXTERIOR ANGLES

1 m∠F + m∠G + m∠H = 180°

m∠F + 90° + 55° = 180°

m∠F + 145 = 180

m∠F + 145 − 145 = 180 − 145

m∠F = 35°

2 m∠C + m∠H + m∠A = 180°

24° + 81° + m∠A = 180°

105 + m∠A = 180

105 − 105 + m∠A = 180 − 105

m∠A = 75°

3 m∠R + m∠S + m∠T = 180°

(y − 3)° + (2y − 5)° + y = 180°

4y − 8 = 180

4y − 8 + 8 = 180 + 8

$\frac{4y}{4} = \frac{188}{4}$

y = 47

m∠R = y − 3   m∠S = 2y − 5

= 47 − 3   = 2(47) − 5

m∠R = 44°   m∠S = 89°

m∠T = y

m∠T = 47°

4 m∠KPL + m∠PKL = m∠KLO

45° + 75° = m∠KLO

120° = m∠KLO

m∠KLP + m∠KLO = 180°

m∠KLP + 120 = 180

m∠KLP + 120 − 120 = 180 − 120

m∠KLP = 60°

5 m∠DBA + m∠ABC = 180°

135° + m∠ABC = 180°

135 − 135 + m∠ABC = 180 − 135

m∠ABC = 180 − 135

m∠ABC = 45°

m∠ABC + m∠BAC + m∠BCA = 180°

45° + 75° + m∠BCA = 180°

$120 + m\angle BCA = 180$

$120 - 120 + m\angle BCA = 180 - 120$

$m\angle BCA = 60°$

6 $m\angle OMC + m\angle MOC = m\angle DCO$

$(4h + 8)° + (5h + 3)° = 146°$

$9h + 11 = 146$

$9h + 11 - 11 = 146 - 11$

$\dfrac{9h}{9} = \dfrac{135}{9}$

$h = 15$

7 $m\angle NOP + m\angle NOR = 180°$

$(5x + 22)° + (6x + 15)° = 180°$

$11x + 37 = 180$

$11x + 37 - 37 = 180 - 37$

$11x = 143$

$\dfrac{11x}{11} = \dfrac{143}{11}$

$x = 13$

$m\angle NOP = (5x + 22)°$

$= 5(13) + 22$

$= 65 + 22$

$m\angle NOP = 87°$

$m\angle NOR = (6x + 15)°$

$= 6(13) + 15$

$= 78 + 15$

$m\angle NOR = 93°$

$\angle NPO \cong \angle NOP$ because $\overline{PN} \cong \overline{ON}$.

$m\angle NPO = 87°$

$m\angle NPO + m\angle NOP + m\angle PNO = 180°$

$87° + 87° + m\angle PNO = 180°$

$174 + m\angle PNO = 180$

$174 - 174 + m\angle PNO = 180 - 174$

$m\angle PNO = 6°$

$m\angle NOP = m\angle y$ (because they are vertical angles)

$87° = m\angle y$

$y = 87$

CHAPTER 12

SIDE-SIDE-SIDE AND SIDE-ANGLE-SIDE CONGRUENCE

1 Using the Side-Angle-Side Congruence Postulate, we can determine that $\triangle RST$ and $\triangle KHG$ are congruent because $\overline{RS} \cong \overline{KH}$, $\overline{ST} \cong \overline{HG}$, and $\angle S \cong \angle H$.

2 Using the Side-Side-Side Congruence Postulate, we can determine that $\triangle ABC$ is congruent to $\triangle CDA$ because $\overline{AC} \cong \overline{AC}$, $\overline{BC} \cong \overline{DA}$, and $\overline{AB} \cong \overline{CD}$.

3 Using the Side-Angle-Side Congruence Postulate, we can determine that $\triangle BCD$ is congruent to $\triangle XZY$ because $\overline{CB} \cong \overline{ZX}$, $\overline{DB} \cong \overline{YX}$, and $\angle B \cong \angle X$.

4 Using the Side-Side-Side Congruence Postulate, we can determine that $\triangle DGH$ is congruent to △HFD because $\overline{GD} \cong \overline{FH}$, $\overline{GH} \cong \overline{FD}$, and $\overline{HD} \cong \overline{HD}$.

5 Using the Side-Angle-Side Congruence Postulate, we can say △OAD is congruent to △OBC because $\overline{BO} \cong \overline{AO}$, $\overline{DO} \cong \overline{CO}$, and ∠COB ≅ ∠DOA because vertical angles are congruent.

6 Using the Side-Side-Side Congruence Postulate, we can determine that △BAC is congruent to △FED because $\overline{AB} \cong \overline{EF}$, $\overline{AC} \cong \overline{ED}$, and $\overline{BC} \cong \overline{FD}$.

7 Using the Side-Angle-Side Congruence Postulate, we can determine that △ABC is congruent to △LMN because $\overline{BC} \cong \overline{MN}$, $\overline{AB} \cong \overline{LM}$, and ∠B ≅ ∠M.

8 Using the Side-Side-Side Congruence Postulate, we can determine that △PQR is congruent to △TSV because $\overline{PR} \cong \overline{TV}$, $\overline{PQ} \cong \overline{TS}$, and $\overline{QR} \cong \overline{SV}$.

9 Gwen is incorrect. In order to use the Side-Angle-Side Congruence Postulate, two sides and the included angle of one triangle must be congruent to two sides and the included angle of the other triangle. ∠T is congruent to ∠H, but they are not the included angles between the two sets of congruent sides. The congruence here is angle-side-side, and that arrangement does *not* prove the triangles to be congruent.

CHAPTER 13

ANGLE-SIDE-ANGLE AND ANGLE-ANGLE-SIDE CONGRUENCE

1 The Angle-Side-Angle Congruence Postulate can be used to prove △QRP is congruent to △CDE.

2 The Hypotenuse-Leg Theorem can be used to prove △ACB is congruent to △ZYX.

3 The Angle-Angle-Side Congruence Theorem can be used to prove △CAB is congruent to △FDE.

4 The Side-Side-Side Congruence Postulate can be used to prove △BAC is congruent to △EDF.

5 None. There is no angle-angle-angle postulate or theorem.

6

Statements	Reasons
1. $\overline{HR}$ bisects ∠CRT ∠CHR ≅ ∠THR	1. Given
2. ∠CRH ≅ ∠TRH	2. Definition of Angle Bisector
3. $\overline{RH} ≅ \overline{RH}$	3. Reflexive Property of Equality
4. △CRH ≅ △TRH	4. Angle-Side-Angle Congruence Postulate

7 ∠QRP ≅ ∠TRS (because they are vertical angles)

$$8y + 6 = 3y + 16$$
$$8y + 6 - 6 = 3y + 16 - 6$$
$$8y = 3y + 10$$
$$8y - 3y = 3y - 3y + 10$$
$$5y = 10$$
$$\frac{5y}{5} = \frac{10}{5}$$
$$y = 2$$

Using the Angle-Angle-Side Congruence Theorem, △PQR ≅ △STR when $y = 2$.

CHAPTER 14

TRIANGLE BISECTORS

1 Point H is the circumcenter of the triangle because it is the point where the three perpendicular bisectors of the sides all meet.

2 Point H is the orthocenter of the triangle because it is the point where the three altitudes of the triangle all meet.

3 Point H is the centroid of the triangle because it is the point where the three medians all meet.

4 Point H is the incenter of the triangle because it is the point where the bisectors of the three interior angles all meet.

5 Point H is the orthocenter because it is the point where the three altitudes all meet.

6 A. $\overline{RS}$ is a median of the triangle because it is the line from a vertex to the midpoint of the opposite side.

B. $\overline{RS}$ is an altitude of the triangle because it is a line segment from a vertex to the opposite side, and perpendicular to that side. An altitude can be outside or inside the triangle (in this case it is outside).

C. $\overline{RS}$ is a perpendicular bisector because it crosses a line segment at a right angle and divides it into two equal parts.

7 The sides marked $(4x - 7)$ and $(2x + 3)$ are the same length due to the Perpendicular Bisector Theorem.

$$4x - 7 = 2x + 3$$
$$4x - 7 + 7 = 2x + 3 + 7$$
$$4x = 2x + 10$$
$$4x - 2x = 2x - 2x + 10$$
$$2x = 10$$
$$\frac{2x}{2} = \frac{10}{2}$$
$$x = 5$$

8 GD = DE by the Incenter Theorem

$$6y - 8 = 5y + 6$$
$$6y - 8 + 8 = 5y + 6 + 8$$
$$6y = 5y + 14$$
$$6y - 5y = 5y - 5y + 14$$
$$y = 14$$

9 Use the Centroid Theorem

$$NM = \frac{2}{3}NG$$
$$10 = \frac{2}{3}NG$$
$$10 \cdot 3 = \frac{2}{3}NG \cdot 3$$
$$30 = 2NG$$

$$\frac{30}{2} = \frac{2NG}{2}$$
$$NG = 15$$

$$NG = NM + MG$$
$$15 = 10 + MG$$
$$15 - 10 = 10 - 10 + MG$$
$$MG = 5$$

10 XU = UZ = UV
XU = UZ
$$12a + 4 = 5a + 18$$
$$12a + 4 - 4 = 5a + 18 - 4$$
$$12a = 5a + 14$$
$$12a - 5a = 5a - 5a + 14$$
$$7a = 14$$
$$\frac{7a}{7} = \frac{14}{7}$$
$$a = 2$$

XU = 12a + 4	UZ = 5a + 18	
= 12(2) + 4	= 5(2) + 18	
XU = 28	UZ = 28	UV = 28

CHAPTER 15

TRIANGLE INEQUALITIES

1 Sides of the triangle from shortest to longest: $\overline{BC}$, $\overline{CA}$, $\overline{BA}$.

2 Sides of the triangle from largest to smallest: $\overline{RS}$, $\overline{RT}$, and $\overline{ST}$.

3 $10 + 18 = 28$, and $28 > 25$, so it is possible to form a triangle. The sum of the lengths of the two shortest sides is greater than the length of the longest side.

4 $8 + 10 = 18$, and $18 > 16$, so it is possible to form a triangle. The sum of the lengths of the two shortest sides is greater than the length of the longest side.

5 $6.6 + 10.4 = 17$, and $17 < 17.5$, so it is not possible to form a triangle. The sum of the lengths of the two shortest sides is less than the length of the longest side.

6 Let x represent the third side of the triangle.

$x + 8.9 > 12.5$
$x + 8.9 - 8.9 > 12.5 - 8.9$
$x > 3.6$

$8.9 + 12.5 > x$
$21.4 > x$
$x < 21.4$

$12.5 + x > 8.9$
$12.5 - 12.5 + x > 8.9 - 12.5$
$x > -3.6$

Since $x > -3.6$ has a negative number, we can ignore this.

$3.6 < x < 21.4$

The length of the third side of the triangle must be greater than 3.6 centimeters and less than 21.4 centimeters.

7 Let x represent the third side of the triangle.

$x + 6\frac{1}{4} > 15\frac{5}{8}$
$x + 6\frac{1}{4} - 6\frac{1}{4} > 15\frac{5}{8} - 6\frac{1}{4}$
$x > 9\frac{3}{8}$

$6\frac{1}{4} + 15\frac{5}{8} > x$
$21\frac{7}{8} > x$
$x < 21\frac{7}{8}$

$15\frac{5}{8} + x > 6\frac{1}{4}$
$15\frac{5}{8} - 15\frac{5}{8} + x > 6\frac{1}{4} - 15\frac{5}{8}$
$x > -9\frac{3}{8}$

Since $x > -9\frac{3}{8}$ has a negative number, we can ignore this.

$9\frac{3}{8} < x < 21\frac{7}{8}$

The length of the third side of the triangle must be greater than $9\frac{3}{8}$ inches and less than $21\frac{7}{8}$ inches.

UNIT 4

Quadrilaterals and Polygons (Chapters 16–19)

CHAPTER 16

PARALLELOGRAMS

1 $\overline{MP}$ = 10 cm $\overline{MR}$ = 10 cm
$\overline{HP}$ = 10 cm $\overline{TH}$ = 14 cm
$\overline{TP}$ = 6 cm

m∠M = 58° m∠R = 122°
m∠H = 58° m∠P = 122°

2 four congruent sides:
square, rhombus

3 exactly one pair of parallel
sides: trapezoid

4 two pairs of parallel sides:
parallelogram, square,
rectangle, rhombus

5 a parallelogram with four right
angles: square, rectangle

6 Property of a parallelogram:
Diagonals bisect each other.
That means $\overline{DE}$ ≅ $\overline{BE}$.

DE = BE
$9z + 8 = 4z + 33$
$9z + 8 - 8 = 4z + 33 - 8$
$9z = 4z + 25$

$9z - 4z = 4z - 4z + 25$
$5z = 25$
$5z \div 5 = 25 \div 5$
$z = 5$

7 Property of a parallelogram:
Opposite angles are congruent.
That means ∠A ≅ ∠C and
∠B ≅ ∠D. Additionally, consecutive
angles are supplementary (180°).

That means m∠A + m∠B = 180°,
m∠B + m∠C = 180°, m∠C + m∠D
= 180°, and m∠D + m∠A = 180°.

m∠A = m∠C
$(2y + 18)° = (y + 40)°$
$2y + 18 - 18 = y + 40 - 18$
$2y = y + 22$
$2y - y = y - y + 22$
$y = 22$

To find the measures of ∠A and
∠C, substitute $y = 22$ into each
expression:

m∠A = m∠C
$[2(22) + 18]° = [(22) + 40]°$
$62° = 62°$

So, m∠A = m∠C = 62°.

To find the measures of ∠B
and ∠D, substitute 62° into the
equations:

$m\angle A + m\angle B = 180°$ and
$m\angle C + m\angle D = 180°$
$62° + m\angle B = 180°$ and $62° + m\angle D$
$= 180°$
$m\angle B = 118°$ and $m\angle D = 118°$

So, $m\angle B = m\angle D = 118°$.

8 Property of a parallelogram: Diagonals bisect each other. That means $\overline{AO} \cong \overline{CO}$ and $\overline{DO} \cong \overline{BO}$.

$AO = CO$
$6x - 5 = 43$
$6x - 5 + 5 = 43 + 5$
$6x = 48$
$6x \div 6 = 48 \div 6$
$x = 8$

$DO = BO$
$3y + 1 = 28$
$3y + 1 - 1 = 28 - 1$
$3y = 27$
$3y \div 3 = 27 \div 3$
$y = 9$

So, ABCD is a parallelogram when $x = 8$ and $y = 9$.

9 Property of a parallelogram: Consecutive angles are supplementary (180°). That means $m\angle C + m\angle D = 180°$.

$m\angle C + m\angle D = 180°$
$(2x + 32)° + (7x - 5)° = 180°$
$9x + 27 = 180$
$9x + 27 - 27 = 180 - 27$
$9x = 153$
$9x \div 9 = 153 \div 9$
$x = 17$

To find the measures of $\angle C$ and $\angle D$, substitute $x = 17$ into each expression:

$m\angle C = (2x + 32)° = [2(17) + 32]° = 66°$
$m\angle D = (7x - 5)° = [7(17) - 5]° = 114°$

So, $m\angle C = 66°$ and $m\angle D = 114°$.

CHAPTER 17

RHOMBUSES, RECTANGLES, AND SQUARES

1 All quadrilaterals are rectangles: FALSE. Quadrilaterals are polygons that contain four sides and four angles. All rectangles are quadrilaterals, but not all quadrilaterals are rectangles. Squares, trapezoids, and rhombuses are also quadrilaterals because they all have four sides and four angles.

2 All squares are rectangles: TRUE.

3 A square and a rectangle have two pairs of adjacent sides that are congruent: FALSE. A square has adjacent sides that are congruent, but a rectangle might not.

4 All rhombuses are not squares: TRUE.

5 Name all possible quadrilaterals that have two pairs of congruent sides.
parallelograms, rectangles, rhombuses, and squares (and kites)

6 Name all possible quadrilaterals that have two pairs of parallel sides.
parallelograms, rectangles, rhombuses, and squares

7 Name all possible quadrilaterals that have four congruent sides and four congruent angles.
squares

8 Because CRST is a rhombus, and a rhombus is a parallelogram, we know that the diagonals bisect each other, which means $\overline{RN} \cong \overline{TN}$.

$RN = TN$
$5w - 6 = 2w + 30$
$5w - 6 + 6 = 2w + 30 + 6$
$5w = 2w + 36$

$5w - 2w = 2w - 2w + 36$
$3w = 36$
$3w \div 3 = 36 \div 3$
$w = 12$

To find the measure of the diagonal $\overline{RT}$, use the Segment Addition Postulate.

$RN + TN = RT$
$(5w - 6) + (2w + 30) = RT$
(Substitute $w = 12$.)
$[5(12) - 6] + [2(12) + 30] = RT$
$54 + 54 = RT$
(Notice each line segment measures 54 units. $108 = RT$)

So, the length of $\overline{RT}$ is 108 units.

9 Use a two-column proof and what you know about parallel lines, parallelograms, and rhombuses to prove GFHJ is a rhombus.

Statements	Reasons
1. GFHJ is a parallelogram.	1. Definition of a Parallelogram (both pairs of opposite sides are parallel; $\overline{FH} \parallel \overline{GJ}$ and $\overline{GF} \parallel \overline{JH}$)
2. $m\angle GHF = m\angle HGJ$	2. Given (both angles measure 36°)

Statements	Reasons
3. m∠GJH = 128°	3. Given
4. m∠GHJ = 26°	4. Triangle Angle-Sum Theorem (the sum of the measures of the interior angles of △GJH must equal 180°) m∠GHJ + 26° + 128° = 180° m∠GHJ + 154° = 180° m∠GHJ + 154° − 164° = 180° − 154° m∠GHJ = 26°
5. ∠GHJ ≅ ∠HGF	5. Alternate Interior Angles Theorem
6. m∠GHJ = m∠HGF	6. Definition of Congruence m∠GHJ = 26° and m∠HGF = 26°
7. m∠FGJ = m∠FHJ	7. m∠FGJ = 26° + 26° = 52° m∠FHJ = 26° + 26° = 52°
8. $\overline{GH}$ bisects ∠GJ and ∠FHJ	8. Definition of Angle Bisector
9. GFHJ is a rhombus	9. Since a diagonal of GFHJ bisects a pair of opposite angles, it is a rhombus.

10 A square is a parallelogram with four right angles and four congruent sides. Therefore, $\overline{KL} \cong \overline{LM}$ and the m∠N = 90°.

KL = LM
$3a + 11 = 10a − 3$
$3a + 11 − 11 = 10a − 3 − 11$
$3a = 10a − 14$
$3a − 10a = 10a − 10a − 14$
$−7a = −14$
$−7a ÷ −7 = −14 ÷ −7$
$a = 2$

To find the lengths of $\overline{KL}$ and $\overline{LM}$, substitute a = 2 into each expression:

KL = 3a + 11 = 3(2) + 11 = 17
LM = 10a − 3 = 10(2) − 3 = 17

So, the lengths of $\overline{KL}$ and $\overline{LM}$ are both 17 units.

To find the value of b, use the equation:

m∠N = 90°
$(6b)° = 90°$
$6b ÷ 6 = 90 ÷ 6$
$b = 15$

So, b = 15.

413

11

Statements	Reasons
1. TUVW is a rhombus. $m\angle TVW = 53°$	1. Given
2. $m\angle TVU = 53°$	2. Each diagonal in a rhombus bisects a pair of opposite angles. So, $m\angle TVU = m\angle TVW$.
3. $m\angle UZV = 90°$	3. Rhombi have diagonals that are perpendicular.
4. $y = 37°$ or $m\angle VUW = 37°$	4. The interior angles of $\triangle UZV$ have measures that sum to $180°$. $y° + 90° + 53°$ $= 180°$ $y + 143° = 180°$ $y + 143° - 143°$ $= 180° - 143°$ $y = 37°$

12 A rectangle is a parallelogram with four right angles.

$$m\angle ABD + m\angle DBC = 90°$$
$$m\angle ABD + 44° = 90°$$
$$m\angle ABD + 44° - 44° = 90° - 44°$$
$$m\angle ABD = 46°$$

A rectangle has opposite sides that are equal in length.

$$AB = CD$$
$$6x - 20 = x + 15$$
$$6x - 20 + 20 = x + 15 + 20$$

$$6x = x + 35$$
$$6x - x = x - x + 35$$
$$5x = 35$$
$$5x \div 5 = 35 \div 5$$
$$x = 7$$

To find the lengths of $\overline{AB}$ and $\overline{CD}$, substitute $x = 7$ into each expression:

$$AB = 6x - 20 = 6(7) - 20 = 22$$
$$CD = x + 15 = 7 + 15 = 22$$

So, the lengths of $\overline{AB}$ and $\overline{CD}$ are both 22 units.

CHAPTER 18

TRAPEZOIDS AND KITES

1 A trapezoid cannot be a parallelogram because it has only one pair of parallel sides.

2 No, Jaquez is not correct. Every rhombus is a kite, but a kite does not have to have four congruent sides like a rhombus does.

3 Since trapezoid ABCD has two pairs of congruent base angles, it is an isosceles trapezoid. That means each pair of base angles is equal in measure, and so the base angle paired with the 128° angle also measures 128°.

Since the figure is a trapezoid, we also know that the top and bottom bases are *parallel*. This means that a top base angle and a bottom base angle are supplementary (by the Same-Side Interior Angles Theorem). Write an equation to find the measure of the top angle. Let x = the unknown base angle measure.

$128° + x° = 180°$
$128 - 128 + x = 180 - 128$
$x = 52$

So, the other two base angles measure 52°.

4 Equation: Length of Midsegment = $\frac{\text{Base 1} + \text{Base 2}}{2}$

Substitute: Midsegment = 58; Base 1 = $x - 16$; Base 2 = $5x$

$58 = \frac{(x - 16) + (5x)}{2}$
$58 = \frac{6x - 16}{2}$
$58(2) = \frac{6x - 16}{2}(2)$
$116 = 6x - 16$
$116 + 16 = 6x - 16 + 16$
$132 = 6x$
$132 \div 6 = 6x \div 6$
$22 = x$

So, $x = 22$.

5 This figure is an isosceles trapezoid because it has only one pair of parallel sides (the top base is parallel to the bottom base) and its legs are congruent.

Because the figure is an isosceles trapezoid, we know that the two top base angles are congruent: $\angle N \cong \angle O$. Therefore, $m\angle N = 114°$.

To find the measures of $\angle M$ and $\angle P$, we can use the Same-Side Interior Angles Theorem:

$m\angle O + m\angle P = 180°$

Letting x stand for $m\angle P$, we can write an equation:

$114° + x° = 180°$
$114 - 114 + x = 180 - 114$
$x = 66$

So, $m\angle N = m\angle O = 114°$, and $m\angle M = m\angle P = 66°$.

6 Given: An isosceles trapezoid. This means the diagonals are congruent.

$6z + 14 = 5z + 22$
$6z + 14 - 14 = 5z + 22 - 14$
$6z = 5z + 8$

415

$6z - 5z = 5z - 5z + 8$

$z = 8$

7   It is given that $\angle S \cong \angle V$. To find the value of h, set the given angle measures equal to each other and solve.

$(4h)° = 148°$

$4h ÷ 4 = 148 ÷ 4$

$h = 37$

8   Because quadrilateral FJHK is a kite, the diagonals are perpendicular. Therefore, $m\angle HEK = 90°$ and $m\angle HEJ = 90°$. It is given that $m\angle KHE = 25°$.

The sum of the measures of the angles of $\triangle HEK$ is $180°$.

Write and solve an equation to find $m\angle HKE$.

$25° + 90° + m\angle HKE = 180°$

$m\angle HKE + 115° = 180°$

$m\angle HKE + 115° - 115° = 180° - 115$

$m\angle HKE = 65°$

The figure shows us that $\overline{JE} \cong \overline{KE}$ and $\overline{JH} \cong \overline{KH}$, and we know that $\overline{HE} \cong \overline{HE}$ by the Reflexive Property of Congruence. So, by the Side-Side-Side Congruence Postulate, $\triangle HEK \cong \triangle HEJ$.

Since congruent triangles have corresponding congruent angles, $\angle HKE \cong \angle HJE$ and $\angle KHE \cong \angle JHE$.

Therefore, $m\angle HJE = m\angle HKE = 65°$, and $m\angle JHE = m\angle KHE = 25°$.

CHAPTER 19

ANGLE MEASURES IN POLYGONS

1   Let n be the number of sides: $n = 12$.

Sum of interior angles =
$(n - 2) \cdot 180°$
$= (12 - 2) \cdot 180°$
$= 1{,}800°$

2   By the Polygon Exterior Angle-Sum Theorem, the sum of the measures of the exterior angles always stays the same no matter how many sides the polygon has. It is equal to $360°$.

3   Let n be the number of sides.

Sum of interior angles $= 1{,}620°$
$1{,}620° = (n - 2) \cdot 180°$
$1{,}620 ÷ 180 = [(n - 2) \cdot 180] ÷ 180$
$9 = n - 2$
$9 + 2 = n - 2 + 2$
$11 = n$

4 By the Polygon Exterior Angle-Sum Theorem, the sum of the measures of the exterior angles always stays the same no matter how many sides the polygon has. It is equal to 360°.

5 A. It's given that the internal angle adjacent to x is congruent to the 30° angle. This means it measures 30°. The interior and exterior angles are supplementary.

$30° + x° = 180°$

$30 - 30 + x = 180 - 30$

$x = 150°$

B. This is a regular triangle: All angles are equal in measure, and all sides are equal in length. Therefore, each angle measures 60°, because the measures of the interior angles of a triangle equal 180°, and $60° + 60° + 60° = 180°$. The interior and exterior angles are supplementary.

$60° + y° = 180°$

$60 - 60 + y = 180 - 60$

$y = 120°$

6 Let n be the number of sides.

Sum of interior angles

$= (n - 2) \bullet 180°$

$= (4 - 2) \bullet 180°$

$= 360°$

$(3x + 97)° + (x + 25)° + 125° + (4x + 9)°$

$= 360°$

$8x + 256 = 360$

$8x + 256 - 256 = 360 - 256$

$8x = 104$

$8x \div 8 = 104 \div 8$

$x = 13$

7 By the Polygon Exterior Angle-Sum Theorem, the sum of the measures of the exterior angles always stays the same no matter how many sides the polygon has. This sum is 360°.

So, write an equation to find the value of a:

$49° + 59° + a° + 60° + (2a)° + 36° = 360°$

$3a + 204 = 360$

$3a + 204 - 204 = 360 - 204$

$3a = 156$

$3a \div 3 = 156 \div 3$

$a = 52$

UNIT 5

Geometric Transformations (Chapters 20–24)

CHAPTER 20

REFLECTIONS

1 To reflect the kite on the coordinate plane across the x-axis, use the rule for reflection over the x-axis: $(x, y) \longrightarrow (x, -y)$.

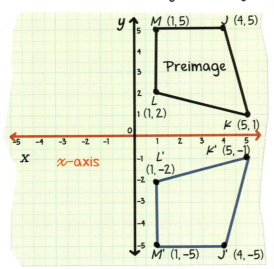

2 To reflect the kite on the coordinate plane across the y-axis, use the rule for reflection over the y-axis: $(x, y) \longrightarrow (-x, y)$.

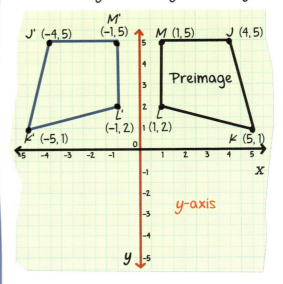

3 To reflect the kite on the coordinate plane across the line $x = -1$, count how many units away from the line of reflection each point is.

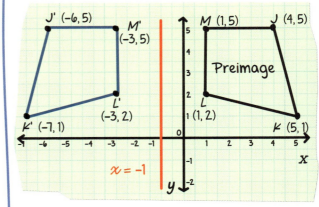

4 To reflect the kite on the coordinate plane across the line $y = -2$, count how many units away from the line of reflection each point is.

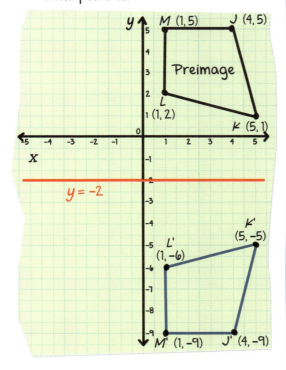

5 To reflect the triangle on the coordinate plane across the line $y = x$, use the rule $(x, y) \longrightarrow (y, x)$.

Image points: $W'(-3, -3)$, $U'(4, -4)$, and $V'(1, -1)$

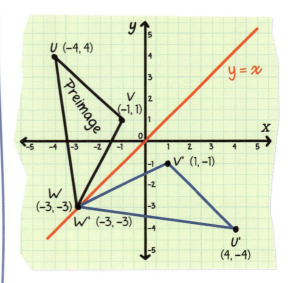

CHAPTER 21

TRANSLATIONS

1 The translation vector is $(5, -4)$.

The translation of the point slides 5 units to the right and 4 units down.

2 This is *not* a translation.

Notice that the orientation of the figure has changed. It appears to be a reflection.

3 This is a translation. The translation vector is $(-5, 0)$.

The translation rule is $(x, y) \longrightarrow (x + -5, y + 0)$.

4 This is a translation. The translation vector is (–6, 2).

The translation rule is
$(x, y) \longrightarrow (x – 6, y + 2)$.

5 This is a translation. The translation vector is (8, –10).

The translation rule is
$(x, y) \longrightarrow (x + 8, y – 10)$.

6 The translation vector is (3, –1).

The translation rule is
$(x, y) \longrightarrow (x + 3, y – 1)$.

Preimage points: X(–9, 6), Y(2, 3), and Z(–2, –8)

Image points: X'(–6, 5), Y'(5, 2), and Z'(1, –9)

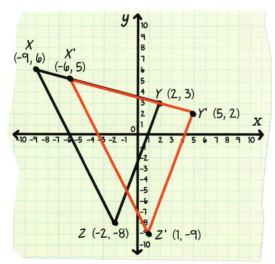

7 The translation vector is (–7, –6).

The translation rule is:
$(x, y) \longrightarrow (x – 7, y – 6)$.

Preimage points: A(1, 3), B(1, 6), C(6, 6), and D(6, 3)

Image points: A'(–6, –3), B'(–6, 0), C'(–1, 0), and D'(–1, –3)

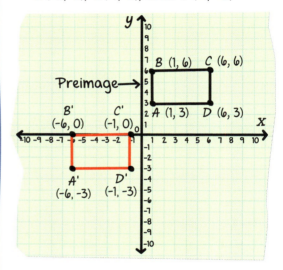

8 The translation vector is (–4, 5).

The translation rule is
$(x, y) \longrightarrow (x – 4, y + 5)$.

Preimage points: M(2, 1), A(2, 4), T(5, 4), and H(5, 2)

Image points: M'(–2, 6), A'(–2, 9), T'(1, 9), and H'(1, 7)

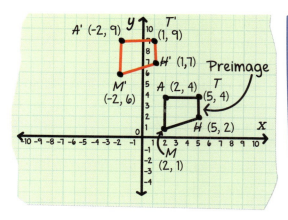

CHAPTER 22

ROTATIONS

1   FALSE. Rotations are rigid motions just like translations and reflections.

2   TRUE.

3   FALSE. The center of rotation can be located outside, inside, or on a figure.

4   FALSE. H and H' are the same distance from the center of rotation, R. This is written as RH = RH'.

5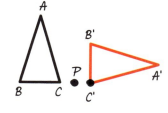

6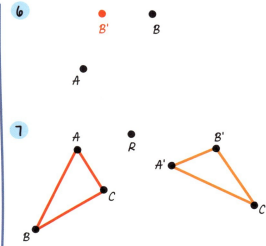

7

8   To rotate the polygon 270° counterclockwise around the origin, follow the rule $(x, y) \rightarrow (y, -x)$.

Preimage points: M(1, –3), A(1, –6), T(4, –6), and H(4, –2)

Image points: M'(–3, –1), A'(–6, –1), T'(–6, –4), and H'(–2, –4)

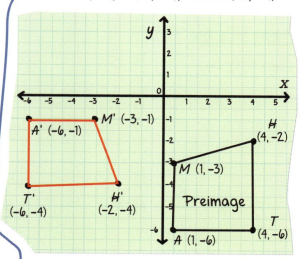

9 To rotate the triangle 90°
counterclockwise around the origin,
follow the rule $(x, y) \rightarrow (-y, x)$.

Preimage points: R(-2, 5), S(-2, 1),
and T(-5, 1)

Image points: R'(-5, -2),
S'(-1, -2), and T'(-1, -5)

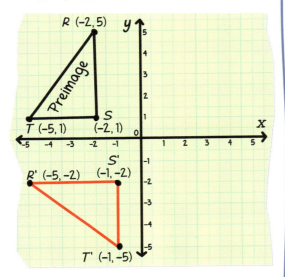

Rotation image points: A'(5, -2)
and B'(1, -6)

To reflect $\overline{A'B'}$ across $y = x$, follow
the rule $(x, y) \rightarrow (y, x)$. Label the
line segment $\overline{A''B''}$.

Reflection image points: A''(-2, 5)
and B''(-6, 1)

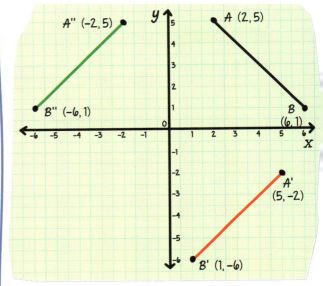

CHAPTER 23

COMPOSITIONS

1 To rotate $\overline{AB}$ 270° counterclockwise
around the origin, follow the rule
$(x, y) \rightarrow (y, -x)$. Label the line
segment $\overline{A'B'}$.

Preimage points: A(2, 5)
and B(6, 1)

2 Rotation about the point
of intersection

3 A composition of two
reflections across two parallel
lines forms a **translation**.

4 FALSE

5 TRUE

6 FALSE

7 A. To find the reflection of the polygon across the y-axis, use the rule $(x, y) \longrightarrow (-x, y)$.

To find the reflection of the polygon across the x-axis, use the rule $(x, y) \longrightarrow (x, -y)$.

Preimage points: R(–4, 2), S(–6, 4), T(–4, 6), and W(–1, 2)

Reflection across y-axis image points: R'(4, 2), S'(6, 4), T'(4, 6), and W'(1, 2)

Reflection across x-axis image points: R"(4, –2), S"(6, –4), T"(4, –6), and W"(1, –2)

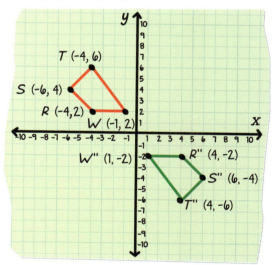

B. A 180° rotation clockwise (or counterclockwise) about the point of intersection (0,0)

maps polygon RSTW to polygon R"S"T"W".

8 Both figures have line symmetry. The equilateral triangle has three lines of symmetry. The star has four lines of symmetry.

CHAPTER 24

CONGRUENCE

1 Not congruent. There is no rigid motion that maps one line segment directly onto the other.

2 The congruence statement is △QRS ≅ △TUV.

3 The congruence statement is △LKM ≅ △JHG.

4 Not congruent. The polygons are not the same shape. There is no rigid motion that maps one figure directly onto the other.

5 Yes. △ABC ≅ △RST.

Rotating △ABC 90° counterclockwise results in △RST.

6 MATH ≇ PNRO. There is no rigid motion that maps one figure directly onto the other.

UNIT 6

Similarity
(Chapters 25–29)

CHAPTER 25

RATIO AND PROPORTION

1 h : l : w
   4 in : 10 in : 3 in

2 $\frac{5}{7} = \frac{50}{75}$

   $375 \neq 350$
   not a true proportion

   $\frac{10}{15} = \frac{20}{30}$

   $300 = 300$
   true proportion

   $\frac{5}{7} = \frac{25}{45}$

   $225 \neq 175$
   not a true proportion

   $\frac{8}{12} = \frac{32}{60}$

   $480 \neq 384$
   not a true proportion

   If the cross products are equal
   to each other, then the two
   ratios are equal and form a
   proportion. If they are not
   equal, then the two ratios
   do not form a proportion.

3 $\frac{x}{14} = \frac{32}{56}$

   $56 \bullet x = 14 \bullet 32$
   $56x = 448$
   $\frac{56x}{56} = \frac{448}{56}$
   $x = 8$

4 $\frac{28}{63} = \frac{4}{x}$

   $28 \bullet x = 63 \bullet 4$
   $28x = 252$
   $\frac{28x}{28} = \frac{252}{28}$
   $x = 9$

5 $\frac{4x}{57} = \frac{8}{6}$

   $4x \bullet 6 = 57 \bullet 8$
   $24x = 456$
   $\frac{24x}{24} = \frac{456}{24}$
   $x = 19$

6 $\frac{7}{11} = -\frac{x}{33}$

   $7 \bullet (-33) = 11 \bullet x$
   $-231 = 11x$
   $\frac{-231}{11} = \frac{11x}{11}$
   $x = -21$

7 $\dfrac{\text{teaspoons of yeast}}{\text{cups of flour}}$

$\dfrac{2}{3} = \dfrac{14}{x}$

$2x = 3 \cdot 14$

$2x = 42$

$\dfrac{2x}{2} = \dfrac{42}{2}$

$x = 21$

The recipe will require
21 cups of flour.

8 $\dfrac{\text{months}}{\text{cost}}$

$\dfrac{24}{x} = \dfrac{8}{305}$

$24 \cdot 305 = 8 \cdot x$

$7,320 = 8x$

$\dfrac{7,320}{8} = \dfrac{8x}{8}$

$x = 915$

The athlete pays \$915 for a
24-month club membership.

CHAPTER 26

DILATIONS

1 A. Enlargement
   B. Reduction
   C. No change
   D. Reduction
   E. Enlargement
   F. Reduction

2 The scale factor is $\dfrac{1}{4}$. The
dilation is a reduction.

3 The scale factor is 3. The
dilation is an enlargement.

4 The scale factor is $\dfrac{1}{2}$. The
dilation is a reduction.

5 $\dfrac{12}{16} = \dfrac{3}{4}$

The scale factor is $\dfrac{3}{4}$. The
dilation is a reduction.

6 $\dfrac{15}{5} = 3$

The scale factor is 3. The
dilation is an enlargement.

7 $\dfrac{12}{6} = \dfrac{16}{8} = \dfrac{8}{4} = 2$

The scale factor is 2. The
dilation is an enlargement.

8

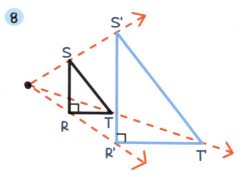

9

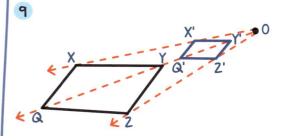

10 M(–4, 8) ⟶ M'(–3, 6)
    A(8, 8) ⟶ A'(6, 6)
    T(–4, –12) ⟶ T'(–3, –9)
    H(8, –12) ⟶ H'(6, –9)

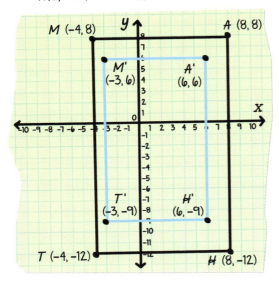

CHAPTER 27

SIMILAR FIGURES

1 Similar figures are dilations of each other but can also be rotated, translated, or reflected because they have the same shape but are not necessarily the same size or set in the same orientation.

2 △BAC ~ △DEC

3 The scale factor of △BAC to △DEC is $\frac{18}{6} = \frac{15}{5} = \frac{12}{4}$ or $\frac{3}{1}$ or 3.

4 $\frac{HG}{DC} = \frac{GF}{CB}$

$\frac{36}{8} = \frac{x}{12}$

$36 \cdot 12 = 8 \cdot x$

$432 = 8x$

$\frac{432}{8} = \frac{8x}{8}$

$x = 54$

5 $\frac{ED}{KL} = \frac{DF}{LJ}$

$\frac{3}{15} = \frac{4}{x}$

$3 \cdot x = 15 \cdot 4$

$3x = 60$

$\frac{3x}{3} = \frac{60}{3}$

$x = 20$

∠D ≅ ∠L
∠E ≅ ∠K
∠F ≅ ∠J
$y = m∠J$

$90° + 53.13° + y° = 180°$
$143.13 + y = 180$
$143.13 - 143.13 + y = 180 - 143.13$
$y = 36.87°$

6 $\frac{GD}{GH} = \frac{42}{12} = \frac{7}{2}$

$\frac{GE}{GF} = \frac{35}{10} = \frac{7}{2}$

$\frac{DE}{HF} = \frac{28}{8} = \frac{7}{2}$

Similarity statement:
$\triangle DGE \sim \triangle HGF$
Scale factor: $\frac{7}{2}$ or 3.5

7 $\frac{CT}{ND} = \frac{11}{44} = \frac{1}{4}$

$\frac{CA}{NM} = \frac{15}{60} = \frac{1}{4}$

$\frac{TA}{DM} = \frac{21}{84} = \frac{1}{4}$

$\angle C \cong \angle N$

$\angle T \cong \angle D$

$\angle A \cong \angle M$

Similarity statement:
$\triangle ACT \sim \triangle MND$
Scale factor: $\frac{1}{4}$ or 0.25

8 $\frac{TE}{GH} = \frac{9}{6} = \frac{3}{2}$

$\frac{EK}{HB} = \frac{12}{8} = \frac{3}{2}$

$\frac{KA}{BR} = \frac{15}{10} = \frac{3}{2}$

$\frac{AT}{RG} = \frac{6}{4} = \frac{3}{2}$

$\angle T \cong \angle G$

$\angle A \cong \angle R$

$\angle K \cong \angle B$

$\angle E \cong \angle H$

Similarity statement: $TEKA \sim GHBR$
Scale factor: $\frac{3}{2}$ or 1.5

9 These polygons are not similar. They do not have corresponding angles that are congruent. (We can also see that the polygons are not similar by observing that corresponding sides are not proportional.)

10 Herman is correct. Triangle DEF and triangle DGF are similar and congruent because all corresponding angles are congruent and all corresponding sides are both proportional and congruent. Note: Congruent figures are always similar.

CHAPTER 28

SIMILAR TRIANGLES

1 To show that the triangles are similar, use the Side-Side-Side (SSS) Similarity Theorem. If the corresponding sides of two triangles are proportional, then the triangles are similar.

2 To show that the triangles are similar, use the Angle-Angle (AA) Similarity Postulate. If two angles of one triangle are congruent to two angles of another triangle, then those two triangles are similar.

3 To show that the triangles are similar, use the Side-Angle-Side (SAS) Similarity Theorem. If two corresponding sides of two triangles are proportional and the included angles of those sides are congruent, then the triangles are similar.

4 To show that the triangles are similar, use the Side-Angle-Side (SAS) Similarity Theorem. If two corresponding sides of two triangles are proportional and the included angles of those sides are congruent, then the triangles are similar.

5 To show that the triangles are similar, use the Side-Side-Side (SSS) Similarity Theorem. If the corresponding sides of two triangles are proportional, then the triangles are similar.

6 Use the Side-Angle-Side Similarity Theorem to determine similarity.
$\angle R \cong \angle Q$
$$\frac{SR}{PQ} = \frac{14}{21} = \frac{2}{3}$$
$$\frac{RT}{QT} = \frac{4}{6} = \frac{2}{3}$$
So, $\frac{SR}{PQ} = \frac{RT}{QT}$

Similarity statement:
$\triangle SRT \sim \triangle PQT$

7 Use the Angle-Angle Similarity Postulate to determine similarity.

$\angle ACD \cong \angle CBD$
$\angle CDA \cong \angle CDB$
Similarity statement:
$\triangle ACD \sim \triangle CBD$

8 $\frac{SK}{RK} = \frac{18}{28}$

$\frac{MK}{NK} = \frac{25}{33}$

So, $\frac{SK}{RK} \neq \frac{MK}{NK}$

Therefore, $\triangle RKN$ and $\triangle SKM$ are not similar.

9 Use the Side-Angle-Side Similarity Theorem to determine similarity.
$\angle P \cong \angle P$
$$\frac{PA}{PQ} = \frac{15}{24} = \frac{5}{8}$$
$$\frac{PB}{PR} = \frac{20}{32} = \frac{5}{8}$$
So, $\frac{PA}{PQ} = \frac{PB}{PR}$

Similarity statement:
$\triangle QPR \sim \triangle APB$

10 $\frac{BA}{ED} = \frac{AC}{DF}$

$\frac{10}{ED} = \frac{30}{540}$

$10 \cdot 540 = ED \cdot 30$

$5{,}400 = 30ED$

$\frac{5{,}400}{30} = \frac{30ED}{30}$

$ED = 180$

The height of the ramp labeled DEF is 180 cm.

CHAPTER 29

PROPORTIONS IN TRIANGLES

1 $\dfrac{RQ}{QS} = \dfrac{RP}{PT}$

$\dfrac{9}{x} = \dfrac{6}{4}$

$9 \bullet 4 = x \bullet 6$

$\dfrac{36}{6} = \dfrac{6x}{6}$

$x = 6$

$RS = RQ + QS$

$RS = 9 + x$

$RS = 9 + 6$

$RS = 15$

2 We can conclude that $\overline{RE} \| \overline{ST}$ using the converse of the Triangle Proportionality Theorem.

3 $\dfrac{SR}{CR} = \dfrac{TE}{CE}$

$\dfrac{24}{36} = \dfrac{y}{48}$

$24 \bullet 48 = 36 \bullet y$

$1{,}152 = 36y$

$\dfrac{1{,}152}{36} = \dfrac{36y}{36}$

$y = 32$

The length of $\overline{TE}$ is 32 cm.

4 $AB + BC = AC$

$2w + w = 60$

$3w = 60$

$\dfrac{3w}{3} = \dfrac{60}{3}$

$w = 20$

$AB = 2w \qquad\qquad BC = w$

$AB = 2 \bullet 20 \qquad\quad BC = 20 \text{ inches}$

$AB = 40 \text{ inches}$

5 $\dfrac{15}{a} = \dfrac{27}{45}$

$15 \bullet 45 = a \bullet 27$

$675 = 27a$

$\dfrac{675}{27} = \dfrac{27a}{27}$

$a = 25$

6 $\dfrac{36 - b}{8} = \dfrac{b}{4}$

$(36 - b) \bullet 4 = 8 \bullet b$

$144 - 4b = 8b$

$144 - 4b + 4b = 8b + 4b$

$144 = 12b$

$\dfrac{144}{12} = \dfrac{12b}{12}$

$b = 12$

7 $\dfrac{FG}{FJ} = \dfrac{GH}{HJ}$

$\dfrac{10}{14} = \dfrac{x + 2}{2x + 1}$

$10 \bullet (2x + 1) = 14 \bullet (x + 2)$

$20x + 10 = 14x + 28$

$20x + 10 - 10 = 14x + 28 - 10$

$20x = 14x + 18$

$20x - 14x = 14x - 14x + 18$

$6x = 18$

$\dfrac{6x}{6} = \dfrac{18}{6}$

$x = 3$

$GH = x + 2$
$GH = 3 + 2$
$GH = 5$
$HJ = 2x + 1$
$HJ = 2(3) + 1$
$HJ = 6 + 1$
$HJ = 7$

8 $\dfrac{YX}{XV} = \dfrac{YZ}{ZV}$

$\dfrac{15}{35} = \dfrac{21}{m}$

$15 \cdot m = 35 \cdot 21$

$15m = 735$

$\dfrac{15m}{15} = \dfrac{735}{15}$

$m = 49$

$XZ = XV + VZ$
$XZ = 35 + 49$
$XZ = 84$

9 $\dfrac{AB}{BD} = \dfrac{AC}{CD}$

$\dfrac{2x+1}{9} = \dfrac{x+3}{6}$

$(2x + 1) \cdot 6 = 9 \cdot (x + 3)$

$12x + 6 = 9x + 27$

$12x + 6 - 6 = 9x + 27 - 6$

$12x - 9x = 9x - 9x + 21$

$\dfrac{3x}{3} = \dfrac{21}{3}$

$x = 7$

10 $AB = 2x + 1 \qquad AC = x + 3$
$AB = 2(7) + 1 \qquad AC = 7 + 3$
$AB = 14 + 1 \qquad AC = 10$
$AB = 15$

UNIT 7
Right Triangles and Trigonometry (Chapters 30–36)

CHAPTER 30

SLOPE AND LINEAR EQUATIONS

1 Slope: $-\dfrac{2}{5}$, y-intercept: $(0, -12)$

2 Slope: 3, y-intercept: $(0, 5)$

3 Slope: $1\dfrac{1}{4}$, y-intercept: $(0, 0)$

4 $\dfrac{y_2 - y_1}{x_2 - x_1} = \dfrac{3 - 8}{-6 - 5} = \dfrac{-5}{-11} = \dfrac{5}{11}$

Slope: $\dfrac{5}{11}$

5 $\dfrac{y_2 - y_1}{x_2 - x_1} = \dfrac{2 - 2}{-4 - 0} = \dfrac{0}{-4} = 0$

Slope: 0

6 $\dfrac{\text{rise}}{\text{run}} = \dfrac{-1}{1} = -1$
Slope: -1

7 The line is horizontal, so the slope is 0.

8 The slope of a line that is parallel to line a is $-\frac{3}{4}$ because parallel lines have the same slope.

CHAPTER 31

THE PYTHAGOREAN THEOREM

1 $a^2 + b^2 = c^2$
$x^2 + 21^2 = 29^2$
$x^2 + 441 = 841$
$x^2 + 441 - 441 = 841 - 441$
$x^2 = 400$
$\sqrt{x^2} = \sqrt{400}$
$x = 20$
The distance from the bottom of the ladder to the building is 20 feet.

2 $a^2 + b^2 = c^2$
$5^2 + 12^2 = x^2$
$25 + 144 = x^2$
$\sqrt{169} = \sqrt{x^2}$
$x = 13$
Note: You can also select a Pythagorean triple to use in your calculation.
Tarik drove 13 miles to return home.

3 $a^2 + b^2 = c^2$
$10^2 + 15^2 = x^2$
$100 + 225 = x^2$
$325 = x^2$

$\sqrt{325} = \sqrt{x^2}$
$x \approx 18.028$

4 $a^2 + b^2 = c^2$
$x^2 + 33^2 = 65^2$
$x^2 + 1{,}089 = 4{,}225$
$x^2 + 1{,}089 - 1{,}089 = 4{,}225 - 1{,}089$
$x^2 = 3{,}136$
$\sqrt{x^2} = \sqrt{3{,}136}$
$x = 56$

5 $a^2 + b^2 = c^2$
$44^2 + 117^2 \stackrel{?}{=} 125^2$
$1{,}936 + 13{,}689 \stackrel{?}{=} 15{,}625$
$15{,}625 = 15{,}625$
The triangle is a right triangle.

6 $a^2 + b^2 = c^2$
$8^2 + 12^2 \stackrel{?}{=} 16^2$
$64 + 144 \stackrel{?}{=} 256$
$208 < 256$
The triangle is obtuse.

7 $a^2 + b^2 = c^2$
$9^2 + 10^2 \stackrel{?}{=} 13^2$
$81 + 100 \stackrel{?}{=} 169$
$181 > 169$
The triangle is acute.

8 $a^2 + b^2 = c^2$
$18^2 + 20^2 \stackrel{?}{=} 30^2$
$324 + 400 \stackrel{?}{=} 900$
$724 < 900$
The triangle is obtuse.

CHAPTER 32

MIDPOINT AND DISTANCE FORMULAS

1 midpoint $= \frac{a+b}{2} = \frac{-5+8}{2} = \frac{3}{2} = 1.5$

2 midpoint $= \frac{a+b}{2} = \frac{-3+7}{2} = \frac{4}{2} = 2$

3 midpoint $= \frac{a+b}{2} = \frac{3.5+15.5}{2} = \frac{19}{2} = 9.5$

4 midpoint $= (\frac{x_1+x_2}{2}, \frac{y_1+y_2}{2})$

$= (\frac{-4+5}{2}, \frac{2+2}{2}) = (\frac{1}{2}, 2)$

5 midpoint $= (\frac{x_1+x_2}{2}, \frac{y_1+y_2}{2})$

$= (\frac{-5+(-1)}{2}, \frac{3+(-3)}{2}) = (-3, 0)$

6 midpoint $= (\frac{x_1+x_2}{2}, \frac{y_1+y_2}{2})$

$= (\frac{4+10}{2}, \frac{1+5}{2}) = (7, 3)$

7 midpoint $= (\frac{x_1+x_2}{2}, \frac{y_1+y_2}{2})$

$0 = \frac{5+x_2}{2}$

$2 \cdot 0 = \frac{5+x_2}{2} \cdot 2$

$0 = 5 + x_2$

$0 - 5 = 5 - 5 + x_2$

$x_2 = -5$

$-2 = \frac{2+y_2}{2}$

$2 \cdot (-2) = \frac{2+y_2}{2} \cdot 2$

$-4 = 2 + y_2$

$-4 - 2 = 2 - 2 + y_2$

$y_2 = -6$

Endpoint P is $(-5, -6)$.

8 $|a - b| = |{-12} - 8| = |{-20}| = 20$

The distance between A and C is 20.

9 $MK = \sqrt{(x_2 - x_1)^2 + (y_2 - y_1)^2}$

$MK = \sqrt{(5 - (-3))^2 + (4 - (-2))^2}$

$MK = \sqrt{8^2 + 6^2}$

$MK = \sqrt{64 + 36}$

$MK = \sqrt{100}$

$MK = 10$

The distance between M and K is 10.

10 $MT = \sqrt{(x_2 - x_1)^2 + (y_2 - y_1)^2}$

$MT = \sqrt{(12 - (-4))^2 + (5 - (-4))^2}$

$MT = \sqrt{16^2 + 9^2}$

$MT = \sqrt{256 + 81}$

$MT = \sqrt{337}$

The length of the diagonal $\overline{MT}$ is $\sqrt{337}$.

CHAPTER 33

COORDINATE TRIANGLE PROOFS

1 Use the distance formula to determine the lengths of the sides of $\triangle LRP$.

$L(-6, -4)$, $R(-3, 4)$

$LR = \sqrt{(x_2 - x_1)^2 + (y_2 - y_1)^2}$

$LR = \sqrt{(-3 - (-6))^2 + (4 - (-4))^2}$

$LR = \sqrt{3^2 + 8^2}$

$LR = \sqrt{9 + 64}$

$LR = \sqrt{73}$

$R(-3, 4)$, $P(5, 0)$

$RP = \sqrt{(x_2 - x_1)^2 + (y_2 - y_1)^2}$

$RP = \sqrt{(5 - (-3))^2 + (0 - 4)^2}$

$RP = \sqrt{8^2 + (-4)^2}$

$RP = \sqrt{64 + 16}$

$RP = \sqrt{80}$

$P(5,0)$, $L(-6, -4)$,

$PL = \sqrt{(x_2 - x_1)^2 + (y_2 - y_1)^2}$

$PL = \sqrt{(-6 - 5)^2 + (-4 - 0)^2}$

$PL = \sqrt{(-11)^2 + (-4)^2}$

$PL = \sqrt{121 + 16}$

$PL = \sqrt{137}$

$\triangle LRP$ is a scalene triangle because all sides have different lengths.

2 Use the slope formula to determine the slope of $\overline{BC}$ and $\overline{AC}$.

$B(-2, 5)$, $C(-4, 2)$

$m = \dfrac{y_2 - y_1}{x_2 - x_1} = \dfrac{2 - 5}{-4 - (-2)} = \dfrac{-3}{-2} = \dfrac{3}{2}$

$A(2, -2)$, $C(-4, 2)$

$m = \dfrac{y_2 - y_1}{x_2 - x_1} = \dfrac{2 - (-2)}{-4 - 2} = \dfrac{4}{-6} = -\dfrac{2}{3}$

If two lines have slopes that are negative reciprocals of each other, then the lines are perpendicular and form a right angle. $\triangle ABC$ is therefore a right triangle.

3 Use the distance formula to determine if two sides of $\triangle RST$ have equal lengths.

$R(6, 7)$, $S(4, 2)$

$RS = \sqrt{(x_2 - x_1)^2 + (y_2 - y_1)^2}$

$RS = \sqrt{(4 - 6)^2 + (2 - 7)^2}$

$RS = \sqrt{(-2)^2 + (-5)^2}$

$RS = \sqrt{4 + 25}$

$RS = \sqrt{29}$

$R(6, 7)$, $T(8, 2)$

$RT = \sqrt{(x_2 - x_1)^2 + (y_2 - y_1)^2}$

$RT = \sqrt{(8 - 6)^2 + (2 - 7)^2}$

$RT = \sqrt{2^2 + (-5)^2}$

$RT = \sqrt{4 + 25}$

$RT = \sqrt{29}$

$\triangle RST$ is an isosceles triangle because sides $\overline{RS}$ and $\overline{RT}$ are equal in length.

4 Use the distance formula to determine the lengths of the sides of the triangle.

$V(0, -5)$, $W(-1, 7)$

$VW = \sqrt{(x_2 - x_1)^2 + (y_2 - y_1)^2}$

$VW = \sqrt{(-1 - 0)^2 + (7 - (-5))^2}$

$VW = \sqrt{(-1)^2 + 12^2}$

$VW = \sqrt{1 + 144}$

$VW = \sqrt{145}$

$V(0, -5)$, $Q(-5, 5)$

$VQ = \sqrt{(x_2 - x_1)^2 + (y_2 - y_1)^2}$

$VQ = \sqrt{(-5 - 0)^2 + (5 - (-5))^2}$

$VQ = \sqrt{(-5)^2 + 10^2}$

$VQ = \sqrt{25 + 100}$

$VQ = \sqrt{125}$

$Q(-5, 5)$, $W(-1, 7)$

$QW = \sqrt{(x_2 - x_1)^2 + (y_2 - y_1)^2}$

$QW = \sqrt{(-1 - (-5))^2 + (7 - 5)^2}$

$QW = \sqrt{4^2 + 2^2}$

$QW = \sqrt{16 + 4}$

$QW = \sqrt{20}$

Use the Pythagorean Theorem to determine if triangle QVW is a right triangle.

$a^2 + b^2 = c^2$

$VQ^2 + QW^2 = VW^2$

$\sqrt{125} + \sqrt{20} \overset{?}{=} \sqrt{145}$

$125 + 20 \overset{?}{=} 145$

$145 = 145$

$\triangle QVW$ is therefore a right triangle.

CHAPTER 34

COORDINATE QUADRILATERAL PROOFS

1 Use the slope formula to find the slope of each side of the quadrilateral.

$F(-4, 5)$, $K(3, 3)$

$m = \dfrac{y_2 - y_1}{x_2 - x_1} = \dfrac{3 - 5}{3 - (-4)} = \dfrac{-2}{7}$

$G(-1, -2)$, $H(6, -4)$

$m = \dfrac{y_2 - y_1}{x_2 - x_1} = \dfrac{-4 - (-2)}{6 - (-1)} = \dfrac{-2}{7}$

$\overline{FK} \parallel \overline{GH}$

F(−4, 5), G(−1, −2)

$m = \dfrac{y_2 - y_1}{x_2 - x_1} = \dfrac{-2 - 5}{-1 - (-4)} = \dfrac{-7}{3}$

K(3, 3), H(6, −4)

$m = \dfrac{y_2 - y_1}{x_2 - x_1} = \dfrac{-4 - 3}{6 - 3} = \dfrac{-7}{3}$

$\overline{FG} \parallel \overline{KH}$

Quadrilateral MATH is a parallelogram because each pair of opposite sides, $\overline{FK}$ and $\overline{GH}$ and $\overline{FG}$ and $\overline{KH}$, have the same slope and therefore are parallel.

2 Use the slope formula to determine if quadrilateral ABCD has one pair of opposite sides that are parallel.

A(−1, 2), B(1, 5)

$m = \dfrac{y_2 - y_1}{x_2 - x_1} = \dfrac{5 - 2}{1 - (-1)} = \dfrac{3}{2}$

C(2, 0), D(4, 3)

$m = \dfrac{y_2 - y_1}{x_2 - x_1} = \dfrac{3 - 0}{4 - 2} = \dfrac{3}{2}$

$\overline{AB} \parallel \overline{CD}$

Use the distance formula to determine if those two sides are congruent.

$AB = \sqrt{(x_2 - x_1)^2 + (y_2 - y_1)^2}$

$AB = \sqrt{(1 - (-1))^2 + (5 - 2)^2}$

$AB = \sqrt{2^2 + 3^2}$

$AB = \sqrt{4 + 9}$

$AB = \sqrt{13}$

$CD = \sqrt{(x_2 - x_1)^2 + (y_2 - y_1)^2}$

$CD = \sqrt{(4 - 2)^2 + (3 - 0)^2}$

$CD = \sqrt{2^2 + 3^2}$

$CD = \sqrt{4 + 9}$

$CD = \sqrt{13}$

Quadrilateral ABCD has one pair of opposite sides that are parallel and congruent.
$\overline{AB} \parallel \overline{CD}$ and $\overline{AB} \cong \overline{CD}$

3 Use the slope formula to determine if both pairs of opposite sides of quadrilateral WXYZ are parallel.

W(−4, 1), X(−3, 4)

$m = \dfrac{y_2 - y_1}{x_2 - x_1} = \dfrac{4 - 1}{-3 - (-4)} = \dfrac{3}{1}$

Z(1, −1), Y(2, 2)

$m = \dfrac{y_2 - y_1}{x_2 - x_1} = \dfrac{2 - (-1)}{2 - 1} = \dfrac{3}{1}$

$\overline{WX} \parallel \overline{ZY}$

W(–4, 1), Z(1, –1)

$$m = \frac{y_2 - y_1}{x_2 - x_1} = \frac{-1-1}{1-(-4)} = \frac{-2}{5}$$

X(–3, 4), Y(2, 2)

$$m = \frac{y_2 - y_1}{x_2 - x_1} = \frac{2-4}{2-(-3)} = \frac{-2}{5}$$

$\overline{WZ} \parallel \overline{XY}$

Quadrilateral WXYZ is a parallelogram because both pairs of opposite sides have the same slope and therefore are parallel.

4 Use the slope formula to determine if quadrilateral MATH has exactly one pair of opposite sides that are parallel.

M(–5, 1), A(5, 1)

$$m = \frac{y_2 - y_1}{x_2 - x_1} = \frac{1-1}{5-(-5)} = \frac{0}{10} = 0$$

T(1, –4), H(3, –4)

$$m = \frac{y_2 - y_1}{x_2 - x_1} = \frac{-4-(-4)}{3-1} = \frac{0}{2} = 0$$

$\overline{MA} \parallel \overline{TH}$

M(–5, 1) T(1, –4)

$$m = \frac{y_2 - y_1}{x_2 - x_1} = \frac{-4-1}{1-(-5)} = \frac{-5}{6}$$

A(5, 1), H(3, –4)

$$m = \frac{y_2 - y_1}{x_2 - x_1} = \frac{-4-1}{3-5} = \frac{-5}{-2} = \frac{5}{2}$$

$\overline{MT}$ is *not* parallel to $\overline{AH}$. Quadrilateral MATH is a trapezoid because it has exactly one pair of opposite sides that are parallel. $\overline{MA} \parallel \overline{TH}$

5 Use the slope formula to determine if quadrilateral RSTV has exactly one pair of opposite sides that are parallel.

R(–9, 1), S(0, 10)

$$m = \frac{y_2 - y_1}{x_2 - x_1} = \frac{10-1}{0-(-9)} = \frac{9}{9} = 1$$

V(–3, 1), T(0, 4)

$$m = \frac{y_2 - y_1}{x_2 - x_1} = \frac{4-1}{0-(-3)} = \frac{3}{3} = 1$$

$\overline{RS} \parallel \overline{VT}$

R(–9, 1), V(–3, 1)

$$m = \frac{y_2 - y_1}{x_2 - x_1} = \frac{1-1}{-3-(-9)} = 0$$

S(0, 10), T(0, 4)

$$m = \frac{y_2 - y_1}{x_2 - x_1} = \frac{4-10}{0-0} = \frac{-6}{0}$$

undefined slope (the zero in the denominator is undefined)

Quadrilateral RSTV is a trapezoid because it has exactly one pair of opposite sides that are parallel. $\overline{RS} \parallel \overline{VT}$

CHAPTER 35

TRIGONOMETRIC RATIOS

1. $\sin 32° = \dfrac{\text{opposite}}{\text{hypotenuse}} = \dfrac{12.2}{27.8} = \dfrac{6.1}{13.9}$

   $\cos 32° = \dfrac{\text{adjacent}}{\text{hypotenuse}} = \dfrac{25}{27.8}$

   $\tan 32° = \dfrac{\text{opposite}}{\text{adjacent}} = \dfrac{12.2}{25}$

2. $\sin x = \dfrac{\text{opposite}}{\text{hypotenuse}} = \dfrac{20}{29}$

   $\cos x = \dfrac{\text{adjacent}}{\text{hypotenuse}} = \dfrac{21}{29}$

   $\tan x = \dfrac{\text{opposite}}{\text{adjacent}} = \dfrac{20}{21}$

3. $\sin x = \dfrac{\text{opposite}}{\text{hypotenuse}} = \dfrac{5}{10} = \dfrac{1}{2}$

   $\cos x = \dfrac{\text{adjacent}}{\text{hypotenuse}} = \dfrac{8.7}{10} = 0.87$

   $\tan x = \dfrac{\text{opposite}}{\text{adjacent}} = \dfrac{5}{8.7}$

4. $\sin x = \dfrac{\text{opposite}}{\text{hypotenuse}} = \dfrac{6}{7.2} = \dfrac{1}{1.2}$

   $\cos x = \dfrac{\text{adjacent}}{\text{hypotenuse}} = \dfrac{4}{7.2} = \dfrac{1}{1.8}$

   $\tan x = \dfrac{\text{opposite}}{\text{adjacent}} = \dfrac{6}{4} = \dfrac{3}{2}$

5. $\sin x = \dfrac{\text{opposite}}{\text{hypotenuse}} = \dfrac{6}{6\sqrt{2}} = \dfrac{1}{\sqrt{2}}$

   $\cos x = \dfrac{\text{adjacent}}{\text{hypotenuse}} = \dfrac{6}{6\sqrt{2}} = \dfrac{1}{\sqrt{2}}$

   $\tan x = \dfrac{\text{opposite}}{\text{adjacent}} = \dfrac{6}{6} = 1$

6. $\sin x = \dfrac{\text{opposite}}{\text{hypotenuse}} = \dfrac{8}{17}$

   $\cos x = \dfrac{\text{adjacent}}{\text{hypotenuse}} = \dfrac{15}{17}$

   $\tan x = \dfrac{\text{opposite}}{\text{adjacent}} = \dfrac{8}{15}$

7. longer leg = shorter leg $\times \sqrt{3}$
   $a = 9 \times \sqrt{3}$
   $a = 9\sqrt{3}$

8. $a = \text{leg} \times \sqrt{2}$
   $a = 9\sqrt{2} \times \sqrt{2}$
   $a = 18$

9. $a = \text{shorter leg} \times 2$
   $a = 7 \times 2$
   $a = 14$

10. $h = \text{shorter leg} \times 2$
    $15 = y \times 2$
    $\dfrac{15}{2} = \dfrac{2y}{2}$
    $y = 7.5$

    $x = \text{shorter leg} \times \sqrt{3}$
    $x = 7.5 \times \sqrt{3}$
    $x = 7.5\sqrt{3}$

11. Adeet:
    $\sin R = \dfrac{\text{opposite}}{\text{hypotenuse}} = \dfrac{DP}{RP}$

    $\cos P = \dfrac{\text{adjacent}}{\text{hypotenuse}} = \dfrac{DP}{RP}$

    $\sin R = \cos P$

Reardon:

$\sin P = \dfrac{\text{opposite}}{\text{hypotenuse}} = \dfrac{RD}{RP}$

$\cos R = \dfrac{\text{adjacent}}{\text{hypotenuse}} = \dfrac{RD}{RP}$

Both students are correct. Each student took a different approach to writing an equation involving a trigonometric relationship.

CHAPTER 36

LAWS OF SINES AND COSINES

① $\dfrac{\sin S}{s} = \dfrac{\sin R}{r}$

$\dfrac{\sin 93°}{x} = \dfrac{\sin 55°}{18}$

$\dfrac{18 \sin 93°}{\sin 55°} = \dfrac{x \sin 55°}{\sin 55°}$

$x = \dfrac{18 \sin 93°}{\sin 55°}$

$x \approx 21.94$

$x \approx 22$

② $\dfrac{\sin D}{d} = \dfrac{\sin C}{c}$

$\dfrac{\sin 65°}{12} = \dfrac{\sin x}{8}$

$\dfrac{8 \sin 65°}{12} = \dfrac{12 \sin x}{12}$

$\sin x = \dfrac{2}{3} \sin 65$

$\sin x = \dfrac{2}{3} \times 0.9063$

$\sin x \approx 0.6042$

$x = \sin^{-1} 0.6042$

$x \approx 37.2$

③ $\dfrac{\sin M}{m} = \dfrac{\sin K}{k}$

$\dfrac{\sin 51°}{6} = \dfrac{\sin 104°}{x}$

$\dfrac{x \sin 51°}{\sin 51°} = \dfrac{6 \sin 104°}{\sin 51°}$

$x = \dfrac{6 \times 0.970}{0.777}$

$x \approx 7.5$

④ $\dfrac{\sin P}{P} = \dfrac{\sin Q}{q}$

$\dfrac{\sin x}{14} = \dfrac{\sin 50°}{16}$

$\dfrac{16 \sin x}{16} = \dfrac{14 \sin 50°}{16}$

$\sin x = \dfrac{14 \sin 50°}{16}$

$\sin x = \dfrac{14 \times 0.766}{16}$

$\sin x \approx 0.67$

$x = \sin^{-1} 0.67$

$x \approx 42.1$

⑤ $c^2 = a^2 + b^2 - 2ab \cos C$

$50^2 = 29^2 + 44^2 - 2(29)(44) \cos x°$

$2{,}500 = 841 + 1{,}936 - 2{,}552 \cos x°$

$2{,}500 = 2{,}777 - 2{,}552 \cos x°$

$2{,}500 - 2{,}777 = 2{,}777 - 2{,}777 - 2{,}552 \cos x°$

$\dfrac{-277}{-2{,}552} = \dfrac{-2{,}552 \cos x°}{-2{,}552}$

$0.10854 \approx \cos x°$

$\cos^{-1} 0.10854 \approx x$

$x \approx 83.8$

⑥ $c^2 = a^2 + b^2 - 2ab \cos C$

$x^2 = 50^2 + 60^2 - 2(50)(60) \cos 115°$

$x^2 = 2{,}500 + 3{,}600 - 2(50)(60) \cos 115°$

$x^2 = 6,100 - 6,000 \times (-0.4226)$

$x^2 = 6,100 + 2,535.71$

$x^2 = 8,635.71$

$\sqrt{x^2} = \sqrt{8,635.71}$

$x \approx 92.9$

7 $c^2 = a^2 + b^2 - 2ab \cos C$

$x^2 = 11^2 + 13^2 - 2(11)(13) \cos 42°$

$x^2 = 121 + 169 - 286 \times 0.7431$

$x^2 = 290 - 212.539$

$x^2 = 77.46$

$\sqrt{x^2} = \sqrt{77.46}$

$x \approx 8.8$

8 $c^2 = a^2 + b^2 - 2ab \cos C$

$9^2 = 15^2 + 13^2 - 2(15)(13) \cos x°$

$81 = 225 + 169 - 390 \cos x°$

$81 - 394 = 394 - 394 - 390 \cos x°$

$\dfrac{-313}{-390} = \dfrac{-390 \cos x°}{-390}$

$\cos x° \approx 0.80$

$x \approx \cos^{-1} 0.80$

$x \approx 36.9$

UNIT 8
Circles
(Chapters 37–44)

CHAPTER 37

CIRCLE FUNDAMENTALS

1 $C = \pi d$ $r = \frac{1}{2}d$

$\dfrac{64\pi}{\pi} = \pi d$ $r = \frac{1}{2}(64)$

$d = 64$ $r = 32$

2 $C = \pi d$

$C \approx 3.14(18.75)$

$C \approx 58.88$

3 $d = 2r$

$d = 2(185)$

$d = 370$

$C = \pi d$

$C \approx 3.14(370)$

$C \approx 1,161.8$

$4 \times 1161.8 = 4,647.2$

Bart walked about 4,647.2 yards.

4 $a^2 + b^2 = c^2$

$8^2 + 12^2 = c^2$

$64 + 144 = c^2$

$208 = c^2$

$\sqrt{c^2} = \sqrt{208}$

$c \approx 14.4222051$

$C = \pi d$

$C \approx 3.14(14.4222051)$

$C \approx 45.29$

5 $C = 2\pi r$

$\dfrac{36\pi}{2\pi} = \dfrac{2\pi \times SP}{2\pi}$

$SP = 18$

$SP = ST + TP$

$18 = ST + 10$

$18 - 10 = ST + 10 - 10$

$ST = 8$

The radius of circle Q is
QS + ST = 3 + 8 = 11.
C = 2πr
C = 2π(11)
C = 22π
The circumference of
circle Q is 22π.

6 Larger circle:
C = 2πr

$$\frac{72\pi}{2\pi} = \frac{2\pi}{2\pi}$$

r = 36

Smaller circle:
r = 36 − 12
r = 24
C = 2πr
C ≈ 2(3.14)(24)
C ≈ 150.72

7 Diameter of the smaller circle:
d = 2r
d = 2(20)
d = 40

Diameter of the larger circle:
d = 2r
d = 2(42)
d = 84

Circumference of the
smaller circle:
C = πd

C ≈ 3.14(40)
C ≈ 125.6

Circumference of the larger circle:
C = πd
C ≈ 3.14(84)
C ≈ 263.76

263.76 − 125.6 = 138.16
The measure is 138.16 inches.

CHAPTER 38

CENTRAL ANGLES AND ARCS

1 Major arc: $\overset{\frown}{QTK}$; more than
one correct answer possible

2 Minor arc: $\overset{\frown}{FQ}$; more than one
correct answer possible

3 Semicircle: $\overset{\frown}{FTW}$; more than
one correct answer possible

4 Sector: KPW; more than one
correct answer possible

5 Diameter: $\overline{FW}$

6 Radius: $\overline{PW}$; more than one
correct answer possible

7 $\overset{\frown}{FQW}$ is a semicircle and therefore
measures 180°.
$m\overset{\frown}{FQW} - m\overset{\frown}{FQ} = m\overset{\frown}{QSW}$

$180° - 53° = 127°$

The measure of $\overset{\frown}{QSW}$ is 127°.

8 $\overset{\frown}{FTW}$ is a semicircle and therefore measures 180°.

$m\overset{\frown}{FTW} - m\overset{\frown}{kW} = m\overset{\frown}{FTK}$

$180° - 27° = 153°$

The measure of $\overset{\frown}{FYK}$ is 153°.

9 A. $m\angle DFC + m\angle CFB + m\angle BFA +$
$\quad m\angle AFD = 360°$

$\quad 21° + 101° + 90° + x° = 360°$

$\quad 212 + x = 360$

$\quad 212 - 212 + x = 360 - 212$

$\quad x = 148$

B. $\ell = \dfrac{x}{360} \times 2\pi r$

$\quad \ell = \dfrac{101}{360} \times 2\pi(12)$

$\quad \ell = \dfrac{101}{360} \times 24\pi$

$\quad \ell \approx 21.1$

The length of $\overset{\frown}{CB}$ is approximately 21.2 inches.

10 $\ell = \dfrac{x}{360} \times 2\pi r$

$\ell = \dfrac{33}{360} \times 2\pi(18)$

$\ell = \dfrac{33}{360} \times 36\pi$

$\ell \approx 10.362$

$\ell \approx 10.4$

The length of $\overset{\frown}{LN}$ is approximately 10.4 feet.

11 $C = \pi d$

$C \approx 3.14(25)$

$C \approx 78.5$

$78.5 \div 2 = 39.25$

$\overset{\frown}{RSW}$ is half of the circumference, so the length of $\overset{\frown}{RSW}$ is 39.3.

CHAPTER 39

RADIANS

1 $90° \times \dfrac{\pi}{180} = \dfrac{90\pi}{180} = \dfrac{\pi}{2}$ rad

2 $350° \times \dfrac{\pi}{180} = \dfrac{350\pi}{180} = \dfrac{35\pi}{18}$ rad

3 $58° \times \dfrac{\pi}{180} = \dfrac{58\pi}{180} = \dfrac{29\pi}{90}$ rad

4 $32° \times \dfrac{\pi}{180} = \dfrac{32\pi}{180} = \dfrac{8\pi}{45}$ rad

5 $145° \times \dfrac{\pi}{180} = \dfrac{145\pi}{180} = \dfrac{29\pi}{36}$ rad

6 $\dfrac{\pi}{8\,2} \times \dfrac{180\;45}{\pi} = \dfrac{45}{2} = 22.5°$

7 $\dfrac{2\pi}{5} \times \dfrac{180\;36}{\pi} = 72°$

8 $\dfrac{9\pi}{4} \times \dfrac{180\;45}{\pi} = 405°$

9 $2\dfrac{3}{4}\pi \times \dfrac{180}{\pi} = \dfrac{11\pi}{4} \times \dfrac{180\;45}{\pi} = 495°$

10 $\dfrac{\pi}{14\,7} \times \dfrac{180\;90}{\pi} = \dfrac{90}{7} \approx 12.857 \approx 12.9°$

CHAPTER 40

ARCS AND CHORDS

1 $4x + 22 = 10x - 2$

$4x - 10x + 22 = 10x - 10x - 2$

$-6x + 22 = -2$

$-6x + 22 - 22 = -2 - 22$

$\dfrac{-6x}{-6} = \dfrac{-24}{-6}$

$x = 4$

2 $3y + 8 = 5y - 4$

$3y - 5y + 8 = 5y - 5y - 4$

$-2y + 8 - 8 = -4 - 8$

$\dfrac{-2y}{-2} = \dfrac{-12}{-2}$

$y = 6$

3 We know that $\overarc{QS} \cong \overarc{MN}$, and that means $\overarc{QS} \cong \overarc{MN}$, so $\overarc{QS} = 88°$. The m$\angle$QRS equals 88° because the measure of an arc is equal to the measure of its central angle.

4 We know that m$\overarc{WZ}$ = m$\overarc{XV}$ because $\overarc{WZ} \cong \overarc{XV}$.

The total degree measure of a circle is 360°, so we know that m$\overarc{WX}$ + m$\overarc{ZV}$ + m$\overarc{WZ}$ + m$\overarc{XV}$ = 360°.

$92° + 24° + $ m$\overarc{WZ}$ + m$\overarc{XV}$ = 360°

$116 + $ m$\overarc{WZ}$ + m$\overarc{XV}$ = 360

$116 - 116 + $ m$\overarc{WZ}$ + m$\overarc{XV}$ = 360 - 116

m$\overarc{WZ}$ + m$\overarc{XV}$ = 244

Since m$\overarc{WZ}$ = m$\overarc{XV}$, we can divide 244 by 2 to find the measure of each arc.

$244 \div 2 = 122$

m$\overarc{WZ}$ = 122°

m$\overarc{XV}$ = 122°

5 $12x + 7 = x + 40$

$12x - x + 7 = x - x + 40$

$11x + 7 = 40$

$11x + 7 - 7 = 40 - 7$

$\dfrac{11x}{11} = \dfrac{33}{11}$

$x = 3$

6 In a circle, if chords are equidistant from the center, they are congruent.

$\overline{KJ} \cong \overline{ST}$

$KJ = 22$

7 $\overline{AC}$ is a perpendicular bisector of $\overline{DE}$, so $\overline{DB} \cong \overline{BE}$.

$\dfrac{1}{2} \overline{DE} = \overline{DB}$ and $\dfrac{1}{2} \overline{DE} = \overline{BE}$

$\dfrac{1}{2}(29) = 14.5$

$DB = 14.5$

$BE = 14.5$

8 m$\overarc{MA}$ = m$\overarc{AT}$

m$\overarc{MA}$ + m$\overarc{AT}$ = m$\overarc{MT}$

$50 + 50 = 100$

The measure of an arc is equal to the measure of its central angle, so m$\overarc{MT}$ = m$\angle$MHT.

m$\overarc{MT}$ = 100°

m$\angle$MHT = 100°

9 If a diameter is perpendicular to a chord, then it bisects the chord and its arc.
$\overset{\frown}{SR} = \overset{\frown}{WR} = 42°$

We know the indicated line R is the diameter because it is a perpendicular bisector of chord PH. The line also bisects chord SW and its arc SW. Therefore, $\overset{\frown}{SR} = \overset{\frown}{WR} = 42$, and $y = 42$.

10 MT is congruent to CU because the two chords are equidistant from the center P.
$20w + 14 = 15w + 79$
$20w - 15w + 14 = 15w - 15w + 79$
$5w + 14 = 79$
$5w + 14 - 14 = 79 - 14$
$\dfrac{5w}{5} = \dfrac{65}{5}$
$w = 13$

MT $= 20w + 14$	CU $= 15w + 79$
MT $= 20(13) + 14$	CU $= 15(13) + 79$
MT $= 274$	CU $= 274$

CHAPTER 41

INSCRIBED ANGLES

1 The measure of the inscribed angle is half the measure of the intercepted arc.

$$m\angle XWY = \tfrac{1}{2} m\overset{\frown}{XZY}$$

$85 = \tfrac{1}{2} m\overset{\frown}{XZY}$
$2 \times 85 = \tfrac{1}{2} m\overset{\frown}{XZY} \times 2$
$m\overset{\frown}{XZY} = 170°$

2 $m\angle ABC = m\angle ADC$
$9x - 34 = x + 22$
$9x - x - 34 = x - x + 22$
$8x - 34 = 22$
$8x - 34 + 34 = 22 + 34$
$\dfrac{8x}{8} = \dfrac{56}{8}$
$x = 7$

$m\angle ABC = (9x - 34)°$
$m\angle ABC = (9(7) - 34)°$
$m\angle ABC = 29°$

$m\angle ADC = (x + 22)°$
$m\angle ADC = (7 + 22)°$
$m\angle ADC = 29°$

3 $m\angle QRS = \tfrac{1}{2} m\overset{\frown}{QS}$
$m\angle QRS = \tfrac{1}{2}(156)$
$m\angle QRS = 78°$

4 The vertices of the triangle are on the circle; therefore, the triangle is inscribed in the circle. $\angle ABC$ is inscribed in a semicircle; therefore, it is a right angle and measures 90°.
$m\angle B = 90°$
$m\angle A = m\angle C$

$m\angle A + m\angle B + m\angle C = 180°$

$3y - 12 + 90 + 3y - 12 = 180°$

$6y + 66 = 180$

$6y + 66 - 66 = 180 - 66$

$6y = 114$

$\dfrac{6y}{6} = \dfrac{114}{6}$

$y = 19$

5 Since $\angle BAC$ and $\angle BDC$ are inscribed in the circle and have the same intercepted arc, those angles are congruent.

$\angle BAC \cong \angle BDC$

$m\angle BAC = 52°$

$m\angle BDC = 52°$

6 $\overset{\frown}{VZW}$ forms a semicircle and therefore measures 180°.

The measure of an inscribed angle is half the measure of its intercepted arc.

$m\angle V = \dfrac{1}{2} m\overset{\frown}{WU}$

$53° = \dfrac{1}{2} m\overset{\frown}{WU}$

$53° \times 2 = \dfrac{1}{2} m\overset{\frown}{WU} \times 2$

$106° = m\overset{\frown}{WU}$

$m\overset{\frown}{UV} = 180 - 106 = 74°$

So, $m\overset{\frown}{VZW} = 180°$, $m\overset{\frown}{WU} = 106°$, and $m\overset{\frown}{UV} = 74°$.

7 $m\angle A + m\angle H = 180°$

$2x + 9 + 3x + 6 = 180$

$5x + 15 = 180$

$5x + 15 - 15 = 180 - 15$

$5x = 165$

$x = 33$

8 $m\angle H + m\angle G = 180°$

$x + 16 + 6x - 4 = 180$

$7x + 12 = 180$

$7x + 12 - 12 = 180 - 12$

$7x = 168$

$x = 24$

$m\angle H = (x + 16)°$

$m\angle H = (24 + 16)°$

$m\angle H = 40°$

$m\angle G = (6x - 4)°$

$m\angle G = (6[24] - 4)°$

$m\angle G = 140°$

$m\angle J + m\angle B = 180°$

$3y + 16 + 2y = 180$

$5y + 16 = 180$

$5y + 16 - 16 = 180 - 16$

$5y = 164$

$y = 32.8$

$m\angle J = (3y + 16)°$

$m\angle J = (3[32.8] + 16)°$

$m\angle J = 114.4°$

$m\angle B = (2y)°$

$m\angle B = (2[32.8])°$

$m\angle B = 65.6°$

9 $m\angle SRU = 90°$, $m\angle S = 90°$,

$m\angle STU = 90°$, $m\angle U = 90°$,

$m\overarc{RST} = 180°$, $m\overarc{TUR} = 180°$

CHAPTER 42

TANGENTS

1 FALSE. Circles can have more than one common tangent.

2 FALSE. A tangent is a line, segment, or ray that intersects a circle in exactly one point.

3 TRUE. S, Y, and M are the points where a line, segment, and ray, respectively, intersect the circle, making them points of tangency.

4 If $\overline{CD} \perp \overline{DA}$ then $\overline{CD}$ is a tangent to circle A.

$a^2 + b^2 \overset{?}{=} c^2$

$12^2 + 35^2 \overset{?}{=} 37^2$

$144 + 1225 \overset{?}{=} 1,369$

$1,369 = 1,369$

Triangle CDA is therefore a right triangle, and $\overline{CD} \perp \overline{DA}$ so $\overline{CD}$ is a tangent to circle A.

5 Line CD is not a tangent of circle A because it intersects the circle at two points, not one.

6 $\overline{PB} \cong \overline{PA}$

$4x - 11 = 2x + 7$

$4x - 2x - 11 = 2x - 2x + 7$

$2x - 11 = 7$

$2x - 11 + 11 = 7 + 11$

$2x = 18$

$x = 9$

7 $a^2 + b^2 = c^2$

$24^2 + 10^2 = x^2$

$576 + 100 = x^2$

$676 = x^2$

$\sqrt{676} = \sqrt{x^2}$

$x = 26$

8 $40 + 90 + x = 180$

$130 + x = 180$

$130 - 130 + x = 180 - 130$

$x = 50$

9 $x + 123 = 180$

$x + 123 - 123 = 180 - 123$

$x = 57$

10 $a^2 + b^2 = c^2$

$x^2 + 63^2 = 65^2$

$x^2 + 3,969 = 4,225$

$x^2 + 3,969 - 3,969 = 4,225 - 3,969$

$x^2 = 256$

$\sqrt{x^2} = \sqrt{256}$

$x = 16$

CHAPTER 43

SECANTS

1 $x = \frac{1}{2}(28 + 132)$

$x = \frac{1}{2}(160)$

$x = 80$

2 $95 = \frac{1}{2}(x + 116)$

$95 \times 2 = \frac{1}{2}(x + 116) \times 2$

$190 = x + 116$

$190 - 116 = x + 116 - 116$

$x = 74$

3 $x = \frac{1}{2}(58 - 20)$

$x = \frac{1}{2}(38)$

$x = 19$

4 $x = \frac{1}{2}(114 - 60)$

$x = \frac{1}{2}(54)$

$x = 27$

5 $180 - x = \frac{1}{2}(16 + 34)$

$180 - x = \frac{1}{2}(50)$

$180 - 180 - x = 25 - 180$

$-x = -155$

$\frac{-x}{-1} = \frac{-155}{-1}$

$x = 155$

6 $8^2 = 4 \times (4 + x)$

$64 = 16 + 4x$

$64 - 16 = 16 - 16 + 4x$

$48 = 4x$

$\frac{48}{4} = \frac{4x}{4}$

$x = 12$

CHAPTER 44

EQUATIONS OF CIRCLES

1 Center: $(3, -2)$

Radius: 7

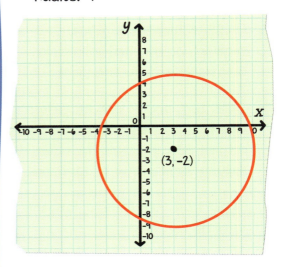

2 Center: (0, 0)
Radius: 8

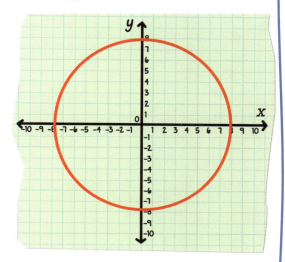

Center (2, −5), radius 4

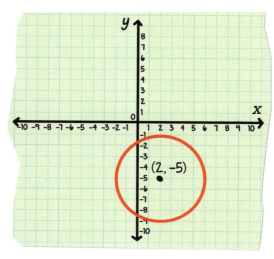

3 $x^2 + y^2 = 144$

4 $(x + 8)^2 + (y − 6)^2 = 100$

5 $x^2 + (y + 3)^2 = 49$

6 $x^2 + y^2 − 4x + 10y + 13 = 0$
$(x^2 − 4x) + (y^2 + 10y) = −13$
$(x^2 − 4x + 4) + (y^2 + 10y + 25) = −13 + 4 + 25$
$(x − 2)^2 + (y + 5)^2 = 16$

7 $x^2 + y^2 + 6x − 8y − 11 = 0$
$(x^2 + 6x) + (y^2 − 8y) = 11$
$(x^2 + 6x + 9) + (y^2 − 8y + 16) = 11 + 9 + 16$
$(x + 3)^2 + (y − 4)^2 = 36$

Center (−3, 4), radius 6

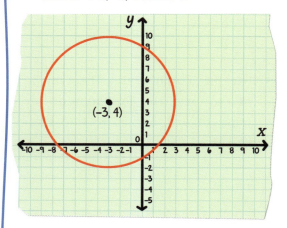

UNIT 9

Area
(Chapters 45–48)

CHAPTER 45

AREAS OF PARALLELOGRAMS AND TRIANGLES

1 $A = bh$
$A = 14 \times 15$
$A = 210 \text{ cm}^2$

2 $A = bh$
$A = 6 \times 12$
$A = 72 \text{ cm}^2$

3 Use the Pythagorean Theorem or recognize the Pythagorean triple of 12, 16, and 20 to find the height of 16 cm.

$A = bh$
$A = 33 \times 16$
$A = 528 \text{ cm}^2$

4 Use the Pythagorean Theorem or recognize the Pythagorean triple of 6, 8, and 10 to find the height of 8 ft.

$A = bh$
$A = 21 \times 8$
$A = 168 \text{ ft}^2$

5 $a^2 + b^2 = c^2$
$12^2 + b^2 = (12\sqrt{2})^2$
$144 + b^2 = 288$
$144 - 144 + b^2 = 288 - 144$
$b^2 = 144$
$\sqrt{b^2} = \sqrt{144}$
$b = 12$
$h = 12$

$A = bh$
$A = 28 \times 12$
$A = 336 \text{ units}^2$

Note: This area can also be found by using the fact that this is a 45–45–90 right triangle.

6 Use the Pythagorean Theorem or recognize the Pythagorean triple of 6, 8, and 10 to find the height of 8 cm.

$A = \frac{1}{2}bh$
$A = \frac{1}{2} \cdot 21 \cdot 8$
$A = 84 \text{ cm}^2$

7 Since the height is *not* given, use what is known about the 30°–60°–90° special right triangle to find the measure.

Let a = shorter leg *or* the base and let b = longer leg *or* the height.

longer leg = shorter leg $\times \sqrt{3}$

$b = a \times \sqrt{3}$

$b = 8 \times \sqrt{3}$

$b = 8\sqrt{3}$

Area $= \frac{1}{2}$ bh

$= \frac{1}{2} \times 10 \times 8\sqrt{3}$

$= \frac{1}{2} \times 80\sqrt{3}$

$= 40\sqrt{3}$

Therefore, the area of this triangle is approximately $40\sqrt{3}$ square units.

8 $A = \frac{1}{2}$ bh

$A = \frac{1}{2} \bullet 22 \bullet 18$

$A = 198$ in²

9 Yes, you can find the height of the triangle using the formula for area.

$A = \frac{1}{2}$ bh

$147 = \frac{1}{2} \bullet 14 \bullet h$

$147 = 7h$

$\frac{147}{7} = \frac{7h}{7}$

$h = 21$ mm

CHAPTER 46

AREAS OF OTHER POLYGONS

1 $A = \frac{1}{2} h(b_1 + b_2)$

$A = \frac{1}{2} \times 15(14 + 26)$

$A = \frac{1}{2} \times 15(40)$

$A = 300$ units²

2 $a^2 + b^2 = c^2$

$a^2 + 7^2 = 25^2$

$a^2 + 49 = 625$

$a^2 + 49 - 49 = 625 - 49$

$a^2 = 576$

$\sqrt{a^2} = \sqrt{576}$

$a = 24$

$h = 24$

$a^2 + b^2 = c^2$

$a^2 + 24^2 = 26^2$

$a^2 + 576 = 676$

$a^2 + 576 - 576 = 676 - 576$

$a^2 = 100$

$\sqrt{a^2} = \sqrt{100}$

$a = 10$

$b_1 = 22$

$b_2 = 10 + 22 + 7 = 39$

$A = \frac{1}{2} h(b_1 + b_2)$

$A = \frac{1}{2} \times 24(22 + 39)$

$A = \frac{1}{2} \times 24(61)$

$A = 732$ ft²

$732 \times \$16 = \$11,712$

The mirrors will cost approximately $11,712.

3 $A = \frac{1}{2}d_1d_2$

$A = \frac{1}{2} \times 18 \times 32$
$A = 288$ cm²

4 $A = \frac{1}{2}d_1d_2$

$A = \frac{1}{2} \times 20 \times 26$

$A = 260$ mm²

5 First, find the length of the other diagonal. Diagonals of a rhombus are perpendicular and form four right triangles. Identify that the side lengths of one of those triangles are a Pythagorean triple of 10, 24, and 26, or use the Pythagorean Theorem to find the measure of the other leg. That leg is 10 feet, which means the missing diagonal is 20 feet.

$A = \frac{1}{2}d_1d_2$

$A = \frac{1}{2} \times 48 \times 20$

$A = 480$ ft²

6 $A = \frac{1}{2}aP$

$A = \frac{1}{2} \times 22 \times 48$

$A = 528$ m²

7 Use 30°-60°-90° special right triangle to find the apothem. 30°-60°-90° triangles have a side ratio of 1:2:$\sqrt{3}$.

longer leg = shorter leg $\times \sqrt{3}$

$a = 12 \times \sqrt{3}$
$a = 12\sqrt{3}$ in
$P = 6 \times 24$
$P = 144$ in

$A = \frac{1}{2}aP$

$A = \frac{1}{2} \times 12\sqrt{3} \times 144 = 864\sqrt{3}$

$A \approx 1,496.49$ in²

Convert inches to feet:
$1,496.91 \div 12 \approx 124.74$ ft²

$124.74 \times 15 \approx 1,871.11$ ft²
Approximately 1,871.11 square feet of the park will contain the stone embellishment.

8 $A = \frac{1}{2}aP$

$172.5 = \frac{1}{2} \times a \times 50$

$172.5 = \frac{1}{2} \times 50a$

$172.5 = \frac{50a}{2}$

$172.5 \times 2 = \frac{50a}{2} \times 2$

$345 = 50a$
$a = 6.9$ m
The apothem is 6.9 m.

CHAPTER 47

AREAS OF CIRCLES AND SECTORS

1 $A = \pi r^2$
$A = \pi (7.5)^2$
$A = 56.25\pi$
$A \approx 56.25 \times 3.14$
$A \approx 176.6 \text{ mm}^2$

2 $A = \pi r^2$
$A = \pi (25)^2$
$A = 625\pi$
$A \approx 625 \times 3.14$
$A \approx 1,962.5 \text{ cm}^2$

3 $A = \pi r^2$
$126\pi = \pi r^2$
$\dfrac{126\pi}{\pi} = \dfrac{\pi r^2}{\pi}$
$126 = r^2$
$\sqrt{126} = \sqrt{r^2}$
$r = \sqrt{126}$
$r \approx 11.2 \text{ mm}$

4 $A = \pi r^2$
$\dfrac{68\pi}{\pi} = \dfrac{\pi r^2}{\pi}$
$68 = r^2$
$\sqrt{68} = \sqrt{r^2}$
$r = 2\sqrt{17}$

$d = 2r$
$d = 2(2\sqrt{17})$
$d = 4\sqrt{17}$
$d \approx 16.49 \text{ ft}$

5 $C = 2\pi r$
$76\pi = 2\pi r$
$r = 38 \text{ cm}$

$A = \pi r^2$
$A = \pi (38)^2$
$A = 1,444\pi$
$A \approx 1,444 \times 3.14$
$A \approx 4,534.2 \text{ cm}^2$

6 $A = \dfrac{\theta}{360°} \times \pi r^2$
$A = \dfrac{84°}{360°} \times \pi (16)^2$
$A \approx 0.2\overline{3} \times 256 \times 3.14$
$A \approx 187.6 \text{ m}^2$

7 $A = \dfrac{\theta}{360°} \times \pi r^2$
$A = \dfrac{240°}{360°} \times \pi (12)^2$
$A \approx \dfrac{2}{3} \times 144 \times 3.14$
$A \approx 301.4 \text{ in}^2$

8 $A = \dfrac{\theta}{360°} \times \pi r^2$
$A = \dfrac{152°}{360°} \times \pi (10)^2$
$A \approx \dfrac{19}{45} \times 100 \times 3.14$
$A \approx 132.6 \text{ mm}^2$

9 $A = \dfrac{\theta}{360°} \times \pi r^2$
$A = \dfrac{100°}{360°} \times \pi (9)^2$
$A \approx \dfrac{5}{18} \times 81 \times 3.14$
$A \approx 70.7 \text{ cm}^2$

10 Area of smaller circle = πr^2
$A = \pi(3)^2$
$A \approx 3.14 \times 9$
$A \approx 28.26$ ft²

Area of the larger circle = πr^2
$A = \pi(7)^2$
$A \approx 3.14 \times 49$
$A \approx 153.86$ ft²

$153.86 - 28.26 \approx 125.6$ ft²

Yes, there is enough paint, because the shaded portion of the design has an area of approximately 125.6 ft².

CHAPTER 48

AREAS OF COMPOSITE FIGURES

1 Area of the rectangle = lw
$A = 22 \times 16$
$A = 352$ cm²

Use the Pythagorean Theorem to determine the height of the triangle.
$a^2 + b^2 = c^2$
$8^2 + b^2 = 17^2$
$64 + b^2 = 289$
$64 - 64 + b^2 = 289 - 64$
$b^2 = 225$
$\sqrt{b^2} = \sqrt{225}$
$b = 15$

height of triangle = 15 cm

Area of the triangle =
$\frac{1}{2} \times$ base $\times$ height
$A = \frac{1}{2} \times 16 \times 15$
$A = 120$ cm²

$352 + 120 = 472$
The area of the shaded figure is 472 cm².

2 $A = lw$
$A = 10 \times 3$
$A = 30$ mm²

$A = lw$
$A = 13 \times 7$
$A = 91$ mm²

$A = lw$
$A = 6 \times 11$
$A = 66$ mm²

$A = lw$
$A = 5 \times 2$
$A = 10$ mm²

$30 + 91 + 66 + 10 = 197$
The area of the shaded figure is 197 mm².

3 $A = lw$
$A = 14 \times 12$
$A = 168$ yd²

$A = lw$

$A = 21 \times 14$

$A = 294$ yd²

$A = lw$

$A = 9 \times 14$

$A = 126$ yd²

Area of the trapezoid $= \frac{1}{2}h(b_1 + b_2)$

$A = \frac{1}{2} \times 8 \times (18 + 21)$

$A = \frac{1}{2} \times 8 \times 39$

$A = 156$ yd²

Area of the semicircle $= \pi r^2$

$A = \frac{1}{2}\pi \times 7^2$

$A = \frac{1}{2} \times \pi \times 49$

$A = 24.5\pi$ yd²

$A \approx 76.9$ yd²

$168 + 294 + 126 + 156 + 76.9 \approx 820.9$
The area of the shaded figure
is approximately 820.9 yd².

4 Area of the rectangle $= lw$

$A = 53 \times 26$

$A = 1,378$ cm²

Area of the pentagon $= \frac{1}{2}aP$

$A = \frac{1}{2} \times 6 \times 75$

$A = 225$ cm²

Area of each triangle $= \frac{1}{2}bh$

$A = \frac{1}{2} \times 19 \times 12$

$A = 114$ cm²

Multiply the triangle's area by two
to determine the sum of the areas
of the two triangles, one on either
side of the pentagon.
$114 \times 2 = 228$ cm²
Add the areas of all the figures
together to determine the total
area of the shaded figure.
$1,378 + 225 + 228 = 1,831$
The area of the shaded
figure is 1,831 cm².

5 Area of the rectangle $= lw$

$A = 32 \times 17$

$A = 544$ ft²

Area of the smaller circle $= \pi r^2$

$A = \pi \times 5.5^2$

$A = \pi \times 30.25$

$A = 30.25\pi$ ft²

Area of the larger circle $= \pi r^2$

$A = \pi \times 8^2$

$A = \pi \times 64$

$A = 64\pi$ ft²

Add the areas of the circles.
$30.25\pi + 64\pi = 94.25\pi$ ft²

Subtract the total area of the circles from the area of the rectangle to find the area of the shaded part of the figure.

$544 - 94.25\pi \approx 544 - 295.9 \approx 248.1$

The area of the shaded figure is approximately 248.1 ft².

6 Area of the rectangle = lw

$A = 70 \times 56$

$A = 3{,}920 \text{ mm}^2$

Area of the kite = $\frac{1}{2} d_1 d_2$

$A = \frac{1}{2} \times 56 \times 70$

$A = 1{,}960 \text{ mm}^2$

Subtract the area of the kite from the area of the rectangle to determine the area of the shaded part of the figure.

$3{,}920 - 1{,}960 = 1{,}960$

The area of the shaded part of the figure is 1,960 mm².

7 Area of the circle = πr^2

$A = \pi(19)^2$

$A = \pi \times 361$

$A \approx 361\pi \text{ in}^2$

Area of the rhombus = $\frac{1}{2} d_1 d_2$

$A = \frac{1}{2} \times 24 \times 38$

$A = 456 \text{ in}^2$

Subtract the area of the rhombus from the area of the circle to

determine the area of the shaded part of the circle.

$361\pi - 456 \approx 1{,}133.5 - 456 \approx 677.5$

The shaded part of the circle has an area of approximately 677.5 in².

8 Use the Pythagorean Theorem to determine the leg/height of the triangle.

$a^2 + b^2 = c^2$

$20^2 + b^2 = 58^2$

$400 + b^2 = 3{,}364$

$400 - 400 + b^2 = 3{,}364 - 400$

$b^2 = 2{,}964$

$\sqrt{b^2} = \sqrt{2{,}964}$

$b = \sqrt{2{,}964}$

leg/height of the triangle $= \sqrt{2{,}964}$

Area of the triangle =

$\frac{1}{2} \times \text{base} \times \text{height}$

$A = \frac{1}{2} \times 20 \times \sqrt{2{,}964}$

$A = 10\sqrt{2{,}964} \text{ cm}^2$

Area of the unshaded sector =

$\frac{\theta}{360°} \times \pi r^2$

$A = \frac{108°}{360°} \times \pi(12)^2$

$A = 0.3 \times \pi \times 144$

$A = 43.2\pi \text{ cm}^2$

Subtract the area of the unshaded sector from the area of the triangle.
$10\sqrt{2,964} - 43.2\pi \approx 544.43 - 135.65 \approx 408.78$
The shaded area of the triangle is ≈ 408.8 cm².

UNIT 10

Surface Area and Volume (Chapters 49–55)

CHAPTER 49

SURFACE AREAS OF PRISMS AND CYLINDERS

1 Use the formula for the surface area of a prism: $SA = 2B + Ph$

B = area of the base = $l \times w$ =
$14 \times 14 = 196$ mm²
P = perimeter of the base =
$14 + 14 + 14 + 14 = 56$ mm
h = height of the prism = 14 mm

$SA = 2(196) + 56(14)$
$= 392 + 784$
$= 1,176$ mm²
$SA = 1,176$ mm²

2 Use the formula for the surface area of a prism: $SA = 2B + Ph$

B = area of the base = $l \times w$ =
$19 \times 11 = 209$ mm²
P = perimeter of the base =
$19 + 19 + 11 + 11 = 60$ mm
h = height of the prism = 17 mm

$SA = 2(209) + 60(17)$
$= 418 + 1,020$
$= 1,438$ mm²
$SA = 1,438$ mm²

3 Use the formula for the surface area of a prism: $SA = 2B + Ph$

B = area of the base = $\frac{1}{2}aP$ =
$\frac{1}{2} \times 8 \times (18 + 18 + 18 + 18 + 18) = 360$ cm²

P = perimeter of the base =
$18 + 18 + 18 + 18 + 18 = 90$ cm
h = height of the prism = 12 cm

$SA = 2(360) + 90(12)$
$= 720 + 1,080$
$= 1,800$ cm²
$SA = 1,800$ cm²

4 Use the formula for the surface area of a prism: $SA = 2B + Ph$

B = area of the base = $\frac{1}{2}bh$ =
$\frac{1}{2} \times 48 \times 7 = 168$ cm²

(Use the Pythagorean triple of 7, 24, and 25 to find half

the base of the triangle. The triangle's base length is 24 cm + 24 cm = 48 cm.)

P = perimeter of the base = 25 + 25 + 48 = 98 cm
h = height of the prism = 95 cm

SA = 2(168) + 98(95)
= 336 + 9,310
= 9,646 cm²
SA = 9,646 cm²

5 Use the formula for the surface area of a prism: SA = 2B + Ph

B = area of the base = $\frac{1}{2}$ bh =
$\frac{1}{2}$ × 30 × 8 = 120 mm²

(Use the Pythagorean triple of 8, 15, and 17 to find half the base of the triangle. The triangle's base length is 15 mm + 15 mm = 30 mm.)

P = perimeter of the base = 17 + 17 + 30 = 64 mm
h = height of the prism = 28 mm

SA = 2(120) + 64(28)
= 240 + 1,792
= 2,032 mm²
SA = 2,032 mm²

6 To find how many square feet of paint the bin will require, find the

surface area of the rectangular prism compost bin.

Use the formula for the surface area of a prism: SA = 2B + Ph

B = area of the base = l × w = 8 × 4 = 32 ft²
P = perimeter of the base = 8 + 8 + 4 + 4 = 24 ft
h = height of the prism = 5 ft

SA = 2(32) + 24(5)
= 64 + 120
= 184 ft²

The compost bin will require 184 ft² of paint.

7 Use the formula for the surface area of a cylinder:
SA = 2πr² + 2πrh

r = radius of the base: 25 m
h = height of the cylinder = 11 m

SA ≈ 2(3.14)(25)² + 2(3.14)(25)(11)
≈ 3,925 + 1,727
≈ 5,652 m²
SA ≈ 5,652 m²

8 Use the formula for the surface area of a cylinder:
SA = 2πr² + 2πrh

r = radius of the base = 8.6 cm
h = height of the cylinder = 31.2 cm

Substitute π = 3.14.
SA $\approx$ 2(3.14)(8.6)² + 2(3.14)(8.6)(31.2)
$\approx$ 464.47 + 1,685.05
$\approx$ 2,149.5 cm²
SA $\approx$ 2,149.52 cm²

9 Use the formula for the surface area of a cylinder:
SA = $2\pi r^2 + 2\pi rh$

r = radius of the base = 4.5 ft
(diameter = 9 ft, radius = $\frac{1}{2}$(9) = 4.5 ft)

h = height of the cylinder = 23 ft

SA $\approx$ 2(3.14)(4.5)² + 2(3.14)(4.5)(23)
$\approx$ 127.17 + 649.98
$\approx$ 777.2 ft²
SA $\approx$ 777.2 ft²

10 Use the formula for the surface area of a cylinder:
SA = $2\pi r^2 + 2\pi rh$

r = radius of the base = 1.5 in
(diameter = 3 in, radius = $\frac{1}{2}$(3) = 1.5 in)

h = height of the cylinder = 6 in

SA $\approx$ 2(3.14)(1.5)² + 2(3.14)(1.5)(6)
$\approx$ 14.13 + 56.52
$\approx$ 70.65 in²

Each label will need 70.65 square inches of paper. Two thousand cans will need 2,000 × 70.65 in² = 141,300 square inches of paper.

The company will need about 141,300 square inches of paper to make 2,000 labels for their tomato soup cans.

CHAPTER 50

SURFACE AREAS OF PYRAMIDS AND CONES

1 Use the formula for lateral area of a regular pyramid: LA = $\frac{1}{2}$ Pℓ
= $\frac{1}{2}$ × (8 + 8 + 8) × 12
= 144 cm²
LA = 144 cm²

2 Use the formula for lateral area of a regular pyramid: LA = $\frac{1}{2}$ Pℓ
= $\frac{1}{2}$ × (9 + 9 + 9 + 9) × 14
= 252 cm²
LA = 252 cm²

3 Use the formula for the surface area of a regular pyramid:
SA = B + $\frac{1}{2}$ Pℓ

B = area of regular hexagonal base = $\frac{1}{2}$ aP

457

$= \frac{1}{2}(14)(20 \times 6) + \frac{1}{2}(20 \times 6)(24)$

$= 840 + 1{,}440$

$= 2{,}280$ in²

SA $= 2{,}280$ in²

4 Use the formula for the surface area of a regular pyramid:
SA $= B + \frac{1}{2}Pl$

To find the slant height (l), use the Pythagorean triple of 5, 12, and 13 or the Pythagorean Theorem: $12^2 + 5^2 = $ slant height²; slant height $= 13$ mm.

$= (10 \times 10) + \frac{1}{2}(10 \times 4)(13)$

$= 100 + 260$

$= 360$ mm²

SA $= 360$ mm²

5 Use the formula for the surface area of a regular pyramid:
SA $= B + \frac{1}{2}Pl$

B $=$ area of regular pentagonal base $= \frac{1}{2}aP$

$= \frac{1}{2}(10)(24 \times 5) + \frac{1}{2}(24 \times 5)(16)$

$= 600 + 960$

$= 1{,}560$ in²

SA $= 1{,}560$ in²

6 Use the formula for the lateral area of a cone: LA $= \pi r l$

To find the slant height (l), use the Pythagorean Theorem:
$10.5^2 + 13^2 = $ slant height²; slant height $= 16.71$ in.

$\approx \pi(13)(16.71)$

$\approx 217.2\pi$ in² or approximately 682 in²

LA $\approx 217.2\pi$ in² or approximately 682 in²

7 Use the formula for the surface area of a cone: SA $= \pi r^2 + \pi r l$

SA $= \pi(13)^2 + \pi(13)(26)$

$= 169\pi + 338\pi$

$= 507\pi$ ft²

SA $= 507\pi$ ft²

8 Use the formula for the surface area of a cone: SA $= \pi r^2 + \pi r l$

The radius is half the diameter (22 m), so $r = 11$.

SA $= \pi(11)^2 + \pi(11)(60)$

$= 121\pi + 660\pi$

$= 781\pi$ m²

SA $= 781\pi$ m²

9 Use the formula for the surface area of a cone: SA $= \pi r^2 + \pi r l$

The radius is half the diameter (28 ft), so $r = 14$.

$SA = \pi(14)^2 + \pi(14)(58)$

$= 196\pi + 812\pi$

$= 1,008\pi$ ft² or approximately 3,165.12 ft²

One square foot of roof replacement costs $40.

$40 × 3,165.12 ft² = $126,604.80

The new roof will cost approximately $126,604.80.

10 To find the slant height of the pyramid, use the equation for surface area: $SA = B + \frac{1}{2}P\ell$

$5,775 \text{ ft}^2 = (35 × 35) + \frac{1}{2}(35 × 4)(\ell)$

$5,775 = 1,225 + 70\ell$

$5,775 - 1,225 = 1,225 - 1,225 + 70\ell$

$4,550 = 70\ell$

$65 \text{ ft} = \ell$

So, the slant height is 65 ft. The slant height of the sculpture is 65 ft.

11 Reardon is correct. The height of a pyramid is always less than its slant height. Therefore, using the height of the pyramid instead of the slant height to calculate the surface area will yield a measure that is less than the actual surface area.

CHAPTER 51

VOLUMES OF PRISMS AND CYLINDERS

1 Use the formula for the volume of a rectangular prism: $V = Bh = (lw)h$

$= 9 × 13 × 4$

$= 468 \text{ mm}^3$

$V = 468 \text{ mm}^3$

2 Use the formula for the volume of a triangular prism:

$V = Bh = (\frac{1}{2} × \text{base} × \text{height})h$

$= (\frac{1}{2} × 21 × 20)(42)$

$= 8,820 \text{ in}^3$

$V = 8,820 \text{ in}^3$

3 Use the formula for the volume of a cylinder: $V = Bh = (\pi r^2)h$

$= \pi × (5.5)^2 × 11$

$= 332.75\pi \text{ ft}^3$

$\approx 1,044.8 \text{ ft}^3$

$V = 332.75\pi \text{ ft}^3$ or about 1,044.8 ft³

4 Use the formula for the volume of a cylinder: $V = Bh = (\pi r^2)h$

$= \pi × (9)^2 × 16$

$= 1,296\pi \text{ in}^3$

$\approx 4,069.4 \text{ in}^3$

$V = 1,296\pi \text{ in}^3$ or about 4,069.4 in³

5 Use the formula for the volume of an oblique cylinder: $V = Bh = (\pi r^2)h$

$= \pi \times (15)^2 \times 32$

$= 7,200\pi$ cm³

$\approx 22,608$ cm³

$V = 7,200\pi$ cm³ or
about 22,608 cm³

6 Use the formula for the volume
of an oblique rectangular prism:
$V = Bh = (lw)h$

$= 4 \times 6 \times 18$

$= 432$ in³

$V = 432$ in³

7 Use the formula for the volume of
a cylinder: $V = Bh = (\pi r^2)h$

The radius is half the diameter
(16 ft), so $r = 8$.

$= \pi \times (8)^2 \times 19$

$= 1,216\pi$ ft³

$\approx 3,818.2$ ft³

$V = 1,216\pi$ ft³ or about 3,818.2 ft³

8 Use the formula for the
volume of a triangular prism:
$V = Bh = (\frac{1}{2} \times base \times height)h$

$= (\frac{1}{2} \times 35 \times 12)(40)$

$= 8,400$ cm³

$V = 8,400$ cm³

9 Use the formula for the volume of
a rectangular prism: $V = Bh = (lw)h$

Given: Volume of water = 45 ft³
Prism length = 6 ft
Prism width = 3 ft

We will solve for h, the height of
the water in the fish tank.

45 ft³ = 6 × 3 × h

45 = 18h

2.5 ft = h

The height of the water
level is 2.5 feet.

10 Use the formula for the volume of
a cylinder: $V = Bh = (\pi r^2)h$

Smaller Cylinder Grain Bin	Larger Cylinder Grain Bin
$= \pi \times (8)^2 \times 26$ $= 1,664\pi$ ft³ $\approx 5,224.96$ ft³	$= \pi \times (15)^2 \times 40$ $= 9,000\pi$ ft³ $\approx 28,260$ ft³

Subtract the smaller bin's volume
from the larger bin's volume.

28,260 ft³ − 5,224.96 ft³ =
23,035.04 ft³

So, the larger bin can hold
23,035.04 cubic feet more grain.

CHAPTER 52

VOLUMES OF PYRAMIDS AND CONES

1. Use the formula for the volume of a square pyramid:

$V = \frac{1}{3} \times$ area of base $\times$ height

$V = \frac{1}{3} \times$ (lw) $\times$ height

$= \frac{1}{3} \times (6.2 \times 6.2) \times 10$

$= 128.1\overline{3}$ cm³

$V \approx 128.1$ cm³

2. Use the formula for the volume of a regular octagonal pyramid:

$V = \frac{1}{3} \times$ area of base $\times$ height

$V = \frac{1}{3} \times (\frac{1}{2} aP) \times$ height

$= \frac{1}{3} \times (\frac{1}{2} \times 12 \times [(8 \times 8)]) \times 18$

$= 2{,}304$ in³

$V = 2{,}304$ in³

3. Use the formula for the volume of a rectangular pyramid:

$V = \frac{1}{3} \times$ area of base $\times$ height

$V = \frac{1}{3} \times$ (lw) $\times$ height

$= \frac{1}{3} \times (16 \times 20) \times 24$ (We can use the Pythagorean Theorem to find the height: $10^2 + h^2 = 26^2$; $h = 24$.)

$= 2{,}560$ mm³

$V = 2{,}560$ mm³

4. Use the formula for the volume of a triangular pyramid:

$V = \frac{1}{3} \times$ area of base $\times$ height

$V = \frac{1}{3} \times (\frac{1}{2} bh) \times$ height

$= \frac{1}{3} \times (\frac{1}{2} \times 18 \times 8) \times 22$

$= 528$ cm³

$V = 528$ cm³

5. Use the formula for the volume of a cone:

$V = \frac{1}{3} \times$ area of base $\times$ height

$V = \frac{1}{3} \times \pi r^2 \times$ height

$= \frac{1}{3} \times \pi \times 14^2 \times 25$

$\approx 1{,}633.\overline{3}\pi$ m³

$\approx 5{,}128.7$ m³

$V \approx 1{,}633.\overline{3}\pi$ m³ or approximately $5{,}128.7$ m³

6. Use the formula for the volume of a cone:

$V = \frac{1}{3} \times$ area of base $\times$ height

$V = \frac{1}{3} \times \pi r^2 \times$ height

$= \frac{1}{3} \times \pi \times 7.5^2 \times 14$

$= 262.5\pi$ cm³

≈ 824.3 cm³

$V = 262.5\pi$ cm³ or approximately 824.3 cm³

7. Use the formula for the volume of a cone:

$V = \frac{1}{3} \times$ area of base $\times$ height

$V = \frac{1}{3} \times \pi r^2 \times$ height

$= \frac{1}{3} \times \pi \times 9^2 \times 40$ (The radius is half the diameter, which is 18 ft, so r = 9. We can use the Pythagorean Theorem to find the height: $9^2 + h^2 = 41^2$; h = 40.)

$= 1,080\pi$ ft³

$\approx 3,391.2$ ft³

V = 1,080π ft³ or approximately 3,391.2 ft³

8 Use the formula for the volume of a frustum:

$V = \frac{1}{3} B_1 h_1 - \frac{1}{3} B_2 h_2$

$V = \frac{1}{3}(LW)H - \frac{1}{3}(lw)h$

$= \frac{1}{3}(36 \times 36) \times 42 - \frac{1}{3}(20.5 \times 20.5) \times 26$

$= 18,144 - 3,642.1\overline{6}$

$\approx 14,501.8$ cm³

$V \approx 14,501.8$ cm³

9 Use the formula for the volume of a frustum:

$V = \frac{1}{3} B_1 h_1 - \frac{1}{3} B_2 h_2$

$V = (\frac{1}{3}\pi R^2 H) - (\frac{1}{3}\pi r^2 h)$ (The base is a circle, so the area = πr².)

$= \frac{1}{3} \times \pi \times 13.5^2 \times 58 - (\frac{1}{3} \times \pi \times 7.6^2 \times 21)$

$= 3,523.5\pi - 404.32\pi$

$= 3,119.18\pi$

$\approx 9,794.2$ cm³

$V \approx 9,794.2$ cm³

10 Use the formula for the volume of a cone:

$V = \frac{1}{3} \times$ area of base × height

$V = \frac{1}{3} \times \pi r^2 \times$ height

$2,034.72 = \frac{1}{3} \times \pi \times r^2 \times 24$ (Substitute the given volume and height. Then solve for the radius.)

$6,104.16 = \pi \times r^2 \times 24$ (Multiply each side of the equation by 3.)

$254.34 = \pi \times r^2$ (Divide each side of the equation by 24.)

$81 = r^2$ (Divide each side of the equation by π = 3.14.)

r = 9 ft (Take the square root of each side of the equation.)
The radius is 9 feet.

11 Use the formula for the volume of a rectangular pyramid:

$V = \frac{1}{3} \times$ area of base × height

$1,320 = \frac{1}{3} \times (180) \times h$ (Substitute the given volume and base area. Then solve for the height.)

$3,960 = 180 \times h$ (Multiply each side of the equation by 3.)

22 cm = h (Divide each side of the equation by 180.)

The height is 22 cm.

CHAPTER 53

SURFACE AREA AND VOLUMES OF SPHERES

1. Use the formula for the surface area of a sphere:
$$SA = 4\pi r^2$$
$$= 4\pi(6.5)^2$$
$$= 169\pi \text{ in}^2$$
$$SA = 169\pi \text{ in}^2$$

2. Use the formula for the surface area of a sphere:
$$SA = 4\pi r^2$$
$$= 4\pi(8)^2 \text{ (The radius is half the diameter, which is 16 ft, so } r = 8.)$$
$$= 256\pi \text{ ft}^2$$
$$SA = 256\pi \text{ ft}^2$$

3. Use the formula for the surface area of a hemisphere:
$$SA = \frac{1}{2}(4\pi r^2) + \pi r^2$$
$$= \frac{1}{2}(4\pi[14]^2) + \pi(14)^2$$
$$= 392\pi + 196\pi$$
$$= 588\pi \text{ cm}^2$$
$$SA = 588\pi \text{ cm}^2$$

4. Find the radius:
$$\text{Circumference} = 2\pi r$$
$$21.5\pi = 2\pi r$$
$$10.75 \text{ cm} = r$$

Use the formula for the surface area of a sphere:

$$SA = 4\pi r^2$$
$$= 4\pi(10.75)^2$$
$$= 462.25\pi \text{ cm}^2$$
$$\approx 1,451.5 \text{ cm}^2$$
$$SA = 462.25\pi \text{ cm}^2 \text{ or approximately } 1,451.5 \text{ cm}^2$$

5. Find the radius:
$$\text{Area} = \pi r^2$$
$$25\pi = \pi r^2$$
$$5 \text{ in} = r$$

Use the formula for the surface area of a hemisphere:

$$SA = \frac{1}{2}(4\pi r^2) + \pi r^2$$
$$= \frac{1}{2}(4\pi[5]^2) + \pi(5)^2$$
$$= 50\pi + 25\pi$$
$$= 75\pi \text{ in}^2$$
$$SA = 75\pi \text{ in}^2$$

6. Find the radius using the formula for the surface area of a sphere:
$$SA = 4\pi r^2$$
$$144\pi = 4\pi(r)^2$$
$$36 = r^2$$
$$6 \text{ yd.} = r$$
Use the formula for the volume of a sphere:

$$V = \frac{4}{3}\pi r^3$$
$$= \frac{4}{3}\pi(6)^3$$
$$= 288\pi \text{ yd}^3$$
$$\approx 904.3 \text{ yd}^3$$

$V = 288\pi$ yd³ or approximately 904.3 yd³

7 Use the formula for the volume of a sphere:

$V = \frac{4}{3}\pi r^3$

$= \frac{4}{3}\pi(11)^3$

$\approx 1{,}774.\overline{6}\pi$ in³

$V \approx 1{,}774.\overline{6}\pi$ in³

8 Use the formula for the volume of a sphere:

$V = \frac{4}{3}\pi r^3$

$= \frac{4}{3}\pi(4.5)^3$ (The radius is half the diameter, which is 9 in, so r = 4.5.)

$= 121.5\pi$ in³

$V = 121.5\pi$ in³

9 Use the formula for the volume of a hemisphere:

$V = \frac{1}{2} \times \frac{4}{3}\pi r^3$

$= \frac{1}{2} \times \frac{4}{3}\pi(11)^3$ (The radius is half the diameter, which is 22 cm, so r = 11.)

$\approx 887.\overline{3}\pi$ cm³

$V \approx 887.\overline{3}\pi$ cm³

10 Find the radius:

Circumference = $2\pi r$

$60 = 2\pi r$

$\frac{30}{\pi} = r$

Use the formula for the volume of a hemisphere:

$V = \frac{1}{2} \times \frac{4}{3}\pi r^3$

$= \frac{1}{2} \times \frac{4}{3}\pi(\frac{30}{\pi})^3$

$= \frac{18{,}000}{\pi^2}$ yd³

$\approx 1{,}825.6$ yd³

$V = \frac{18{,}000}{\pi^2}$ yd³ or about 1,825.6 yd³

11 Use the formula for the volume of a sphere:

$V = \frac{4}{3}\pi r^3$

$= \frac{4}{3}\pi(8)^3$ (The radius is half the diameter, which is 16 ft, so r = 8.)

$\approx 682.\overline{6}\pi$ ft³

If the balloon deflates at 28 ft³ per minute, then the balloon will collapse entirely in: $682.\overline{6}\pi$ ft³ ÷ 28 ft³ per minute ≈ 76.6 minutes.

The balloon will collapse entirely at approximately 76.6 minutes.

12 Find the radius:

Area = πr^2

$56.25\pi = \pi r^2$

7.5 in = r

Use the formula for the surface area of a hemisphere:

$SA = \frac{1}{2}(4\pi r^2) + \pi r^2$

$= \frac{1}{2}(4\pi[7.5]^2) + \pi(7.5)^2$

$= 112.5\pi + 56.25\pi$

$= 168.75\pi \text{ in}^2$

$\approx 529.9 \text{ in}^2$

SA $= 168.8\pi \text{ in}^2$ or
approximately 529.9 in^2

CHAPTER 54

VOLUMES OF COMPOSITE FIGURES

1 The composite figure is made up of a pyramid and a prism. The outside faces, including the base of the figure, make up the surface area.

Use the equation: total surface area $= \frac{1}{2}P\ell + Ph + lw$
$= \frac{1}{2}(28 + 28 + 24 + 24)(9) +$
$(28 + 28 + 24 + 24)(13) + 28 \times 24$
$= 468 + 1,352 + 672$
$= 2,492 \text{ cm}^2$
Surface area $= 2,492 \text{ cm}^2$

2 The composite figure is made up of a cylinder and a cone.

The outside faces, including the area of the circle at the left end of the cylinder, make up the surface area.

Use the equation: total surface area $= 2\pi rh + \pi r^2 + \pi r\ell$

$= 2 \times \pi \times 5 \times 13.5 + \pi \times 5^2 + \pi \times 5 \times 13$
(Use the Pythagorean Theorem to find the slant height: $5^2 + 12^2 = c^2$; $c = 13$; slant height $= 13$ in.)
$= 135\pi + 25\pi + 65\pi$
$= 225\pi \text{ ft}^2$
$\approx 706.5 \text{ ft}^2$
Surface area $= 225\pi \text{ ft}^2$ or approximately 706.5 ft^2

3 The composite figure is made up of a hemisphere and a prism. πr^2 is deleted because the great circle is the area of overlap.

Use the equation: total surface area $= \frac{1}{2}(4\pi r^2) + 2B + Ph$

$= \frac{1}{2}(4\pi[5]^2) + 2(10)(16) +$
$(10 + 10 + 16 + 16)(8)$
$= 50\pi + 320 + 416$
$\approx 50(3.14) + 320 + 416$ Use $\pi = 3.14$.
$\approx 893 \text{ ft}^2$
Surface area $\approx 893 \text{ ft}^2$

4 The composite figure is made up of a hemisphere and a cone. So, add the volumes of each figure.

Use the equation: total volume $= \frac{1}{2}(\frac{4}{3}\pi r^3) + \frac{1}{3}\pi r^2h$

$= \frac{1}{2}(\frac{4}{3}\pi[11]^3) + \frac{1}{3}\pi(11^2)(16.5)$

$\approx 887.\overline{3}\pi + 665.5\pi$

= 1,552.83$\overline{3}$π in³ or approximately 4,875.9 in³

Volume = 1,552.83$\overline{3}$π in³ or approximately 4,875.9 in³

5 **One way:** The composite figure is made up of three prisms.
So, add the volumes of each.

Use the equation: total
volume = Bh + Bh + Bh
= Left Prism + Middle Prism + Right Prism
= (5 x 11 x 5) + (5 x 6 x 5) + (5 x 11 x 5)
= 275 + 150 + 275
= 700 cm³

Another way: Find the volume of the entire prism and subtract from it the area of the prism that is cut out.

= (15 x 11 x 5) − (5 x 5 x 5)
825 − 125 = 700
= 700 cm³
Volume = 700 cm³

6 To find the volume of the solid, subtract the volume of the cylinder from the volume of the rectangular prism.

Use the equation: total
volume = Bh − πr²h
= (3 x 16 x 9) − π(1.5)²(9)

= 432 − 20.25π ≈ 368.4 cm³
Volume = approximately 368.4 cm³

CHAPTER 55

SOLIDS OF REVOLUTION

1 cone

2 hemisphere

3 cylinder

4 Volume of cone = $\frac{1}{3}$πr²h
= $\frac{1}{3}$π(36)²(15) (Use the Pythagorean Theorem to find the height:
36² + h² = 39²; height = 15 cm)
= 6,480π
≈ 20,347.2 cm³
Volume ≈ 20,347.2 cm³

5 Volume of cylinder = πr²h
= π(5.8)²(9.6)
= 322.944π
≈ 1,014 in³
Volume ≈ 1,014 in³

6 To find the volume of the sphere that is shaded, subtract the volume of the smaller sphere from the volume of the larger sphere.

Volume of sphere = $\frac{4}{3}$πr³
Volume = $\frac{4}{3}$π(10)³ − $\frac{4}{3}$π(2)³
= 1,333.$\overline{3}$π − 10.$\overline{6}$π

$= 1,322.\overline{6}\pi$

$\approx 4,153.2 \ ft^3$

Volume $\approx 4,153.2 \ ft^3$

7 Volume of cylinder $= \pi r^2 h$

$= \pi (11)^2 (14)$

$= 1,694\pi \ in^3$

Volume $= 1,694\pi \ in^3$

8 Volume of cone $= \frac{1}{3}\pi r^2 h$

$= \frac{1}{3}\pi (3)^2 (4)$

$= 12\pi \ units^3$

Volume $= 12\pi \ units^3$

9 Volume of sphere $= \frac{4}{3}\pi r^3$

$= \frac{4}{3}\pi (6)^3$

$= 288\pi \ units^3$

Volume $= 288\pi \ units^3$

10 Volume of cylinder $= \pi r^2 h$

$= \pi (3)^2 (10)$

$= 90\pi \ units^3$

Volume $= 90\pi \ units^3$

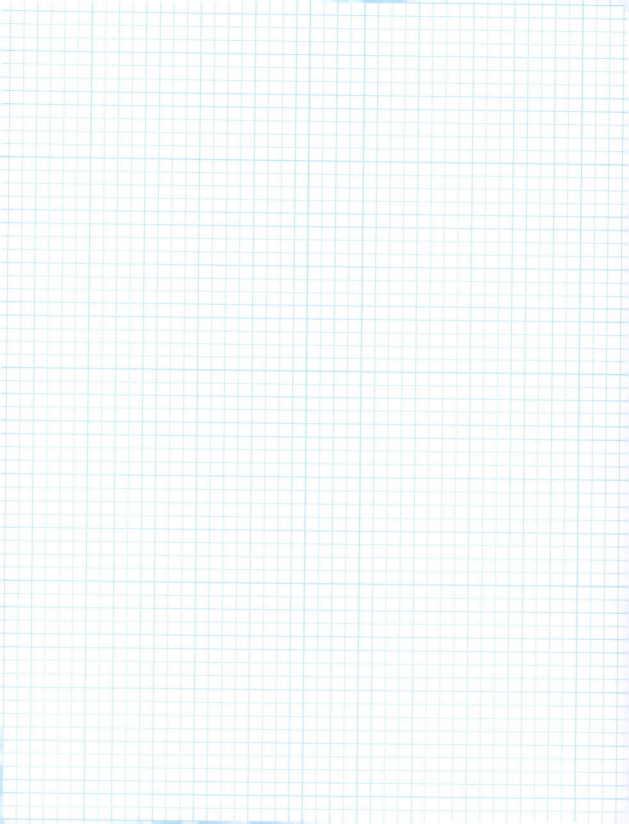

Everything You Need to Ace Geometry is right here!

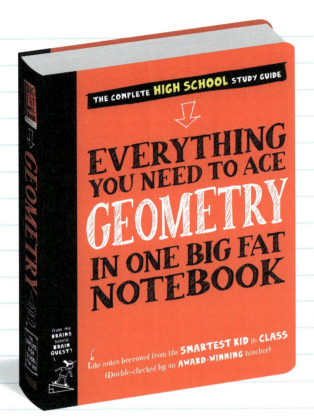

This **Big Fat Notebook** makes all the stuff you need to know sink in with key concepts reinforced through **mnemonic devices, easy-to-understand definitions, doodles, and diagrams.**

Continue to ace high school math and science with these **BIG FAT NOTEBOOKS:**

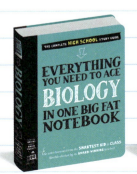
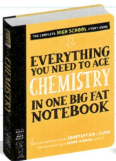
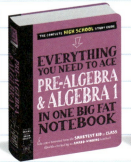
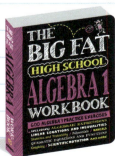